Table of Contents

STATE SECRETS: CHINA'S LEGAL LABYRINTH

Acknowledgments   v

Abbreviations   vi

Translator's Note   vii

Introduction   1

Section I: Into the Legal Labyrinth   5

A. The International and Domestic Legal Framework   5

1. International Norms and Standards   5
   PRC Obligations Under International Law   7
2. The PRC State Secrets Framework   9
   Overview   9
   The State Secrets Law   10
3. Enforcement of the State Secrets System   17
   Sanctions   17
   State Secrets and State Security   21
4. Derogations from Procedural Protections   23

B. Impact of the System on Human Rights   24

1. Impact on the Rule of Law   25
   Stripping Procedural Protections   27
   Intimidation of and Attacks on Defense Lawyers   31
   Lack of Independent Review   31
2. Lack of Transparency and Accountability   32
   Cover-ups   34
   Corruption and Official Malfeasance   37
   Detention, Torture, and the Death Penalty   38
3. Undermining Independent Civil Society   44

C. Reform Efforts   47

    1. Open Government Information (OGI): Local Initiatives   48
    2. The Right to Know   50
    3. The Declassification of State Secrets   52
    4. Reforms of the State Secrets System   53
       Declassification of Natural Disaster Casualties   53
       Criminal Justice Reforms   55
    5. The Limits of Reforms   56
    6. Conclusion   57

D. Recommendations   58

Introduction and Section I Notes   61

Section II: State Secrets Laws and Regulations of the PRC   79

Editors' Introduction   79

A. Main Statutes, Regulations, and Supreme Court Interpretation Governing the State Secrecy System in China   81

    1. Law on the Protection of State Secrets of the People's Republic of China   81
    2. Measures for Implementing the Law on the Protection of State Secrets of the People's Republic of China   94
    3. The Supreme People's Court Interpretation of Certain Issues Regarding the Specific Application of the Law When Trying Cases of Stealing, Gathering, Procuring or Illegally Providing State Secrets or Intelligence Outside of the Country   112

B. Selected Provisions of Major Laws Involving State Secrets   117

    State Security Law of the People's Republic of China   118
    Criminal Law of the People's Republic of China   120
    Criminal Procedure Law of the People's Republic of China   122

C. Four Classified Regulations Pertaining to Law Enforcement and the Judiciary   125

    1. Regulation on State Secrets and the Specific Scope of Each Level of Secrets in Public Security Work   125
    2. Regulation on State Secrets and the Specific Scope of Each Level of Secrets in the Work of the People's Procuratorates   138
    3. Regulation on State Secrets and the Specific Scope of Each Level of Secrets in the Work of the People's Courts   143

4. Regulation on State Secrets and the Specific Scope of Each Level
   of Secrets in Judicial Administration Work   152

**D. Regulation on the Protection of State Secrets
in News Publishing**   160

**E. Selection of State Secrets Provisions
Regulating Specific Activities**   168

Appendices   187

Editors' Introduction   188

I. Official Documents   189

II. Cases Involving State Secrets   213

III. Incidents of Official Cover-Ups   236

Appendices Notes   243

Glossary   249

I. General Terms   249

II. State Bodies   250

III. PRC State Secrets Laws and Regulations Cited in this Report   251

Bibliography   255

Acknowledgments

Human Rights in China (HRIC) would like to thank the Chinese legal and policy experts who provided invaluable comments and suggestions on working drafts of this report. Special thanks to: Jerome A. Cohen, Fu Hualing, Liu Baopu, Christine Loh, Andrew Nathan, and others who wish to remain anonymous.

Abbreviations

CAT	Convention Against Torture and Other Cruel, Inhuman or Degrading Treatment or Punishment
CEDAW	Convention on the Elimination of All Forms of Discrimination Against Women
CERD	International Convention on the Elimination of All Forms of Racial Discrimination
CPC	Communist Party of China
CPL	Criminal Procedure Law
CRC	Convention on the Rights of the Child
HRIC	Human Rights in China
ICCPR	International Covenant on Civil and Political Rights
ICESCR	International Covenant on Economic, Social and Cultural Rights
MOJ	Ministry of Justice
MPS	Ministry of Public Security
NAPSS	National Administration for the Protection of State Secrets
NGO	Non-governmental organization
NPC	National People's Congress
OGI	Open Government Information
PRC	People's Republic of China
RTL	Reeducation Through Labor
SARS	Severe Acute Respiratory Syndrome
SCMP	South China Morning Post
SEPA	State Environment Protection Administration
SEZ	Special Economic Zone
SPC	Supreme People's Court
SPP	Supreme People's Procuratorate
UNDP	United Nations Development Programme
UDHR	Universal Declaration of Human Rights
UN	United Nations
WHO	World Health Organization
WTO	World Trade Organization
XUAR	Xinjiang Uyghur Autonomous Region

Translator's Note

In this report, we have attempted, as much as possible, to use the English names of government bodies in the People's Republic of China as found on their Web sites or in official publications. The difficulty in doing this in regard to state secrets bodies, however, is that firstly, state secrets bodies at the provincial and municipal levels (all called 保密局 in Chinese, or "protection of state secrets bureau") often do not have English translations of their names; and secondly, if they do have English names, there is a lack of consistency in the way the name is translated. For example, the Guangdong Province state secrets body (广东省国家保密局) calls itself the "Administration for the Protection of State Secrets of Guangdong Province," but the equivalent Jiangxi Province state secrets body (江西省国家保密局) calls itself the "Jiangxi State Secrecy Bureau."

Furthermore, there is a lack of consistency in the way foreign NGOs refer to these bodies, particularly the national-level state secrets organ (国家保密局), which many organizations refer to simply as the State Secrets Bureau—but whose official English name is the "National Administration for the Protection of State Secrets." Therefore, in the text of this report, we have chosen to use the national body's official name, or its abbreviation, NAPSS. State secrets bodies at the provincial and municipal level are translated as "bureau" and at levels lower than the municipal level, "department."

A phrase found in a number of the laws and regulations in Section II: State Secrets Laws and Regulations of the PRC is the rather vague term 国家保密工作部门. This literally translates as "National Protection of State Secrets Work Department," but it does, in fact, also refer to the "National Administration for the Protection of State Secrets." Therefore, when translating this term in the various laws and regulations in Section II, because it is not the official name of the body in Chinese (国家保密局) but rather a generic term, we have used the more generic-sounding "national State Secrets Bureau." When there is mention of a 保密工作部门 at the provincial or municipal level, we have simply used the lower-case "state secrets bureau."

In translating the different classification levels of secrets that exist in China, we have opted to use the following terms: The highest level of secret (绝密) is "top-secret," the next highest level (机密) is "highly secret" and the lowest level (秘密) is "secret." The purpose of translating the classification levels in this way is to reflect the comment element in the Chinese terms (密) and to provide the reader with an immediate grasp of the hierarchy between the three.

The glossary at the end of this report contains a full list of terms related to state secrets in Chinese and English, as well as a bilingual list of government bodies and state secrets laws and regulations cited in this report.

All of the laws, regulations and other documents presented in both Section II and in the Appendices of this report are original English translations produced by HRIC.

Introduction

Since the People's Republic of China (PRC) introduced economic reforms in the late 1970s, its exponential growth and the lucrative potential of its huge market have shaped how international business, media, and governments engage with the PRC, often to the detriment of human rights concerns. Despite this reported economic growth, the Communist Party of China's (CPC) post-Tiananmen "bargain" of silence—don't ask, get rich—is breaking down under the pressures of endemic corruption, growing social inequalities and unrest, and serious environmental, public health and social welfare challenges.

The PRC ruling elite[1] maintains political and social control in this volatile domestic landscape through a comprehensive and non-transparent state secrets system, which is largely shielded from the international spotlight. The development of the state secrets system as a sword and a shield, together with an effective security apparatus, serves to strengthen the one-party rule of the CPC and undermines the foundations for good governance, an independent rule of law and sustainable development.

This report describes and examines the PRC state secrets system and shows how it allows and even promotes human rights violations by undermining the rights to freedom of expression and information. The PRC state secrets system, implemented through a CPC-controlled hierarchy of government bodies, is comprised of state secrets laws and regulations that work in tandem with the PRC's state security, criminal procedure and criminal laws, to create a complex, opaque system that controls the classification of—and criminalizes the disclosure or possession of—state secrets. By guarding too much information and sweeping a vast universe of information into the state secrets net, the complex and opaque state secrets system perpetuates a culture of secrecy that is not only harmful but deadly to Chinese society.[2]

> **The development of the state secrets system as a sword and a shield, together with an effective security apparatus, serves to strengthen the one-party rule of the CPC and undermines the foundations for good governance, an independent rule of law and sustainable development.**

In 2003, when Hong Kong officials tried to confirm reports concerning Severe Acute Respiratory Syndrome (**SARS**), a Guangdong health official told them that there was a legal requirement at that time that infectious diseases had to be classified as state secrets. The control of critical information and lack of transparency continued to plague the response to the SARS epidemic, which spread and, to date, has infected thousands and killed nearly 800 worldwide.

On November 13, 2005, an explosion at a petrochemical plant in Jilin released more than 100 tons of toxic chemicals, including benzene, into the environment, which subsequently poisoned the **Songhua River.** Ambiguity in the regulations concerning reporting on industrial/pollution accidents and questions concerning the classification of this information added to the confusion in reporting the incident. Only ten days after the explosion and one day after the water was shut off in Harbin did the State Environment Protection Administration (SEPA) admit serious pollution of the river. Eventually water was cut off to nine million residents in Harbin, and the polluted water flowed across the Russian border.

Tan Kai (谭凯), a computer repair technician from Zhejiang, was formally indicted on April 29, 2006 on charges of "illegally obtaining state secrets," ostensibly for information he had obtained while doing routine file back-ups for his clients, in particular for work he did in 2005 for an employee of the Zhejiang Provincial Party Committee. However, Tan is also an environmental activist and on November 15, 2005 the Zhejiang provincial government declared Green Watch—the organization Tan helped found—an illegal organization, calling into question the real reason he was prosecuted. Tan was sentenced to 18 months' imprisonment on August 11, 2006 by the Hangzhou Municipal People's Intermediate Court on the state secrets charge.

Lu Jianhua (陆建华), a prominent sociologist with the Chinese Academy of Social Sciences, was reportedly sentenced to 20 years for "leaking state secrets" in a case linked to that of Hong-Kong based reporter **Ching Cheong** (程翔), who was sentenced in August 2006 to five years for "spying." Lu was well known for the essays he wrote and his appearances on TV talk shows and often assisted Ching with articles on the political and social situation in China that were published in the Singapore newspaper *The Straits Times*. Some Chinese officials claimed that three of these articles, published in 2004, contained state secrets.

These are all examples of how the PRC's state secrets system is used as both a **shield**—classifying a broad range of information and keeping it from the public view, and a **sword**—using it as a means to crack down on individuals who are critical of the government. The initial suppression of information about the spread of SARS and the Songhua River case also reflect some of the critical development, governance, and human rights issues at stake under the PRC's regime of information control. In addition to the impact on the rights of Chinese people, this regime has significant consequences for other diverse stakeholders, including the media, scholars and researchers, the business community, Chinese officials and international policymakers. The free flow of accurate, transparent, and reliable data and information has an important impact on each and all of their interests, activities and goals.

Despite the tremendous pressures and need for more information access, the PRC ruling elite remains committed to the existence of the state secrets system and exerts considerable effort to maintain it. However, the sheer volume of material that is classified by the state secrets system does not mean that the system is successful at ensuring total information control.

Section I, Part A of this report outlines the **international and domestic legal framework of the PRC's state secrets system,** including a review of the main laws and regulations and an examination of the implementation of this system, together with its impact on criminal procedural protections. The state secrets system allows large amounts of information to be classified as state secrets, employs extensive technological, police and social controls to monitor the flow of information, and places it all under political reins. In this complex, arbitrary and encompassing system, anything and everything can be determined to be a state secret, especially under the retroactive classification that the system allows.

> In this complex, arbitrary and encompassing system, anything and everything can be determined to be a state secret, especially under the retroactive classification that the system allows.

Section I, Part B examines the **impact of the state secrets system, focusing on several key impact points: governance, development, the rule of law and human rights.** Combined with the one-party regime, and the absence of an independent and transparent rule of law in the PRC, the state secrets system allows further consolidation of political and social control by the ruling elite. Tight control over this system by the government bureaucracy, headed by the National Administration for the Protection of State Secrets (hereinafter NAPSS), gives the CPC leadership the power to classify any information it desires as a state secret and thereby keep or—even if it is already public—remove it from circulation. This information includes the state secrets laws and regulations themselves, and without public dissemination of these laws, it is exceptionally difficult for individuals to know for sure when they are violated. Instead of the "harmonious society"[3] being called for by Chinese leaders, what remains is a controlled society where critical voices pay a heavy price.

Section I, Part C describes and assesses some **government reform efforts,** including the Open Government Information (OGI) effort started in 2002. This OGI effort continues to develop, and reflects some desire to make government information available. However, greater superficial openness does not necessarily mean that the government is adopting the oversight, monitoring, and accountability mechanisms necessary to implement these initiatives in a way that are not constrained by the overriding imperative to maintain political power at all costs. The state secrets system itself undermines these reform efforts.

Section I, Part D presents **HRIC's recommendations** for reforms of the state secrets system to better protect the rights to freedom of expression and information. Governments have an obligation under international law and norms to facilitate transparency and access to information. Without access to information, other rights are easily infringed, including the right to education, health and criminal procedural protections. Without a transparent and accountable legal system, the PRC has a rule *by* law, not a rule *of* law. While recognizing the limits of any legislative reforms in the absence of political reforms, HRIC presents recommendations for substantive revisions, as well as suggestions for more accessible and clear legislation that defines the relationship it has to the implementing bodies—the public security apparatus, administrative agencies and the courts. HRIC also presents recommendations aimed at promoting the PRC's compliance with and implementation of its international human rights obligations.

Section II presents **state secrets laws, regulations and implementation measures, as well as other relevant provisions of the state security law, criminal law and criminal procedure law.** These documents are presented both in Chinese and in English translation. With this report, HRIC is providing in English, for the first time, an extensive collection of the documents and regulations that help to describe and define the PRC state secrets system. A fundamental principal of rule of law is that law must be promulgated and accessible. In preparing this report, sustained effort has been made to identify law as currently effective and amended, but a fundamental flaw in the PRC state secrets framework is the absence of coherent systems permitting timely access to governing law.[4]

As examples of the impact of the state secrets system on individuals, on the whole society, and on the legal system, we also present, in the **Appendices,** information on individual state secret cases and information on governmental cover-ups. A rare selection of official charts and documents related to the state secrets system are also included in the Appendices. Taken as a whole, this report provides a useful and constructive resource for advancing greater transparency, accountability, and protection for human rights in the PRC.

Into the Legal Labyrinth

A.
The International and Domestic Legal Framework

1. INTERNATIONAL NORMS AND STANDARDS

In the past two decades, the PRC has become an increasingly active member of the international community, signing and ratifying numerous human rights treaties, including those related to torture, discrimination, economic, social, and cultural rights, and rights of women and children.[5] The discussion below outlines international norms and standards relevant to freedom of information; the rights to access and disseminate information; and appropriate guidelines for balancing national security and state secrecy concerns with the freedoms and rights of citizens and the government's development and economic policy goals.

The rights to access and impart information are interrelated in nature, and make up a key component of the right to freedom of expression.[6] These rights are protected in numerous international treaties and declarations,[7] and ongoing elaboration of these rights by interpretive bodies and special procedures of the former Commission on Human Rights, and the current Human Rights Council, emphasize their fundamental importance in society, facilitating equitable development and access to all human rights.[8] Therefore, freedom of expression and access to information is an "essential test right," reflecting a country's standard of fair play, justice and honesty.[9]

Freedom of expression and access to information is an "essential test right," reflecting a country's standard of fair play, justice and honesty.

While the rights to freedom of expression and information can be legitimately restricted, these restrictions must be narrowly tailored and specific in order to prevent abuse. Restrictions on information are permissible, but they must be provided by law and serve one of the enumerated purposes in the International Covenant on Civil and Political Rights (ICCPR), including the protection of national security, to respect the rights or reputations of others, or for the protection of public order (*ordre public*), public health or morals.[10] Freedom of expression can only be restricted in the most serious cases of a direct political or military threat to the entire nation[11]—and as a result, peaceful expression is always protected.[12] Even where a purpose is legitimately invoked, any restrictions must be proportional and necessary, and must be the least restrictive means of achieving that purpose.[13]

International law and norms also specifically address the issue of State classification of information, and the criminalization of leaking such information. The need to protect national security while balancing the need to protect human rights is a problematic issue for nation states around the globe. While not a legally binding treaty, "The Johannesburg Principles on National Security, Freedom of Expression and Access to Information" (hereinafter, Johannesburg Principles) have become a widely accepted norm and are arguably considered customary international law. In addition to the proportionality and narrowly tailored requirements for such restrictions—including on information relating to national security[14]—the Johannesburg Principles dictate that "no person may be punished on national security grounds for disclosure of information if:

- the disclosure does not actually harm and is not likely to harm a legitimate national security interest, or

- the public interest in knowing the information outweighs the harm from disclosure."[15]

If information has already been made generally available—by means lawful or unlawful—the *public's right to know* overrides any invoked justification for stopping further publication of the information.[16] In the classification of information, the State must adopt a means for independent review of the denial of access to information on national security grounds to ensure that the purpose is not abused by authorities. Finally, international law requires an actual finding of objective harm before an individual can be imprisoned for leaking classified information.[17]

PRC Obligations Under International Law

The rights to freedom of expression and to access and disseminate information have specific implications for a framework that classifies wide ranges of information like the PRC state secrets system. The PRC is a State Party or signatory to numerous international human rights treaties where these rights are specifically set forth. The PRC's obligations include those of constitutional protection, legislative enactment, and implementation and monitoring of specific rights.[18] These obligations exist in spite of the many challenges facing all law reform efforts in China: the lack of independent courts, transparency, accountability, and widespread corruption in the legal system.

The PRC Constitution and other domestic laws include provisions protecting freedom of expression and the right to, for example, criticize the government. However, the state secrets framework, with its severe restrictions on information and the criminalization of possessing and disclosing information, undermines both domestic law and the PRC's international legal obligations. The internal contradictions and tensions in domestic law provisions, and the failure to consistently implement international norms, also undermine the development of a functioning and coherent rule of law.

The state secrets framework, with its severe restrictions on information and the criminalization of possessing and disclosing information, undermines both domestic law and the PRC's international legal obligations.

CASE STORY

Tohti Tunyaz

Tohti Tunyaz (图尼亚孜), an ethnic Uyghur, was arrested on February 6, 1998 after returning to China to collect research materials for his Ph.D. thesis. Tunyaz, who wrote under the pen-name Tohti Muzart, enrolled at the University of Tokyo's graduate school in 1995 and was preparing a thesis about China's policies toward the country's ethnic minorities. He was charged with "illegally procuring state secrets" and sentenced to five years in prison, plus seven years for "inciting splittism," with a combined sentence of 11 years' imprisonment. Reportedly, the documents in question were historical records from 50 years ago that he obtained from a library worker and photocopied. On the latter charge, he allegedly published a book in Japan in 1998 entitled *The Inside Story of the Silk Road*. According to the Chinese government, the book advocates ethnic separation, but neither the book nor its manuscript was submitted to the court, one source says. Furthermore, Tunyaz's supervisor, Professor Sato Tugitaka at the University of Tokyo, claims that this book simply does not exist.[19]

Tunyaz appealed to the Xinjiang Uyghur Autonomous Region (XUAR) Higher People's Court, which upheld his sentence of 11 years' imprisonment with two years' subsequent deprivation of political rights on February 15, 2000. However, the Higher Court later amended the charge from stealing state secrets to illegally acquiring them. He is being held at Urumqi No. 3 Prison in the XUAR and is due for release on February 10, 2009.

In May 2001, the UN Working Group on Arbitrary Detention concluded that his imprisonment was arbitrary and in violation of his rights to freedom of thought, expression and opinion. Successive presidents of the University of Tokyo have written letters to Chinese leaders to ask for Tunyaz's release, saying that, for example, "Tohti was critical of the independence movement. He did not plan to publish a book. His arrest is based on misunderstandings." On November 29, 2005, he was visited by the UN Special Rapporteur on Torture and Other Cruel, Inhuman, or Degrading Treatment or Punishment, Manfred Nowak, during his mission to China between November 20 and December 2, 2005. Tunyaz told the Special Rapporteur that he had been held in a pretrial detention facility for more than two years. He was put in a solitary confinement cell, interrogated daily and was unable to communicate with his family.[20]

Tohti Tunyaz

2. THE PRC STATE SECRETS FRAMEWORK

Overview

The protection of state secrets has long been considered a priority by the PRC and the CPC, both because it is a part of a broader political culture of secrecy, and because it is a key tool for maintaining political control. The legal framework originated in the Provisional Regulation on Protecting State Secrets promulgated in June of 1951,[21] which stipulated that Party members as well as non-Party members had the responsibility to safeguard state secrets.

The current state secrets framework includes the 1988 Law on the Protection of State Secrets of the People's Republic of China[22] (hereinafter, State Secrets Law), and the 1990 Measures for Implementing the Law on the Protection of State Secrets of the People's Republic of China[23] (hereinafter, Implementation Measures). The State Secrets Law sets forth the meaning, scope, and classification of state secrets, and the security system and its procedures. All state organs, armed forces, political parties, organizations, enterprises, institutions, and citizens have an obligation to protect state secrets. The Implementation Measures significantly expand the scope of the state secrets system by providing for *retroactive classification* based upon specified "consequences" (后果) and *pre-emptive classification* based upon determination of *potential harm* if disclosed.

In addition, related provisions in the State Security Law (1993)[24] and the Criminal Law (1979, amended 1997, 1999, 2001, 2002, 2005)[25] further stipulate specific administrative and criminal sanctions for violations of state secrets or state security provisions. The Criminal Procedure Law (1997)[26] sets forth relevant procedures for investigation, prosecution, and defense of state secrets and state security cases. This framework is further complemented by numerous laws and regulations that are not primarily a part of the state secrets framework, but include references to state secrets and to obligations not to divulge them, governing, for example, the work of lawyers,[27] of accountants,[28] and the use of the telecommunications network.[29]

Under this state secrets system, all information falls under one of the following:

- **already classified** (and marked as such),

- **subject to classification** when state secrets "arise,"

- **retroactively classified** based upon harm perceived to have occurred,

- **pre-emptively classified** based upon determination of potential harm,

- **intelligence** (concerns state secrets, but not yet made public or classified), or

- **internal *(neibu)*/work secrets** of a work unit or organization.

As elaborated below, these categories of information are malleable and subject to arbitrary and politicized manipulation. Furthermore, the distinction drawn between domestic disclosure and external disclosure outside the country, and the crime of "endangering state security," sweeps *intelligence* (情报), into the state secrets net with attendant criminal liability for its disclosure. Thus, the state secrets framework presents problems of over-classification, subjectivity and arbitrariness that impact a range of individual rights and issues of transparency and governance. The restriction of rights to freedom of expression and information are therefore restricted in ways that are neither narrowly tailored nor specific, as required under international law.

The State Secrets Law

The State Secrets Law, which came into effect on May 1, 1989, was passed for the purpose of "protecting state secrets, safeguarding state security and national interests and ensuring the smooth progress of reform, of opening to the outside world, and of socialist construction."[30] As the primary legislation governing the management of state secrets in the PRC, the State Secrets Law stipulates procedures for making classification determinations and lays out the basic scope of information to be protected.

Scope of State Secrets

The State Secrets Law defines state secrets as "matters that are related to state security and national interests."[31] The State Secrets Law, Article 8 sets forth six types of state secrets matters, and a seventh catch-all provision, as follows:

- major policy decisions on state affairs,

- building of national defense and activities of the armed forces,

- diplomatic activities, activities related to foreign countries, as well as commitments to foreign countries,

- national economic and social development,

- science and technology,

- activities for safeguarding state security and investigation of criminal offenses, and

- other matters that are classified as state secrets by the national State Secrets Bureau (NAPSS).[32]

> The state secrets framework presents problems of over-classification, subjectivity and arbitrariness.

Some specificity is delineated under each broad category by regulations issued by the NAPSS and other departments. *State secrets in criminal investigations* include, for example, "Important internal directives, decisions, plans and proposals used by the Supreme People's Court and higher people's courts in trying cases of very high significance."[33] Specific information that are state secrets are also delineated in numerous regulations, and includes *information in news publishing, information about strikes, data on numbers of people fleeing from famine, and unemployment rates.* (See Section II for examples of regulations that lay out specifics on what information is classified.)

In addition, *intelligence*, while not identified as falling within the scope of state secrets, has been treated almost interchangeably with state secrets, especially in the context of external disclosures or the charge of endangering state security. The disclosure of "intelligence" has also been incorporated into Article 111 of the Criminal Law, and is a matter distinct from leaking state secrets.[34] Defined tautologically as "matters that concern state security and interests which have either not yet been made public, or should not be made public, according to relevant regulations," "intelligence" is a legally operative term, vague enough to be used to expand the scope of protected materials beyond documents classified in accordance with the formal state secrets system.[35] Its definition relies on the examination of what should be public, and in this respect courts and legislators fail to provide a clear interpretation.[36] Described in a legal treatise, however, the scope of "intelligence" is about as wide as state secrets, covering "important political, economic, military, scientific and technological information."[37]

Categories of Classification and Levels of Harm

The State Secrets Law, Article 9 classifies state secrets in three hierarchical categories linked to levels of potential harm to state security and national interests if disclosed:

- "top secret" (绝密) if disclosure would cause *extremely serious harm*;

- "highly secret" (机密) if disclosure would cause *serious harm*; and

- "secret" (秘密) if disclosure would cause *harm*.

The State Secrets Law, Article 14 stipulates that specific measures for determining the time period for keeping state secrets classified shall be formulated by the NAPSS, and Articles 15 and 16 stipulate that classification levels and the length of classification may be altered by the organ that originally made such determinations, and that automatic declassification occurs when the original time period expires.[38] Various units and departments that encounter potential state secrets make initial determinations or can seek clarification from bureaus higher in hierarchy, after which the information is treated as a state secret, pending final determination by the relevant bureau. Once information is determined to be a state secret, however, there is no corresponding avenue for the review or appeal of classification.

CASE STORY

Zhang Shanguang

Zhang Shanguang (张善光), a workers' rights advocate and formerly a secondary school teacher, was sentenced to ten years in prison for "illegally providing intelligence to overseas organizations" under Article 111 of the Criminal Law on December 27, 1998. The court used the terms "intelligence" and "state secrets" interchangeably to describe Zhang's offense of providing a Hong Kong-based reporter for Radio Free Asia with information about a protest and a kidnapping case in Xupu County in Hunan Province. Zhang was first detained on July 21, 1998 after his home was raided by police, who confiscated documents and his personal computers. He was formally arrested on August 28, 1998. The court stated that the interview with the reporter for Radio Free Asia violated the terms of his probation, which had not yet concluded. The verdict also claimed that he provided the interviewer with intelligence, because the case Zhang described had not yet been made public by public security officials, even though it was common knowledge among citizens in the area.

Zhang appealed the conviction immediately. While the law stipulates that the appeal must be heard within 45 days, Zhang was forced to wait nearly a year and a half before officials suddenly announced that the court was upholding the original verdict. While judging the appeal, the court did not conduct any investigation nor ask Zhang a single question about his case. Prior to this imprisonment, he had spent seven years in jail after the June 4, 1989 government crackdown for his role in organizing the Hunan Workers' Autonomous Federation in May of that year. He is currently being held at the Hunan No. 1 Prison. He suffers from tuberculosis and is reportedly in very poor medical condition.

Information on the above case is taken from HRIC's human rights database or website.

Zhang Shanguang

How information is treated once it is classified is also laid out in the law: information is not only marked with its corresponding category, but further provisions in the State Secrets Law and the Implementation Measures govern, for example, who can access and transport the information and how they should be trained, as well as how state secrets are to be made, received, dispatched, transmitted, used, copied, excerpted, preserved and destroyed.[39]

In addition to information that is already classified, classification of information is carried out when the state secret "arises."[40] This may mean, for example, in the work of the people's courts, where a criminal case is being tried, the people's courts must determine whether it is a case of significance and the extent to which that matter should be classified, if at all.[41]

To aid units and offices in which state secrets matters arise, numerous regulations on the specific scope of information that is considered a state secret—and which are classified as top secret, highly secret, or secret—exist. In the Regulation on State Secrets and Specific Scope of Each Level of Secrets in Judicial Administration Work, for example, overall programs and plans for nationwide prison and reeducation through labor (RTL) work are to be considered top secret, whereas nationwide and provincial statistics on the number of executions is considered highly secret.[42]

Expansion of the Scope of Classification: Consequences（后果）

The Implementation Measures, promulgated in 1990 by the NAPSS, provides for retroactive classification of information not already enumerated or classified as a state secret, if disclosure of information *could* result in any one of the eight "consequences"[43] deemed to cause harm to the security and interests of the state.[44] In addition to retroactive classification, the Implementation Measures also provide for *pre-emptive* classification of information based on a perceived *potential harm*, further expanding the scope of information that can be classified.

These provisions in the State Secrets Law and the Implementation Measures allow for serious abuse by authorities because of a lack of clear and specific definitions, the role of subjective perceptions, and extensive use of state security rationale for restricting access to information. Taken together, these elements have the potential to sweep any information, whether or not it is already in the possession of the government, under the veil of state secrets protection.

Eight potential consequences of disclosure that can be invoked to support classification of information: (Implementation Measures, Article 4)

———

Endangering the ability of the state to consolidate and defend its power
（危害国家政权的巩固和防御能力）

———

Affecting national unity, ethnic unity or social stability
（影响国家统一、民族团结和社会安定）

———

Harming the political or economic interests of the state in its dealings with foreign countries
（损害国家在对外活动中的政治、经济利益）

———

Affecting the security of state leaders or top foreign officials
（影响国家领导人、外国要员的安全）

———

Hindering important security or defense work of the state
（妨害国家重要的安全保卫工作）

———

Causing a decrease in the reliability, or a loss of effectiveness to, the measures used to safeguard state secrets
（使保护国家秘密的措施可靠性降低或者失效）

———

Weakening the economic and technological strength of the state
（削弱国家经济、科技实力）

———

Causing state organs to lose the ability to exercise their authority according to law.
（使国家机关依法行使职权失去保障）

Neibu *Information and "Work Secrets"*

In addition to information classified as "state secrets," a vast array of information is also considered *neibu* ("internal"). *Neibu* information is treated as equivalent to "work secrets," which includes the ways that different departments carry out their work. "Work secrets" and *neibu* information are not specifically classified as state secrets, but they should not be publicly disseminated because if disclosed, they "could bring indirect harm to the work of [the] organ or unit."[45] The internal use by government departments of "work secrets" in the course of their duties is not classified by degrees but is formulated to conform to the measures of each individual unit, and the general practice is to mark them as "*neibu*."[46] State secrets regulations issued by individual ministries and departments often identify specific categories of information for internal departmental use only and prohibit their disclosure without prior approval.[47]

The Implementation Measures clearly mark *neibu* matters as a separate and distinct category of information lying outside the scope of state secrets protection and correspondingly, state secrets criminal prosecutions,[48] though in practice, there is no bright line separating what is legitimately "state secrets" and what is "*neibu*" information. This lack of a bright line distinction is played out in the cases of individuals charged with crimes of disclosing state secrets, where a charge of disclosing state secrets is applied even where the information is *neibu* information. For example, in Zheng Enchong's case, the trial court applied a *neibu* provision of a state secrets regulation issued by the Ministry of Public Security to support its certification that Zheng's handwritten account of police deployment in a labor incident amounted to a state secret. This provision refers to "opinions currently being drafted regarding proposed changes to organs and their personnel" and concerns *neibu* information not legally classifiable as a "state secret."[49]

These broad and all-encompassing provisions on classification provide numerous bodies at all levels of government, in essence, the ability to classify any information they deem necessary as state secrets.

These broad and all-encompassing provisions on classification provide numerous bodies at all levels of government, in essence, the ability to classify any information they deem necessary as state secrets.

Organs and Bodies Responsible for Classification

The primary responsibility for the administration of the state secrets framework and the designation of state secrets falls to the NAPSS, a functioning organ of the State Council,[50] with the exception of the administration of military secrets, which is the responsibility of the Central Military Commission.[51] The PRC Constitution notes that the responsibility for keeping state secrets falls to all Chinese citizens, though personnel in state secrets departments are governed with specific sets of regulations.[52]

The NAPSS has authority over the drafting of state secrets laws and regulations, is responsible for inspecting and classifying state secrets protection work on a national level, and organizes the implementation of the framework, including technology in the service of state secrets work.[53] The NAPSS has authority at the national level, and as a government organization is separate from the subordinate party organization of the Central Committee of the CPC—the Central Committee for the Protection of State Secrets. State secrets bodies and Party committees are then established in provincial and city level governments, as well as in other substantive organs according to their functions.[54] As a result, both state secrets bureaus and offices within other departments at every level have the authority to designate state secrets, and the responsibility to protect them.[55]

The state secrets system is the operational means for various central state agencies to route and maneuver information within their respective departments. Through the enabling mechanisms of the state secrets laws, state (and Party) organs are able to codify their systems for information distribution by issuing their own regulations classifying specific types of information—from religious affairs to family planning to land management.[56]

These numerous bureaus have responsibilities to designate and protect secrets in accordance with the State Secrets Law. However, all state organs and units at all levels of government have responsibility for the primary classification where state secrets matters "arise."[57] Corresponding to a traditional hierarchy, central state organs are responsible for guiding secrets protection work in their own scope of work,[58] while departments at the county level and above actually administer (through setting up bodies or designating personnel) the daily work of protecting state secrets within their own organs or units."[59]

3. ENFORCEMENT OF THE STATE SECRETS SYSTEM

The emphasis in Chinese domestic law is on the role of the individual to protect state secrets. For instance, the Chinese Constitution includes the right to freedom of speech,[60] but it also imposes an obligation on all citizens to "keep state secrets."[61] As a corollary to the duty of all citizens, the State Secrets Law and the Implementation Measures have a detailed system of reward and sanction for people who contribute to the protection of state secrets, or who steal or disclose state secrets.[62]

Sanctions

There are three types of sanctions for disclosure, illegally obtaining or holding of state secrets:

- **criminal** sanctions for intentional or negligent disclosure under circumstances deemed "serious," illegally obtaining state secrets, and unlawfully holding state secrets;

- **administrative** sanctions when disclosure is not deemed serious enough to warrant criminal punishment; and

- **Party** sanctions for Party members.

The Implementation Measures, Article 35, elaborates on "disclosing," "leaking," or "divulging" state secrets to include: "allowing a state secret to be known by any individual that is not allowed to know such information;" and allowing information "to go beyond the specified group of individuals allowed access" and "to not be able to prove that such a disclosure of information did not take place."

Criminal Responsibility: Domestic Versus External Disclosure

The State Secrets Law and the Criminal Law draw distinctions between intentionally or negligently disclosing information domestically, and disclosing information outside the country. While individuals can incur criminal sanctions for intentionally or negligently disclosing state secrets domestically under "serious circumstances" (情节)[63], "serious circumstances" are not required to trigger criminal sanctions for individuals who provide this information to individuals or organizations outside the country.[64]

CASE STORY

Rebiya Kadeer

An advocate for women's and Uyghur minority rights in China, **Rebiya Kadeer** (热比亚卡德尔), was also a successful entrepreneur who founded and directed a trading company in the Xinjiang Uyghur Autonomous Region (XUAR). In recognition of her work and accomplishments, the Chinese government appointed her to the Chinese People's Political Consultative Conference and to the Chinese delegation that participated in the 1995 UN World Conference on Women. Kadeer was also a standing member of the XUAR Chamber of Commerce and additionally founded the Thousand Mothers Movement to promote women's rights in 1997.

Kadeer frequently sent newspaper clippings from XUAR newspapers to her husband, who had left China for the U.S. in 1996. In August 1999, Kadeer was on her way to a meeting with visiting U.S. Congressional staff, carrying copies of local newspapers and other information concerning human rights abuses in the XUAR, when she was detained. Kadeer was sentenced to eight years' imprisonment in 2000 for "illegally providing state secrets overseas."

International human rights activists and organizations, as well as the U.S. government and over 100 members of Congress, advocated on Kadeer's behalf. After the Chinese authorities reduced her sentence by one year in 2004, she was given early release in 2005. Ignoring warnings from Chinese government officials urging Kadeer not to discuss sensitive issues after her release, she continues to advocate for Uyghur human rights, and several of her family members in the XUAR have since been detained.

According to Kadeer's family and news reports, in May 2006, the XUAR authorities formally detained two of her sons and were keeping one of her daughters under house arrest for alleged tax evasion, after seriously beating one son in front of his children.[65] On November 27, 2006, two of her sons were fined for tax evasion, one of whom was also sentenced to seven years in prison.[66] The previous day, another son currently held under subversion charges was taken from the Tianshan District Detention Center on a stretcher, in apparent need of medical attention; it is feared that he was beaten and tortured as a result of Kadeer being elected president of the World Uyghur Congress on November 26, 2006.[67] He was formally sentenced to nine years in prison and three years' deprivation of political rights for "instigating and engaging in secessionist activities" by the Intermediate People's Court of Urumqi on April 17, 2007.[68]

Rebiya Kadeer

Furthermore, forbidden information in the context of external disclosure includes intelligence. The State Secrets Law specifies that any individual who "steals, gathers, procures or illegally provides state secrets *or intelligence outside the country* shall be held criminally responsible in accordance with the law."[69] Article 111 of the Criminal Law stipulates the punishment for committing the crime of "stealing, gathering, procuring, or unlawfully providing state secrets *or intelligence* for an organ, organization or individual *outside the territory of China*"[70] and the sentence length is determined by the severity of the circumstances (italics added).

In 2001, the Supreme People's Court also issued an Interpretation of Certain Issues Regarding the Specific Application of the Law When Trying Cases of Stealing, Gathering, Procuring or Illegally Providing State Secrets or Intelligence Outside of the Country (hereinafter, SPC Interpretation of Certain Issues) (see Section II, page 112, for the full text). Article 2 sets forth three circumstances that would make the crime one committed under "*especially serious circumstances,*" thereby subjecting the individual to a sentence of between ten years and life imprisonment:

- stealing, gathering, procuring or illegally providing *top-secret level* state secrets;

- stealing, gathering, procuring or illegally providing *three or more highly-secret level state secrets*;

- stealing, gathering, procuring or illegally providing *state secrets or intelligence* that causes *especially serious harm* to state security interests.

The SPC Interpretation of Certain Issues thus not only brings intelligence fully within the net of state secrets, but also invokes a level of harm used in the classification of state secrets—"especially serious harm"—to the determination of what constitutes a crime with attendant criminal liability, including the death penalty if there are "especially deplorable circumstances."

The crime of "illegally obtaining state secrets" by stealing, gathering or procuring is set forth in the Criminal Law, Article 282, with a sentence of a fixed-term imprisonment of no more than three years, public surveillance or deprivation of political rights. If circumstances are deemed to be serious, then the sentence is not less than three years, but not more than seven years. The SPC Interpretation of Certain Issues also states that a defendant can be held criminally liable if he knew or *should have known* that the disclosure to overseas organizations or individuals of unmarked matter would have a bearing on state security or interests.[71]

Finally, the Criminal Law, Article 282, also specifies that individuals can be sentenced for "unlawfully holding" documents, materials or other objects classified as "top secret" or "highly secret" and "refus[ing] to explain" their source or purpose.[72] This infraction can lead to sentences of up to three years' imprisonment, criminal detention, or public surveillance.[73] Individuals charged with removing secrets have the burden of proving that they did not disclose the information to someone who is not authorized for access.[74] The State Security Law, Article 20 makes it a crime for an individual or organization to hold any documents, materials, or other articles classified as state secrets.

Criminal Penalties for State Secrets Crimes

CRIME	PENALTY	UNDER PARTICULAR CIRCUMSTANCES
Illegally stealing, gathering or procuring state secrets[75]	Not more than 3 years' criminal detention, public surveillance or deprivation of political rights	*Serious circumstances:* 3–7 years' imprisonment
Unlawfully holding documents, materials or other objects classified as "top secret" or "highly secret" and refusing to explain their source or purpose[76]	Not more than 3 years' criminal detention or public surveillance	
Stealing, gathering or illegally providing state secrets or intelligence outside the country[77]	5–10 years' imprisonment Property and belongings can also be confiscated[78]	*Minor circumstances:* not more than 5 years' criminal detention, public surveillance or deprivation of political rights *Especially serious circumstances:* 10 years to life imprisonment *If especially serious harm to the state and the people is caused, or if circumstances are especially serious:* death penalty[79]
Violations of the State Secrets Law by state personnel under serious circumstances and either intentionally or negligently disclosing state secrets[80]	Not more than 3 years' imprisonment	*Especially serious:* 3–7 years' imprisonment
Violations of the State Secrets Law by non-state personnel[81]	Not more than 3 years' imprisonment	*Especially serious:* 3–7 years' imprisonment

In the State Secrets Law, individuals who disclose state secrets, whether intentionally or through negligence, under circumstances that are deemed to be serious, shall be held criminally responsible. And if disclosures are made that are deemed "not serious enough for criminal punishment," administrative sanctions may be imposed.[82]

Administrative and Party Sanctions

Much as in the classification of state secrets, the kind of administrative sanction applied is closely related to the level of actual or perceived harm surrounding the circumstances during which the infraction occurred. The Implementation Measures state that for disclosure of secret, highly secret, or top secret state secrets under minor circumstances, lenient administrative sanctions may be applied.[83] And numerous other regulations have been issued to address specific circumstances or particular areas of work. The unauthorized disclosure of "work secrets" is limited to administrative punishment.[84]

Party members are specifically governed by additional rules. If committed under circumstances deemed to be "minor," the loss of secret documents or the disclosing of state secrets can lead to warnings or the termination of Party duties; if the circumstances are deemed to be relatively serious, individuals may have their Party membership rescinded.[85]

State Secrets and State Security

The state secrets framework has a significant relationship with the State Security Law (1993), and where state security concerns are invoked in the language of state secrets crimes or in the particular circumstances of a case, the penalties that can be applied increase in severity.

The SPC Interpretation of Certain Issues states that the actions punishable under Article 111 of the Criminal Law are in fact "acts endangering state security" as defined in the State Security Law.[86] Article 1 of the State Secrets Law emphasizes its purpose in "safeguarding state security," and Article 8, which delineates the scope of state secrets, includes references to secrets in building the national defense. This relationship between state secrets and state security can also be found in the State Security Law, which includes numerous references to the possession and disclosure of state secrets and the impact on state security.[87]

Under the State Security Law and the Criminal Law, association or collusion with overseas individuals, organizations, or groups brings state secrets offenses within the scope of "endangering state security."[88] Article 111 is an endangering state security crime, but includes the disclosing of any state secrets or intelligence, and in criminal proceedings against individuals, as in the case of Zhang Shanguang, the exact provision invoked is often unclear or changeable. And as seen in various cases, the information transmitted—or which has been attempted to be transmitted—does not necessarily need to be connected to intelligence or espionage.[89] Like other criminal offenses in the PRC, subjective and objective requirements must be met in order to establish the offense of illegally providing state secrets outside the country. Actual or successful transmission is not necessary to the determination of the crime, as long as the individual carried out one of the acts of stealing, gathering or procuring state secrets for individuals or organizations overseas.

Especially Serious Circumstances

Crimes of endangering state security, including that in Article 111 of the Criminal Law, are a particular subset of offenses eligible for the death penalty, as laid out in Article 113 of the Criminal Law.[90] These include the serious crimes of subversion, defecting to the enemy, sabotage, and espionage. Where *"especially serious harm"* is caused to the state as a result of the crime, the death penalty can be imposed.[91]

Some direction towards defining "especially serious circumstances" is given by the Supreme People's Court in its Interpretation of Certain Issues, which considers: the nature of the secrets involved; the number of incidents; and the consequences of their disclosure.

- Any disclosure of "top secret" level secrets or of three "highly secret" state secrets to anyone outside the country constitutes "especially serious circumstances" and can be punishable by imprisonment of ten years to life, plus confiscation of property.

- The disclosure of state secrets or "intelligence" to anyone outside the country is considered to be a crime committed under serious circumstances if "especially serious harm" to state security or interests has been caused.[92]

- Where the harm caused to the state and the people is considered to be "especially serious," and where the circumstances of the crime are deemed be "especially reprehensible," a death penalty can be imposed.[93]

- Because the provision separates the disclosing of information from harm that results, it is clear that the "especially serious consequences" provision can be invoked regardless of finding objective harm.[94]

4. DEROGATIONS FROM PROCEDURAL PROTECTIONS

While the Criminal Law and the State Security Law elaborate on what constitutes a crime in relationship to the State Secrets Law, the Criminal Procedure Law (CPL) includes provisions that allow for derogations from procedural protections in cases involving state secrets. The CPL, promulgated in 1997, provides for greater procedural protections including right to counsel and limits on detention,[95] but there are at least three procedural derogations for cases where state secrets are involved: limits on defendants' access to evidence, the right to counsel, and an open trial.

Evidence involving state secrets shall be kept confidential,[96] and where cases involve state secrets, a suspect must obtain approval from the investigative organ before appointing a lawyer, and before the lawyer can meet with the criminal suspect he must also obtain approval from the investigative organ.[97] Finally, cases involving state secrets are not heard in public.[98] Cases "involving state secrets" have been officially defined as those where case *details* or the *nature* of the case involve state secrets.[99] As such, cases in which defendants are charged with state secrets crimes would certainly fall into the category of cases "involving state secrets," but so do cases where the Procuratorate or others invoke state secrets matters in the evidence.

B.

Impact of the System on Human Rights

The state secrets framework is broad in both implementing structure (multiple bodies at all levels of government have responsibilities and authority on state secrets) and substance (large categories of information are classified or can be classified). The PRC falls far below the international standard on the protection of the right to freedom of expression and information due to the comprehensive amount of information that can be classified, the subjective and arbitrary means by which information is classified, and the serious criminalization of disclosing that information.

Furthermore, where the international legal framework places a burden on the state to show that there is a legitimate need to restrict information,[100] the emphasis in Chinese domestic law places the burden on the individual to protect classified information even if it has not been already designated as such through the state secrets bureaus. While the delineated purposes enumerated in Article 1 of the State Secrets Law tie in somewhat with legitimate restrictions of the right to freedom of expression under the ICCPR, the provision that state secrets include "other matters that are classified as state secrets" by the NAPSS[101] allows numerous bodies at all levels of government the ability to classify any information they deem necessary as state secrets.

The impact of this legal and enforcement framework suggests that not only are individuals impacted by the serious criminal sanctions levied for "disclosing state secrets," but the public interest is undermined where there is so little transparency and freedom of expression is violated. The all-encompassing, circular, and vague classification of information and criminalization of disclosure and possession of that information—with or without knowledge of doing so—creates a chilling effect on the culture of human rights, in particular on three specific areas critical to protection for human rights: the rule of law, transparency and accountable governance, and participation of civil society.

The all-encompassing, circular, and vague classification of information and criminalization of disclosure and possession of that information—with or without knowledge of doing so—creates a chilling effect on the culture of human rights.

1. IMPACT ON THE RULE OF LAW

The state secrets system enables both abusive discretionary prosecutions and restrictions on procedural protections, and undermines even further the independence, fairness, and predictability of the legal system. The problem of lack of predictability results not only from subjectivity in the process and the role of CPC intervention, but also from the possibility of information being classified after public dissemination, the lack of a clear process by which the fact of classification is disseminated, and the lack of a coherent structure of responsibility over classification.

The classification of information that relies on subjective determinations of perceived (not actual) harm is arbitrary and open to abuse. A great deal of uncertainty exists as to the status of information, which runs counter to the need for any rule of law to be predictable. As a result, the development of a rule of law in China—where the implementation of predictable and transparent rules is enforced by independent and impartial institutions—is undermined. However, the key obstacle to a rule of law is the subjection of law, courts, and the legal profession to one-party rule.

An independent judiciary is indispensable to the rule of law, but where institutions and processes remain controlled by one central governing institution, it is vulnerable to abuse. The CPC, which continues to block the judiciary from developing a truly independent role, is able to wield its influence on the judiciary in a number of ways, including in the nomination of judges and prosecutors. Intervention in the judiciary's daily work is most directly exercised by the CPC through political-legal committees (政法委员会), which are responsible for implementing Party policy in legal affairs. Routine cooperation between the police, prosecutors and judges creates obstacles for a fair trial for individuals, particularly in sensitive cases, such as state secrets cases.[102]

> **The state secrets system enables both abusive discretionary prosecutions and restrictions on procedural protections, and undermines even further the independence, fairness, and predictability of the legal system.**

Not only are citizens not able to predict what conduct is proscribed under the State Secrets Law, but they also have no means of knowing which law they have violated until they are prosecuted, and even then may not be notified of charges in a timely way. **Zheng Enchong's case** demonstrates that there is no clear perimeter to the State Secrets Law and that Chinese citizens are not fairly advised as to what information is proscribed from dissemination. Thus, any information, regardless of how it is obtained, can place an individual at risk of criminal prosecution. The appellate ruling upholding Zheng's conviction demonstrates that "public" exposure of information, and indeed many other intuitive barriers to secrecy, such as prior publication, widespread dissemination, or sheer remoteness to state security concerns, has little relevance to the status of information as a government secret.

CASE STORY

Shi Tao

Shi Tao (师涛) was a freelance writer, journalist, and head of the news division at the daily *Dangdai Shangbao* (Contemporary Business News) in Changsha, Hunan Province. He had also written numerous essays for overseas Internet forums, including one entitled "The Most Disgusting Day," in which he criticized the Chinese government for the March 28 detention of Ding Zilin, a Tiananmen Mothers activist whose son was killed during the 1989 democracy movement.

On April 20, 2004, Shi attended a *Dangdai Shangbao* staff meeting in which the contents of a CPC Central Propaganda Bureau document about security concerns and preparation for the upcoming 15th anniversary of the June 4th crackdown were discussed. That evening, Shi used his personal Yahoo! e-mail account to send his notes about this meeting to the New York-based Web site, Democracy Forum. As a result, he was detained on November 24, 2004 and was tried for "illegally providing state secrets overseas" under Article 111 of the Criminal Law on April 27, 2005. Because the document was certified a "top secret" state secret, he was sentenced to ten years' imprisonment.

In his eloquent appeal, Shi wrote: "We give up our life and property in order for the government to 'maintain secrecy,' ordinary citizens become targets of punishment, the news media is surgically operated on, and the people's 'right to know' is treated like a joke. And the government just goes on in its own way, making mistake after mistake. This is the greatest hidden danger of China's stability work." His appeal for a re-examination of the case was denied.

In his brief for the appeal that he lost, Shi Tao described the harassment that can be leveled at journalists who circumvent the system of information control. "[The government has] expended vast amounts of manpower, materials and financial resources on the long process of placing me under control and surveillance, tailing me, tapping my phone, and finally capturing me and throwing me into prison . . . it's impossible for [my family and friends] to comprehend the tremendous psychological pressure that I've been under. Although being in prison is surely terrible, losing one's sense of privacy and safety is even more terrifying."

Information on the above case is taken from HRIC's human rights database. See also "Case Highlight: Shi Tao and Yahoo!" on HRIC's website.

Shi Tao

Examples of how individuals' rights are violated are the cases of **Rebiya Kadeer, Zhang Shanguang** and **Zheng Enchong,** who were all found guilty of violating state secrets provisions with information that was arguably already in the public domain and widely circulated. **Tohti Tunyaz, Song Yongyi** and **Xu Zerong** were prosecuted under state secrets charges because of historical information that, even if classified, had passed the 30-year time limit and should have been declassified based on the Regulation on Time Limits for Classified State Secrets.[103]

In all of these cases, the "sensitive nature" of the information—which ranged from labor protests and ethnic minority policies to the Cultural Revolution and other historical government policies—seems less based on the actual harm that the public dissemination of the information could or did cause than it does on a desire of the authorities to prevent or further limit this dissemination to keep it hidden. This arbitrary information classification has a systemic impact, including a chilling effect on academic research, policy debate and human rights defense, by dissuading individuals from participating in any of these activities.

Stripping Procedural Protections

When state secrets are implicated in criminal prosecutions, the Criminal Procedure Law and related regulations contain numerous provisions to limit suspects' and defendants' rights, impacting some of the most fundamental individual rights, as well as the foundation for building a rule of law.

It is common practice in China to deny the right to counsel to individuals charged not only with state secrets offenses, but all crimes of endangering state security, including subversion. When disputes arise, they are overwhelmingly resolved in favor of police discretion to deny access to legal counsel. For example, despite over four months of repeated requests, Liaoyang labor activist **Yao Fuxin** (姚福信) was only allowed to meet with his lawyer Mo Shaoping five days before his trial. Although Mo had been requesting a meeting with Yao since July 2002, he was told by the Liaoyang Public Security Bureau that it had the right to deny Yao meetings with his lawyer because the case "involved state secrets."[104] Yao was ultimately convicted on May 9, 2003 of subversion, another state security crime, as well as illegal assembly and demonstration.

CASE STORY

Zheng Enchong

Zheng Enchong (郑恩宠) is a lawyer who had for years represented Shanghai residents who had been displaced as a result of urban redevelopment. While working for the Shanghai Min Jian Law Firm, where he practiced property law, Zheng publicly advocated for an amendment to China's Constitution to clarify ownership rights relating to land and residential property. Even after authorities revoked his license to practice law in July 2001, he continued to assist displaced residents in disputes with real estate developers about forced clearance and compensation. In 2003, Zheng advised six families in a lawsuit against the Shanghai Jing'an District Property Development Bureau, claiming that it was colluding with wealthy property developer Zhou Zhengyi in a major redevelopment project. This case attracted significant media coverage because of Zhou's close relationship with senior officials in the central government.

In one instance, Zheng faxed his personal account of police action against a worker demonstration at a Shanghai food plant and a public copy of a news article covering protests by a group of displaced residents to Human Rights in China (HRIC) in New York. He was detained and arrested as a result of this action. After a closed trial, the Shanghai State Secrets Bureau decided that both documents had contained state secrets and Zheng was convicted of "illegally providing state secrets outside of the country." However, prior to the faxing, both documents had already been circulated through the public domain and had never been marked as "state secrets." Despite having acknowledged that the circumstances of his crime were "relatively minor," the court sentenced Zheng to three years' imprisonment and additionally, one year's deprivation of political rights, in October 2003.

Although there have been numerous appeals to the central government on his behalf, including those launched by international human rights organizations, Zheng's appeals were denied at a closed hearing in December 2003. According to information received by Human Rights in China, Zheng was subject to physical abuse at Tilanqiao Prison, had limited and monitored contact with his family there, and had no access to legal counsel. He was released from prison on June 5, 2006 after serving the three-year sentence but was again detained briefly on July 12, 2006 on suspicion of "impeding officials of state organs in the execution of their duties . . . during a period of deprivation of political rights." Zheng continues to face excessive limitations on his movements and ability to seek employment.

Information on the above case is taken from HRIC's human rights database and website.

Zheng Enchong

Investigation stage: In conducting criminal investigations relating to state secrets, police are afforded an extraordinary amount of discretion not only in handling specific state secrets offenses, but also in all cases where state secrets are involved. Cases "involving state secrets" have been officially defined as those where case *details* or the *nature* of the case involve state secrets.[105] To begin with, authorities can detain anyone suspected of intentionally or negligently divulging state secrets related to state security for 15 days prior to initiating a criminal investigation.[106]

Despite cautionary admonitions to the contrary, police routinely stretch the meaning of "involving state secrets" into a convenient pretext to deny or compromise the defendants' lawful right to obtain legal advice.[107] While access to evidence in cases where the defendant is charged with state secrets will be restricted, evidence in other cases may also be restricted under this provision, because there is nothing to suggest that only state secrets crimes fall under the term "involving state secrets."

The Ministry of Public Security has also declared that information concerning current investigations (including investigation plans, methods applied, reconnaissance, pre-trial and technical confirmation work) warrant protection as secret matters from the "secret" up to "top secret" level.[108] Suspects are also frequently denied approval of the legal representation they and their families choose, or the lawyers are then denied the ability to meet with the suspect during detention.

Trial stage: The Criminal Procedure Law denies suspects open trials in cases involving state secrets, a rule that is applied extensively beyond state secrets prosecutions themselves. In many cases, individuals charged with state security crimes, most commonly incitement to subversion, were also denied an open trial.[109] The closed trial mandated by the state secrets system undermines the right of an individual to a fair trial by shielding the process and by denying family members, defense witnesses, and sometimes even defense lawyers, from attending the proceedings.

Where a case involves state secrets, the right to counsel at trial is also negatively impacted in several ways. The role of defense lawyers is made difficult by official practice that continues to limit access to clients in detention and to restrict lawyers' ability to review evidence and cross-examine witnesses who fail to appear in court. Lawyers are also frequently not allowed to attend trials, and suspects who complain about the representation provided by court-appointed lawyers are usually rebuffed by the courts.

> Police are afforded an extraordinary amount of discretion not only in handling specific state secrets offenses, but also in all cases where state secrets are involved.

CASE STORY

Chen Guangcheng

Chen Guangcheng (陈光诚), born in 1971 and blind since childhood, is a self-taught lawyer and activist in Shandong Province who has fought for multiple rural causes, the most famous of which was a class-action lawsuit he filed against the city of Linyi over an official policy of forced abortions and sterilizations.

A few days after he met with Beijing lawyers and journalists in September 2005, Chen was abducted by Shandong authorities and returned to Linyi, where he was placed under house arrest. Despite acknowledgements in official media the same month that family planning abuses in Linyi had taken place and were being investigated, Chen was beaten by local officials when he attempted to meet with visiting lawyers in October 2005. Local authorities told the lawyers, who were also attacked by unidentified assailants, that Chen's case now involved state secrets.

Chen was taken into custody in March 2006, and for three months his status and whereabouts were not disclosed and his lawyers had no access to him. In June, Chen was charged with "damaging public property and gathering people to block traffic" and was sentenced to four years and three months' imprisonment in August 2006. Chen lodged an appeal of the conviction. In October 31, 2006, the court overturned the verdict and ordered a new trial by the county court in Yinan in Shandong Province. On December 1, 2006, the court of the first instance upheld the original verdict. Another appeal was rejected on January 12, 2007, and reports continue to surface of Chen's lawyers being harassed and hindered in their work.

Information on the above case is taken from HRIC's human rights database and website.

Chen Guangcheng

Intimidation of and Attacks on Defense Lawyers

The impact of the state secrets system on the role of lawyers is compounded by increasing threats and intimidations made against lawyers, often with the complicity of the government during all stages of the process, as well as provisions in the law that target lawyers specifically. Article 306 of the Criminal Law allows prosecutors to charge lawyers with "fabricating evidence" and "perjury" as they carry out their client's defense.[110] Reports are also increasing of lawyers who were themselves detained just before trials so that they were unable to represent their clients in court. All of these hindrances are only exacerbated when state secrets are involved. In the case of **Chen Guangcheng** (see box), his legal team was variously detained under suspicion of theft or beaten up by thugs just days before Chen's trial.

In another example of problems facing lawyers, although her conviction was eventually overturned on appeal, attorney **Yu Ping** was originally found guilty of intentionally disclosing state secrets simply for disclosing court documents to her client's family.[111] Taken as a whole, the state secrets system and the related provisions in the Criminal Procedure Law undermine individual human rights, as well as the rule of law.

Lack of Independent Review

The inability of defendants to appeal state secrets classification decisions exacerbates the procedural deficits created by the system. In state secrets prosecutions, state secrets bureaus are responsible for appraising the status and classification level of information.[112] They are not required to articulate why information is classified as a state secret, or to establish that information was protected prior to the initiation of prosecution, which violates international standards on access to information. Where courts are required to examine and apply the state secrets framework in criminal prosecutions, they are not authorized to question the classification of information. Because courts do not have the authority to review the classification which shapes the whole process, the courts' role is quite limited. In the absence of an appeals process, courts accept classifications on their face value and use them as the basis for conviction. In documented state secrets cases, "state secrets" cover any information that any government entity wants to, or has been asked to, classify as a "state secret."

> Because courts do not have the authority to review the classification which shapes the whole process, the courts' role is quite limited.

2. LACK OF TRANSPARENCY AND ACCOUNTABILITY

China is required by international obligations, including under the UN Convention Against Corruption, to take measures to enhance transparency and accountability in public administration.[113] These measures include ensuring that the public has effective access to information and "respecting, promoting and protecting the freedom to seek, receive, publish, and disseminate information" concerning corruption.[114]

The information classified in the regulations of various ministries, including the Ministry of Public Security, the Supreme People's Court and the Ministry of Justice, provides an examination of the type and content of information the political elite considers important and potentially harmful to the continued stability of its rule. The very existence of these regulations casts doubts on the transparency of information flow in China and the accuracy of information that is released to the public.

The great elasticity of state secrets protections has contributed to a widespread culture of secrecy in the official handling and dissemination of information. The government has control over 80% of relevant (有用) information in society.[115] This bottleneck of information is exacerbated by the lack of any independent supervisory mechanisms or precise classification standards.

Good governance, supported by the respect for human rights, enables governments to frame policies that will enact change, but it cannot be achieved in a society where there is no transparency or accountability. Good governance is "necessary for sustainable social and economic development in which government, businesses and civil society work together to address challenges."[116] Where states face challenges in development and in the implementation and respect for human rights, good governance is necessary to effectively address those challenges and frame solutions.[117] To the CPC, however, good governance has long rested on the principle of maintaining social stability and keeping a tight rein on information dissemination—including classifying critical information such as statistics related to health, the judicial system and the environment—in order to ensure political control.

AIDS activist Wan Yanhai spent a month in custody on state secrets charges for making public a government report on the spread of AIDS in Henan Province and posting it on the Web on August 17, 2002.

Prior to 2003, Chinese officials denied that **avian flu** was present in China. A monitoring and information dissemination system on the disease was only created in early 2004. A letter to the *New England Journal of Medicine* by eight Chinese researchers revealed in June 2006 that a 24-year-old Beijing man classified as having died of SARS in November 2003 in fact died of H5N1 avian influenza, two years before the mainland reported any human bird flu infections. In 2006, the WHO was still criticizing the PRC for providing samples too slowly, and attempts to cover up the spread of the disease continued with a farmer in Shandong reporting that officials told him not to talk about a recent cull of 8,000 chickens because of state secret concerns.

The Ministry of Health was criticized for withholding information of a **bacterial meningitis outbreak** until the epidemic had affected 24 provinces, with 546 reported cases and a death toll of 16. Cases of meningitis had been reported since November 2004; however, not until the end of January 2005 did the Ministry of Health issue an emergency notice calling on the whole country to step up preventive measures against the disease.

In July 2005, villagers in **Taishi Village** in Guangdong Province pressed for the removal of their village chief, who was charged with embezzling public funds. The villagers blocked the village office where the evidence in account books was kept, but officials seized the account books during a confrontation. Thugs suspected of having connections with the authorities were hired to guard the entrances to the village and foreign journalists and grassroots activists who tried to enter the village were beaten up. Villagers who contacted activists and reporters continued to be harassed in 2006, and a reporter from the *South China Morning Post* was detained for 8 hours and strip-searched, allegedly for not carrying an identification document, when she tried to report on the one-year anniversary of the Taishi incident.

In January 2006, villagers were negotiating with the Sanjiao Township government for reasonable compensation after farmland was confiscated in order to build a highway and a factory. The protest turned violent on January 14, 2006, when several thousand policemen indiscriminately attacked between 10,000 and 20,000 people. Villagers said that a **15-year-old schoolgirl was beaten to death**; her family later allegedly received 130,000 *yuan* from the local government to say that their daughter had died after a heart attack. The government news service, Xinhua, reported that no one had died in the protest.

INFORMATION COVER-UPS

This is a brief selection of incidents of official cover-ups. For a more extensive list, see Appendices III: Incidents of Official Cover-Ups, page 236.

Cover-ups

The numerous incidences of enforced media silences and cover-ups that have been documented[118] have a direct, fundamental impact on the lives of people in China, and increasingly, globally.[119] Some—including disease outbreaks, environmental accidents and industrial accidents—are tied explicitly to state secrets. Others may not have been directly driven by specific state secrets regulations, but all are representative of government information control, of which state secrets plays an integral part.

To maintain control over the media, specific regulations on state secrets in the work of the media have been passed, such as the 1992 Regulation on the Protection of State Secrets in News Publishing.[120] However, recent regulations released in 2006 governing foreign media, including regulations created specifically for the 2008 Olympics, seemingly contradict both each other and the earlier regulations. In order to address growing international pressure in the lead-up to the Olympic Games, the 2006 regulations purportedly relax requirements for journalists working in China.[121] However, three problems remain: the media regulations still contain wording that is ambiguous; these regulations remain under the overall umbrella of the state secrets system, which is dedicated to information control; and despite reported attempts to relax controls through national regulations, local authorities still operate independently, as witnessed by continuing harassment of and violence directed at Chinese journalists investigating stories at local levels.[122]

Pollution accidents: The toxic spill in the Songhua River in November 2005 was only one of many cover-ups of pollution accidents, including cadmium pollution in the North and Xiang rivers, which prompted the central government to issue guidelines for the prompt reporting of such incidents in February 2006.[123] Ultimately, this new reporting structure and the declassification of death tolls from natural disasters are surgical moves. The NAPSS declined to define "natural disasters" and warned that only government agencies would be able to release (and collect) these statistics—signaling that it was not ready to release its hold on information. And how these guidelines will coordinate with the proposed new "Draft Law on Emergency Response" now working its way through a reviewing process remains unclear. But the limited sections of the draft that have been publicly released to date offer more restrictions on news reporting, not less.[124] The legislation is reportedly to be issued and made public in 2007.[125]

Public health outbreaks: Many factors have contributed to the PRC's mishandling of the SARS outbreak in China, but the culture of secrecy was a defining factor in the spectacular failure of transparency and accountability that many argue was partially responsible for the spread of the epidemic globally.[126] The classification of public health work was likely unclear both externally and within China, despite the report that Chinese officials told the United Nations Development Programme (UNDP) that the 1996 Regulation on State Secrets and on the Specific Scope of Each Level of Secrets in Public Health Work—which classified information related to infectious diseases—had been invalidated in 2001. Questions concerning the classification of the SARS information and the slow reporting of information between local and national bureaucracies arguably slowed the government's response considerably.[127]

The Chinese government claimed that in light of the SARS implosion in 2003, the longstanding culture of secrecy promoted in the handling of matters of public health—emergency or otherwise—had been replaced by greater transparency and accountability. The impact of the system in that case, however, is clear: the failure to control the disease, the number of deaths, and the health-related consequences for millions inside and outside China.

In addition, whereas the government states that it is heralding in a system that is transparent, the prosecution of journalists who exposed the SARS cover-up and the evolving Chinese response to the avian flu continue to reflect examples of poor or questionable governance at both national and local levels. In these failures of governance, secrecy continues to be relied upon as a method of maintaining social order and control, to the detriment of the public. Like SARS, the lack of information on the transmission routes of a disease, and the cover-up of official complicity in the sale of HIV-contaminated blood, had serious human rights impacts on the 69,000 people infected by the blood transfusions and donations.[128] The AIDs pandemic also raises the pervasive problem of official corruption and malfeasance.

CASE STORY

Liu Fenggang

Xu Yonghai

Zhang Shengqi

Protestant house church leaders **Liu Fenggang** (刘凤钢), **Xu Yonghai** (徐永海) and **Zhang Shengqi** (张胜棋) were initially detained on state secrets charges between October and November 2003. They were charged under Article 111 of the Criminal Law with "providing state secrets to foreign organizations," and tried in secret on March 16, 2004 by the Hangzhou Intermediate People's Court in Zhejiang Province.

Liu Fenggang, a Beijing-based Christian, was accused of carrying out research for a report that exposed Chinese government repression of the clandestine Catholic Church. Xu Yonghai, a former psychiatric doctor at Beijing Pingan Hospital, was tried for having printed the report, and Zhang Shengqi, a computer firm employee, for undertaking to post it on the Internet and to send it electronically to organizations abroad. However, their lawyer pointed out that the State Secrets Bureau certificate produced as evidence by the procuratorate had not been signed, and therefore was invalid.

As a result, the court placed Liu and Xu under "residential surveillance" starting on May 14, but no verdict was given until August 6, 2004. The court took no account of the invalid State Secrets Bureau certificate, and sentenced Liu to three years in prison and Xu to two years, as well as imposing a one-year prison sentence on Zhang Shengqi. In addition, the court did not include the period Xu and Liu had spent under residential surveillance as time served, with the result that the period from May 14 until August 6 was effectively added to their sentences.

Zhang Shengqi and Xu Yonghai were released on February 7, 2005 and January 29, 2006, respectively.[129] Despite the release, Xu's freedom continued to be restricted by Chinese security agents. Liu Fenggang was released in February 2007.

Unless otherwise indicated, information on the above case is taken from HRIC's human rights database and website.

Liu Fenggang

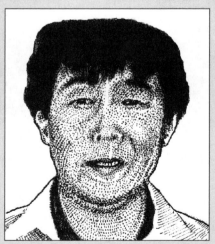
Xu Yonghai

Zhang Shengqi

Corruption and Official Malfeasance

State secrets regulations provide a pretext for information cover-ups, including information that deals with official corruption and that may embarrass officials if made public. More than anything, state secrets regulations provide a lawful pretext for suppressing the dissemination of information that would benefit citizens in their mobilization against corruption, official malfeasance, and infringement of their legitimate rights. In the context of a legal system that currently offers little meaningful protection of individual rights, the open flow of information is critical.

In place of accountability to the general public, authorities often choose to protect the activities of others in government, generating "perverse incentives" for government officials to distort information in order to portray themselves favorably and preserve their position in power. This includes a built-in disincentive to report official malfeasance. This system of misguided and harmful incentives is in conflict with China's own international obligations on transparency and good governance, including obligations under China's WTO accession and the UN Convention Against Corruption.

This system of impunity among officials also has a detrimental impact on the ability of central government officials to implement greater transparency and to actually respond to environmental and public health concerns as they arise, as well as conduct effective emergency management. Rural farmers in Henan Province, who depended on donating blood to secure income but were not informed of the risks of HIV infection, provide one example. Because officials responsible for the cover-up were not punished but actually promoted, years later, media attempting to access some of the hardest-hit villages were closely monitored and the farmers themselves were denied many of the benefits of treatment, support, and compensation despite (and perhaps because of) international scrutiny.[130]

> This system of misguided and harmful incentives is in conflict with China's own international obligations on transparency and good governance.

The state secrets framework supports that system of official impunity and cover-up of information, in that it provides catch-all clauses under which information can be classified. The complex system of classification and de-classification and the participation of multiple actors at multiple levels of government also impacts transparency, in that there is no clarity on whether specific information is classified or has been declassified. The organizational imperative is therefore to keep information secret—with serious impacts where dissemination or withholding of that information affects the interest of the public.

Detention, Torture, and the Death Penalty

Detention facilities: In a regulation jointly issued by the Ministry of Justice (MOJ) and the NAPSS, virtually all information relating to the administration of prisons, juvenile detention centers, and systems of administrative punishment such as reeducation through labor (RTL) is classified as "top secret" or "highly secret."[131] This includes the rules, plans, methods, crackdown countermeasures and manpower allocation in penal institutions.[132] Basic statistics on the number of people in detention are "secrets," while "undisclosed" statistics on numbers of people arrested and processed through the various forms of sentencing are classified as "work secrets" that cannot be disclosed without authorization.[133]

New regulations issued by the MOJ on February 14, 2006 prohibit beating or subjecting inmates in prison or RTL to corporal punishment and other abuses. Prison and RTL police who engage in these prohibited behaviors will be subject to punishment up to dismissal or investigated for criminal responsibility. However, these regulations lack mechanisms for victims to enforce the prohibition against police abusers.[134]

Provisions that classify as secret information on the management of RTL centers and other sites used for administrative detention are of great cause for concern, as they heap greater secrecy protection on a system already notorious for its lack of transparency and accountability. Information about this behemoth administrative system that incarcerates an estimated 300,000 people in around 300 camps is classified alongside that of prisons and detention areas. However, while prisons incarcerate people who have been convicted through a formal criminal process, international monitoring efforts have found uniformly that in an overwhelming majority of cases, the RTL system provides no formal procedures or protections for individuals before they can be sentenced and imprisoned for up to three years, in violation of both the ICCPR and Universal Declaration of Human Rights (UDHR).[135]

Torture in prisons and detention facilities: As confirmed by the Special Rapporteur's report on torture on his mission to China, **torture remains endemic and a serious problem.**[136] However, information about the use of torture in PRC detention facilities and its use to extract confessions is considered classified; this lack of transparency contributes to the violation of the fundamental right to be free from torture, which is a non-derrogable right and is binding on all states.[137] As a signatory to the ICCPR and a party to the UN Convention Against Torture (CAT), torture is prohibited in Chinese written law: the use of torture or coercive methods to gather evidence is strictly forbidden, and the Criminal Law makes it a crime for certain state actors, such as judicial officers and police officers, to abuse or torture individuals detained under their supervision.[138] A significant gap between the Chinese law and the international standard can be seen, however, as evidence procured through torture, coercion, intimidation, entrapment or deceptive practice can be introduced as long as it does not form the *basis* for conviction.[139] Further, no law or regulation absolutely excludes evidence obtained through torture from making its way through Chinese courts, a common practice that should raise serious questions in light of an alarmingly high nationwide conviction rate of nearly 98 percent.[140]

Despite the letter of the law, torture remains a systemic problem in the PRC criminal system. Chinese academics and several government officials have admitted that torture still persists, including Wang Zhenchuan, Deputy Procurator-General of the Supreme People's Procuratorate, who admitted as recently as November 19, 2006 that "nearly every wrongful verdict in recent years" involved illegal interrogation. Wang went on to call for protecting suspects' rights by eliminating illegal interrogation by atrocious torture.[141]

However, victims of official misconduct in criminal investigations have no means of pursuing allegations of torture and other abuse, since much of the work and information in criminal investigations remain state secrets.[142] In addition, the classified status of information about the use of torture to extract confessions leaves victims no recourse for seeking redress without inviting additional risk of criminal sanctions.[143] In the case of Nie Shubin, for example, media coverage brought the news to light that he had been sentenced to death and executed based on a confession obtained through torture. Yet his family, in seeking to overturn his conviction in a court of appeal, was denied access to the original case documents.[144]

CASE STORY

Zhao Yan

Prior to joining the *New York Times* as a researcher in Beijing, **Zhao Yan** (赵岩) was a journalist who wrote extensively about rural issues and government corruption and advocated for farmers' rights.

In September 2004, Zhao was detained in connection with a *New York Times* article which predicted the resignation of Jiang Zemin from his last major post as head of the military. He was held in detention for over 19 months without trial and was arrested on suspicion of leaking state secrets to the newspaper. The case against Zhao was thought to rely almost entirely on a memo that he wrote in July 2004 speculating a "possible dispute between Jiang and his successor, President Hu Jintao, over promotions for two top army generals."

On August 25, 2006, Zhao was unexpectedly cleared of the state secrets charge held against him and he was spared what would have been a minimum of ten years' imprisonment for disclosing information that was considered "top secret." The Beijing court, instead, sentenced him to three years in prison on an unrelated charge of fraud. Zhao's release is scheduled for September 2007 because the two years he has already served in detention will count against his term. The Beijing Higher People's Court rejected Zhao's appeal on December 1, 2006.

Information on the above case is taken from HRIC's human rights database and website.

Zhao Yan

In his first mission to the PRC in 2005, the UN Special Rapporteur on Torture reported that physical and mental coercion is widely used in the PRC to extract confessions and other evidence, and is more prevalent during the early states of criminal investigations.[145] Foreign Ministry spokesman Qin Gang said at the time that "China cannot accept the allegation that torture is widespread in China still," and added that China had made "effective efforts" in outlawing torture.[146] Unfortunately, the official reaction to the Special Rapporteur's report was not constructive—this indefensible position in the face of facts and official recognition of the problem undermines the PRC's credibility by not fully admitting its extent and pervasiveness. As an obstacle to obtaining information that is necessary to analyze both the problem and possible solutions, the state secrets system contributes to the ongoing persistence of torture.

Death penalty: Statistics on capital punishment in China are a closely guarded secret;[147] with the most diligent outside monitoring efforts producing only piecemeal figures that confirm a fraction of what is estimated to be the number of people executed annually.[148] State secrets laws include no less than eight separate provisions for classifying death penalty-related information, and these provisions maximize government control over the nature and tenor of facts and statistics that are actually released.[149] The broadest classification places figures on the ratification and execution of death sentences nationwide at the top-secret level, while other figures cover the number of new prisoner executions, intermediate courts' ratification of death sentences, military statistics, and information on the use of executed criminals' corpses and organs.[150]

In March 2004, Luo Gan, a member of the Standing Committee of the Political Bureau of the CPC Central Committee and Secretary of the Committee of Political and Legislative Affairs, ordered fewer executions whenever possible, a policy directive that contradicts official statements that the use of the death penalty had already declined dramatically since the revision of the Criminal Law in 1997.[151] The number of 1,770 *known* executions carried out in the PRC in 2005 accounted for more than 80% of the 2,148 executions worldwide that year.[152]

As an obstacle to obtaining information that is necessary to analyze both the problem and possible solutions, the state secrets system contributes to the ongoing persistence of torture.

CASE STORY

Li Changqing

Huang Jingao

In January 2006, journalist **Li Changqing** (李长青) was sentenced to three years' imprisonment for two acts, neither of which involves information that would legitimately be considered secret. According to his lawyer, Li, who was the deputy news director of the *Fuzhou Daily,* was formally arrested on suspicion of "incitement to subvert state power" but ultimately tried for "fabricating and spreading false and alarmist/terrorist information" under Article 291 of the Criminal Law.[153] The cited basis for this charge was Li's unauthorized report of an outbreak of dengue fever that infected more than 100 people in Fujian in 2004.[154] Though the provincial government acknowledged the outbreak soon after Li's report (which he claims he did not write but only contributed to) appeared on the overseas Web site Boxun, Li was convicted in January 2005. His appeal was rejected and the sentence was upheld in March 2006.

His arrest, however, was based on his public support and assistance of whistleblower **Huang Jingao** (黄金高), the former Party Secretary of Lianjiang County in Fujian. Huang's open letter from August 11, 2004, posted on the *People's Daily* Web site, detailed being obstructed in his attempts to report corrupt colleagues who confiscated land from farmers and sold it at below-market prices to real estate developers in exchange for bribes.[155] Huang's whistle-blowing act generated widespread public support in a virtual instant, but the campaign of retaliation against him took a year to complete: his letter was taken down a few days later, he was dismissed from his post, put under surveillance, taken into custody, smeared in the official press, and finally sentenced to life imprisonment on November 10, 2004 on 50 counts of corruption for accepting $715,000 in bribes. Li Changqing was not spared in this retaliation campaign: he was taken into custody a few months after Huang. Both Li and his lawyer, Mo Shaoping, insisted that he was being punished for his support of Huang and his allegations.[156] Essentially, Li Changqing was both a whistle-blower and a supporter of one, and his acts of exposure, on topics of vital interest to the public, were well within the ambit of his professional duties as a journalist.

Li Changqing

Huang Jingao

While there is an international move towards a moratorium on the application of the death penalty,[157] its application is not prohibited under international law but is considered an "extreme exception"[158] to the right to life. This exception can only be applied where the defendant has had a fair trial. This kind of fair trial is unlikely where state secrets provisions have been invoked if the defendant has limited access to his lawyer, the evidence and the outside world. Transparency and access to information are "fundamental due process safeguards that prevent the arbitrary deprivation of life."[159] Accordingly, the impact of the state secrets system is that it undermines fair and just procedures, denies human dignity and prevents any informed public debate about capital punishment.[160]

Propping up an authoritarian one-party system, the state secrets system denies the very transparency and accountability necessary for good governance. While the authorities have put significant emphasis on ending corruption and have made several, very visible, crackdowns on officials charged with corruption, broader support for an agenda promoting good governance—and transparency—is absent. In its efforts to maintain control, the PRC government classifies the very information that would not only allow more fair and independent analysis of policy-making decisions, but would assist in creating solutions to address the problems challenging the government, including corruption. Without transparency, secrecy, corruption and impunity flourish.

The impact of the state secrets system is that it undermines fair and just procedures, denies human dignity and prevents any informed public debate about capital punishment.

3. UNDERMINING INDEPENDENT CIVIL SOCIETY

The open dissemination and publication of information is a critical tool for lawyers, journalists, human rights defenders and other civil society actors for spreading awareness, educating the public and advocating for issues that affect them. The impact of the state secrets system in China is to undercut that openness and participation and discourage the transfer of, or access to, information and ideas. Many of these individuals have been detained and harassed by authorities because they raise issues that are critical of the government. Some, like Shi Tao and Zheng Enchong, are themselves charged with crimes of leaking state secrets. Their cases and others are examples of how the state secrets law is used to harass and imprison individuals who are engaged in lawful activities, either through self-expression or by bringing attention to serious social problems. The targeting of these individuals with crimes of disclosing state secrets—and other crimes, from subversion to blackmail and corruption—not only violates their individual human rights to expression, but also China's obligations to promote access to information and transparency under international law.

As soon as civil society responses are deemed threatening to the Party, as in the activities of human rights defenders, for example, this space is constricted through intimidation, detentions, and crackdowns on individual activists and grassroots organizations.

Various state secrets regulations also indicate which social groups the Chinese authorities are concerned about, and correspondingly, to what extent they are willing to utilize state secrets protection to suppress them. The founding of independent political groups, illegal religious activities, illegal publications and the activities of illegal organizations are at the heart of official preoccupation with potential dissent. These groups include "ethnic separatist organizations" (民族分裂组织), "hostile religious forces" (宗教敌势力), "reactionary secret societies" (反动会道门), and "foreign hostile organizations or social groups" (境外敌组织或社团).[161] Although these organizations are not identified by name in any regulations, the framework as it is laid out would suggest that the names or identities of these groups are also a state secret,[162] though in criminal prosecutions, the State Security Bureau confirms the status of those organizations and groups.[163] Under the MPS Regulation, information about campaigns against certain politically sensitive groups is classified as "top secret."[164]

Despite the expanding social roles of, and indeed expectations placed on, non-state actors in Chinese public and private life, the delineated space for that role is small and constrained. Even when space appears to be expanding in certain non-sensitive areas, such as health, the environment, or women's rights, as soon as civil society responses are deemed threatening to one-party rule—as in the activities of human rights defenders, for example—this space is constricted through intimidation, detentions and crackdowns on individual activists and grassroots organizations.[165]

Whistleblowers: By attempting to make information public, whistleblowers often run up against not only policies designed to deny this information, but also officials with their own, often contradicting, agendas seeking to control information flow. In November 2005, whistleblower **Qiao Songju** (乔松举) was detained six weeks after reporting the death of 200 geese in Anhui Province to the Ministry of Agriculture based on information from a friend of his father. Authorities subsequently destroyed over 100,000 geese, and local officials, who were allegedly angry over the poor compensation received, detained Qiao on charges of blackmail.[166] Despite the seeming confirmation of bird flu that this culling represented, Qiao was later sentenced to 3.5 years in prison and fined 30,000 *yuan* for deceiving authorities and blackmailing vaccine sellers.[167] Reports state that local authorities were disturbed by Qiao's interference and the inadequate compensation received for the lost birds, and they therefore punished Qiao. This represents another case of the government restricting information to the public by targeting an individual who sought to increase access to information.

Environmentalists: The continued degradation of the environment in China seemingly demands that civil society, government and international bodies work together to effectively address the issue. However, the PRC government seeks instead to control civil society groups and limit their activity. **Tan Kai** (谭凯) and fellow environmental activists organized an environmental watchdog group called Green Watch (绿色观察) to monitor the situation in Huashui Town in Dongyang City, Zhejiang Province. In April 2005, local residents complained that pollution from a chemical factory was destroying crops and causing birth defects, and protests culminated in a violent conflict with local police on April 10, in which more than 400 police officers were reportedly deployed and many people injured. Although five members of Green Watch were summoned and questioned by the Hangzhou Public Security Bureau on October 19, only Tan was detained. Tan, a computer repair technician, was formally indicted on April 29, 2006 of charges of "illegally obtaining state secrets," ostensibly for information he had obtained while doing routine file back-ups for his clients. However, the fact that on November 15, the Zhejiang provincial government had declared Green Watch an illegal organization calls into question the real reason for his prosecution.

Journalists: Journalists often run afoul of state secrets regulations, but the type of information reported in these cases goes beyond obvious sensitive areas and has included reports on economic information, natural disasters, industrial accidents and advance release of policy speeches. **Xi Yang** (席扬) was a *Ming Pao* newspaper reporter and a mainland-born Hong Kong resident. He was accused of spying and stealing state financial and economic secrets related to an article he wrote discussing Bank of China international gold policy and strategies. The information in Xi's report was considered a "state financial secret" because it had not yet been officially released. Detained by state security agents on September 27, 1993 in Beijing, he was convicted of "stealing and gathering state secrets" and sentenced to 12 years' imprisonment with two years' deprivation of political rights on March 28, 1994 by the Beijing No.1 Intermediate People's Court. Xi was eventually released on parole in January 26, 1997 due to satisfactory behavior.

The state secrets system—in both its norms and implementation—violates a comprehensive range of human rights in China. The state secrets framework is used as both a shield to conceal information and a sword to punish individuals who criticize the government. The lack of political will on the part of the CPC to relinquish control and implement effective reforms has a significant impact on protecting rights in practice.

While the PRC's use of human rights language has grown in sophistication over the years and it increasingly references international human rights law in its reports to UN treaty bodies, in government-issued white papers, and to the press, actual enactments are less prominent. The very rights that the PRC undertakes to uphold through the international framework are undermined by the comprehensive state secrets system.

The state secrets system denies the right to freedom of expression and right of access to information by: classifying information that does not meet narrow international criteria for withholding; classifying information that is necessary for the protection of public health and the environment; allowing information to be classified even after wide public distribution; allowing information on official misconduct and malfeasance to be classified; and allowing state secrets charges to be used as a tool to silence dissent.

C.

Reform Efforts

Calls for greater government transparency, accountability and information access in the PRC have increased in recent years in response to both domestic and international pressures. In large part, this may be a result of the government-delayed disclosure of accurate information on SARS in 2003. This lack of transparency also affects China's international obligations. China's accession requirements to the WTO call for greater transparency in the country's trade rules and requirements. Moreover, the classification of certain statistics as state secrets, such as those on kidnapping and trafficking, induced abortions, infanticide and the gender ratio, prevents a comprehensive and accurate assessment of China's domestic implementation of its human rights commitments at human rights treaty body reviews.[168]

In the aftermath of the Shanghai corruption scandal and the purge of Party leader Chen Liangyu in October 2006, greater government transparency and accountability are increasingly affirmed as key components of China's national anti-corruption strategy. The reform efforts of President Hu Jintao thus seek to increase government transparency and accountability by promoting Open Government Information (OGI) initiatives. New initiatives are variously referred to as Regulations on Government Information Disclosure in the Chinese media and as Freedom of Information Regulations by Western commentators. Greater emphasis is being placed on individuals' "right to know" and on increasing citizen involvement in government affairs. However, due to the exclusion of state secrets from disclosure provisions, these reforms will not effectively address the problem at the heart of the state secrets system: the deadly control over information that maintains an authoritarian one-party rule.

1. OPEN GOVERNMENT INFORMATION (OGI):

LOCAL INITIATIVES

China's first Open Government Information (OGI) reform initiative in 2002, the Guangzhou Municipal Regulation on Open Government Information, introduced to Chinese governance the novel presumptions that government information should be made public and that government agencies are obligated to disclose such information upon request.[169] Since then, similar regulations have been enacted steadily in at least 31 provincial and municipal jurisdictions across China,[170] with notable achievements such as an online OGI legislation adopted by the Special Economic Zone (SEZ) of Shenzhen on April 1, 2004, which required government agencies to disseminate information online.[171] Fundamentally, OGI initiatives reflect two innovative ideas in the Chinese context: first, individuals and organizations have the right to request government information; and, second, government agencies have an obligation to disclose such information, within the limits of those defined as permissible for disclosure, when requested.

Particular focus was placed on the Shanghai Municipal Regulation on Open Government Information when it was adopted in 2004 and labeled as "the most sophisticated approach" of all OGI initiatives in the PRC.[172] It built upon the Guangzhou regulation, while the drafting process itself was marked by a relatively open consultative process that sought public comments.[173] In addition, the Shanghai government launched unprecedented organizational, training and preparatory work to ensure that the regulation was effectively implemented and that the presumption of disclosure prevails in practice.[174]

Following Shanghai's OGI initiative in 2004, some of the achievements at the local level include examples from Guangzhou and Chengdu, where recent measures have been adopted to formalize the methods to request government information disclosure. For instance, the Guangzhou municipal government announced at a press conference in December 2006 that the Guangzhou Municipality's Measures on Applying for the Disclosure of Government Information would take effect on May 1, 2007. These measures stipulate that, apart from eight matters such as state secrets and information on the integrity of leading Party members, all other information can be disclosed to the public according to the law.[175] If such information is not made public, citizens can file complaints, make reports, and even sue government officials. Initial media coverage of these measures have labeled it as the country's first comprehensive and systematic local government regulation to standardize the work of applying to the government to disclose information to the public.[176]

Similarly, on November 30, 2006 the Chengdu municipal government promulgated the Chengdu Municipal Measures for Disclosing Government Information in Response to Requests by Application, which took effect on the same date.[177] The Chengdu measures state that if citizens wish to know information on government matters that has not yet been made public, they may file an application free of charge with the relevant administrative body or unit, and that such requests would be normally dealt with within five working days, as compared to 15 working days in the Shanghai OGI Regulation. Commentaries on the Chengdu OGI have welcomed efforts by the Chengdu local government to protect citizens' right to information by stipulating in the measures that any unit or individual that violates the measures may be held liable according to law.[178]

Reports emerged in December 2006 indicating that the State Council was currently drafting a regulation governing the release of government information at the national level, with the goal to "promote government transparency and the public right to know while allowing the state to protect secrets."[179] In January 2007, it was reported that China's State Council had approved a draft of a national regulation on open government information and that the State Council had committed itself to the promulgation and implementation of this regulation after further revisions to the draft. But continuing the policy of secrecy, officials at the time declined to respond to requests for details of the new rules or to disclose when they might be publicly available.[180] In April 2007, the state media Xinhua released the text of a national OGI regulation to take effect one year later, on May 1, 2008.[181] Contradicting the stated goals of a more transparent government, the release of the national OGI regulation showed that while it was passed on January 17, 2007 by the State Council, it was signed by Premier Wen Jiabao on April 5, 2007 and only became widely available two weeks later, on April 24, 2007.

2. THE RIGHT TO KNOW

At the core of all OGI initiatives is the "right to know" (知情权), which came into greater prominence when it was listed as one of the civil and political rights in China's 2003 White Paper on its human rights cause and progress.[182] The White Paper states that Chinese citizens enjoy the freedom of information, which, similar to the "right to know," is not a right that is specifically enumerated in the Chinese Constitution or any domestic law.[183] The rights to know and to information are not absolute, and OGI regulations specify the types of information that are barred from public disclosure. Although the scope of exemptions for open government disclosure may differ across different jurisdictions, in general the following four types of information are barred: state secrets, commercial secrets, personal private details and other information exempted from disclosure by the provisions of laws and regulations.

Whereas the recent OGI regulation passed by Guangdong Province in 2005 only had these four basic categories for information restrictions, other regulations may broaden the scope of exemptions. A number of jurisdictions have also chosen to exclude potentially wide swaths of additional information, including work secrets, matters under investigation, and other 'harmful information' from declassification, and consequently permanently from public view. For example, the Guangzhou OGI regulation also restricts "government information currently under deliberation or discussion," which also appears in Article 10(d) of the Shanghai OGI Regulation of 2004. The Shanghai OGI Regulation also added a category on "information relating to administrative enforcement, the disclosure of which might influence enforcement activities such as examination, investigation or gathering of evidence, or which might endanger an individual's life or safety." However, what is significant about the Shanghai OGI Regulation is that it specifically stipulates that all the information restrictions, except state secrets and information prohibited from disclosure by laws and regulations, are subject to a balancing test and may be later released if they meet certain conditions.[184]

While the new national OGI regulation legally obliges "[a]ll levels of people's governments and all government departments at or above the county level [to] establish comprehensive systems for the work of making government information public by administrative organs,"[185] it, however, does not significantly expand the 2003 White Paper's inclusion of the right to information. The national OGI regulation states that it will "fully make use of government information as a service for the people, their lives, production and economic and social activities."[186] Citizens, legal entities and other organizations' access to information classified as state secrets remains very limited, because of state secrets' very broad and arbitrary scope.

Article 14 of the national OGI regulation requires administrative organs to "establish comprehensive systems for examining and checking that state secrets are protected in government information that is made public" and that such information "accords with the Law on the Protection of State Secrets of the PRC and other related laws and regulations."[187] This, however, does not address what administrative organs should do in the event of a conflict between the two systems on state secrets and OGI. For instance, statistical information on induced abortions, infanticide and the gender ratio—which are all relevant for a full and accurate assessment of China's family planning policy—are all labeled as state secrets,[188] at the same time that the new national OGI, Article 12, specifically calls for people's governments in villages and townships to "focus on making public . . . [i]nformation on the implementation of family planning policies."[189]

The national OGI regulation creates a detailed system by which the authorities may release government information, which only further consolidates their control over information flow. In addition, the main person responsible in the information disclosing administrative organ could be punished by law and also investigated for criminal liability in certain circumstances for not protecting state secrets.[190] By placing heavy penalties on administrators, in effect the new national OGI regulation bolsters the state secrets system, where non-disclosure is the default for any information labeled as endangering "state security, public security, economic security or social stability."[191] The new regulation continues to deny state secrets to the public, and prevents a critical and transparent assessment of the state secrets legal labyrinth. Due to the fact that state secrets continue to fall outside the scope of local and national OGI initiatives for increasing transparency, efforts to declassify state secrets have given a unique insight to this very wide scope of state secrets classification and how it undermines efforts for a more open and transparent government in China.

3. THE DECLASSIFICATION OF STATE SECRETS

In August 2005, NAPSS vice-minister Shen Yongshe stated that "protecting state secrets and advancing open information are complementary."[192] In particular, the declassification drive of government information in Guangzhou as part of its OGI initiative presents a specific example of the potential scale of this over-classification of state secrets. The city of Guangzhou, a provincial capital, had been aggressively accumulating secret information in the course of its administration and, by 2000, had accumulated a considerable body of state secrets. In 1995, the city classified 19,000 items, and the amount grew to more than 48,000 classified items by 2000. In the span of four months, from September to December 2002, the Guangzhou State Secrets Bureau declassified more than 100,000 state secrets, approximately 97 percent of all the state secrets held by the municipal government at that time.[193]

Though the declassification of state secrets should be automatic（自行解）when the designated time period expires according to the State Secrets Law,[194] in practice Guangzhou only achieved its massive declassification by expunging a large number of mistaken classifications. These included items that no longer held practical value for keeping secret, and other information that would not endanger or may, in some cases, benefit state security and interests but were barred from public distribution as a result of their classification.[195] The wide and seemingly arbitrary scope of classifying information as state secrets, as shown by Guangzhou's declassification drive in 2002, has renewed calls for revisions to the State Secrets Law.

From September to December 2002, the Guangzhou State Secrets Bureau declassified more than 100,000 state secrets.

4. REFORMS OF THE STATE SECRETS SYSTEM

In addition to the OGI initiatives for increasing government transparency and accountability, there have been discussions of reforming the state secrets system itself. Domestic commentaries have focused on the fact that the vast number of secret documents has not only increased the cost of keeping them secret, but has also weakened the authority of the state secrets system while systematically obstructing the government from making its information more accessible to the public.[196] However, after years of speculation over the breadth of its revision, and despite it being cited as a priority for 2006, a draft revision of the State Secrets Law or a timetable for the discussion on its revision has yet to emerge or be confirmed publicly.[197] In December 2006, one *Legal Daily* article commented that a draft revision of the State Secrets Law has been completed and was soon to be submitted to the State Council, without specifying the date.[198] No official reason has been given for this legislative delay, though the draft Law on Government Information Disclosure, which was submitted to the Legislative Affairs Office of the State Council after the 2003 SARS outbreak, was reportedly placed on hold due to the disputed scope of declassification.[199]

Declassification of Natural Disaster Casualties

Despite the absence of legislative revisions to the state secrets system, a significant change took place on September 12, 2005 when the NAPSS held a press conference and announced that, in order to facilitate emergency response to natural disasters, **death tolls** resulting from such incidents would no longer be classified as a state secret.[200] In announcing the declassification, NAPSS spokesperson Shen Yongshe stated that this line-item declassification was in the interests of conducting effective emergency relief work, doing state secrets protection work well and advancing openness in government departments, and was also in the interests of the people's "right to know."[201] This was widely heralded in domestic and international media as the first instance where the state secrets bureaucracy publicly announced a declassification measure to the press. According to Shen, the NAPSS started to develop links between media and the public relatively late, but it has started to do this, and these will gradually become standardized.[202]

Despite it being cited as a priority for 2006, a draft revision of the State Secrets Law or a timetable for the discussion on its revision has yet to emerge or be confirmed publicly.

The declassification of death tolls resulting from natural disasters was announced in the Notice Regarding the Declassification of Statistics on Casualties Caused by Natural Disasters and Related Information (Document 116 [2005] of the Ministry of Civil Affairs), which was drafted by the General Office of the Ministry of Civil Affairs and issued jointly by the Ministry of Civil Affairs and the NAPSS on August 8, 2005.[203] Document 116 removed "statistics on casualties caused by natural disasters" from the scope of "secret level" state secrets as stipulated in Article 3 of the 2000 Regulation on State Secrets and the Specific Scope of Each Level of Secrets in Civil Affairs Work (Document 71 [2000] issued by the Ministry of Civil Affairs and the NAPSS), which stipulated that "statistics and other related information on individuals who flee from famine, beg for food, or die as a result of natural disasters at the national, provincial, autonomous region and directly-administered municipality level" are a "secret-level" state secret.[204]

It was also reported that the release of Document 116 on August 8, 2005 had special significance because the date marked the 30th anniversary of the dam burst at Zhumadian in Henan Province; therefore, as an NAPSS official pointed out, the declassification of this information actually has its roots in the history of natural disasters and disaster relief work. According to information that is now public, from August 8 to September 5, 1975, following a series of typhoons, a large number of dams burst at the Banqiao Reservoir in Zhumadian, Henan Province, resulting in vast flooding that spread 150 kilometers east to west and 75 kilometers north to south.[205] Three days after Beijing announced that casualty figures from natural disasters were no longer state secrets, Xinhua reported that at least 26,000 people were killed by this dam breach in 1975 and acknowledged that "the figure might be even bigger."[206]

> "If a dyke breach causes flooding or a coal mine collapses, there could be both natural and man-made causes. So there is undoubtedly some flexibility in the system of making information public."

Some have questioned the effectiveness of such disclosure of natural disaster causalities in contributing to government transparency and the ability of the press to independently cover such incidents. In particular, Document 116 does not specify how to distinguish between natural disasters and man-made disasters, leading one legal scholar to note the superficiality of the declassification: "If a dyke breach causes flooding or a coal mine collapses, there could be both natural and man-made causes. So there is undoubtedly some flexibility in the system of making information public."[207]

In addition, the release of natural disaster casualty figures runs contrary to newer proposals on the "emergency response" legislation, which aims to better manage emergency responses but contains detrimental clauses that fine media outlets for reporting on disasters without official authorization.[208] It remains to be seen whether the declassification of natural disaster casualties as state secrets actually means that the press is allowed to cover these stories independently or whether they are only allowed to cite official figures and must still seek official authorization. The public announcement by the NAPSS seemingly acknowledges the "right to know;" however, implementing this into an official policy of transparency and expanding its implementation will require a sustained, concerted effort on the part of Chinese government officials, and will also require revision of the state secrets system, which currently violates this right.

Criminal Justice Reforms

Following public concerns that the high number of **death penalty sentences** may be in large part the result of coerced interrogations and the lack of independent review of any torture claims, recent reforms include: a Ministry of Public Security move in May 2006 to *promote* audio and video taping of interrogations;[209] provincial higher courts granting public hearings to all death penalty cases on appeal starting in July 2006, which extends beyond current protections in the Criminal Procedure Law;[210] and the approval by the National People's Congress (NPC) of an amendment to the country's Organic Law of the People's Courts in October 2006 to allow the Supreme People's Court to reclaim its authority to review all death sentences starting from January 1, 2007, which the NPC had extended to intermediate courts in 1983.[211] All these reforms, however, will not be able to bring about an accountable and transparent criminal justice system if the number of executions continues to remain secret.

All these reforms, however, will not be able to bring about an accountable and transparent criminal justice system if the number of executions continues to remain secret.

The scale and implementation of the death penalty in China continues to be one of the most profound gaps in public knowledge about the Chinese justice system. The secrecy surrounding the practice of capital punishment undermines the government's own attempt to review the impartiality of the practice and prevents genuine and meaningful reforms of China's criminal justice system.

5. THE LIMITS OF REFORMS

Despite these numerous and varied attempts to increase governmental transparency and accountability, all will fall short of their stated goals unless the state secrets system is given a systemic overhaul. State apparatus that allows the NAPSS to maintain ultimate control over this classified information, to the exclusion of the judiciary and other branches of the government, will impede any efforts to promote greater transparency and accountability.

Although the official policy of OGI is seemingly aligned with the recognized goal of good governance, OGI initiatives fall short of their intended aims for several reasons:

All OGI regulations to date exclude all state secrets from disclosure, completely sidestepping the serious issues presented by the existing wide and opaque scope of state secrets. While the legislative reform efforts attempt to address limited aspects of the abuses of information control, by allowing large classes of information to remain secret, the state secrets system will continue to shield much of the administrative work behind closed doors.

Despite these numerous and varied attempts to increase governmental transparency and accountability, all will fall short of their stated goals unless the state secrets system is given a systemic overhaul.

With this ultimate control over state secrets and no viable means to challenge it in the judicial realm, any reform efforts, like the declassification of causality figures from natural disasters, will remain intermittent, superficial and lacking in real effects of implementation. This contradiction will become more apparent in light of increasing reform efforts towards administration openness, such as the goals of the 2006–2010 Five-Year Audit Development Program, which categorically excludes information labeled as state secrets while aspiring to increase government transparency by disclosing all audit report results.[212]

However, even though the long-term effectiveness of OGI in promoting a genuine culture of openness in China's bureaucracy is undermined by the wide scope of the state secrets system, these initiatives, nonetheless, may raise public demands for greater administration transparency, accountability and responsiveness. In so doing, these OGI initiatives contribute to actively fostering a culture of information and governmental participation based on the practice of information disclosure by default. Without really addressing the systemic problems of the "culture of secrecy" style of administration, as best exemplified by the wide scope and arbitrary nature of China's state secrets system, the goal of a more open and transparent governance to combat corruption will continue to be in tension with the ruling elite's political imperative to maintain control over information and stability at any cost.

6. CONCLUSION

Despite repeated official reaffirmations of the policy supporting the rule of law and, after almost 30 years of legal reform, the combined impact of the various state secrets laws and regulations presents a serious impediment to creating a functioning, impartial judiciary, a fair system for trying individuals subject to criminal and administrative punishment, and official accountability and transparency through strengthened legal processes. Commentators have also not hesitated to link openness and transparency in information, especially government-controlled information, to economic and social development.[213] Some have even argued that open government information regulations do not sufficiently address the challenges of the state secrets system, which stands to be a liability in the drive to sustain economic growth and development.[214]

Piecemeal tinkering with a closed one-party controlled system will not be enough to promote genuine progress towards an independent rule of law, good governance and human rights protections. Efforts to encourage police and security officers to alter interrogations methods—without allowing information on interrogations methods, results and other data to be made public—lack any real incentives for compliance. Without access to and disclosure of information, no real accountability can be guaranteed.

The state secrets system continues to seriously deny the right to freedom of expression and information by classifying too much information as secret and maintaining a culture of secrecy that has a chilling effect on the rule of law and independent civil society, and undermines any reform efforts towards these goals.

While every system must grapple with the balance between national security, protection of state secrets and protection of rights, the ruling elite in the PRC does not allow any dissent or criticism and has demonstrated its capacity for violent crackdown and suppression. Rather than a rule of law, the ruling elite uses law, and even new legislation couched behind reform rhetoric, to affirm its *rule by law* and maintain power and social control.

> **Piecemeal tinkering with a closed one-party controlled system will not be enough to promote genuine progress towards an independent rule of law, good governance and human rights protections.**

D.
Recommendations

The state secrets system needs comprehensive reform to both bring it into line with international norms and the PRC's obligations, and to advance good governance, the rule of law, and protect human rights. HRIC offers the following recommendations to bring the state secrets system in China in line with international and domestic human rights standards. HRIC recognizes the structural, ideological and cultural challenges that legal reform efforts in China presents, and the even greater implementation difficulties. However, the failure of the current state secrets system to protect even basic rights to information, freedom of expression and freedom of association is exacting a heavy human and social price. The following recommendations reflect not only recommendations from international monitoring bodies and the international human rights community, but also domestic calls for reform from Chinese lawyers, jurists, scholars, officials and NGOs.

The international community, which includes international organizations, governments, multinational corporations and civil society groups, has a critical role in the promotion of rights protections inside China. The international community should continue to engage the Chinese government in substantive dialogue on the issue of human rights and political reforms to increase transparency and accountability, through monitoring and pressure, while continuing to cooperate in providing technical assistance and capacity-building initiatives, but such assistance should be linked with human rights benchmarks. HRIC urges international policy-makers to consider the recommendations below as they engage in international cooperation and multi-lateral and bilateral processes.

RECOMMENDATIONS FOR THE PRC GOVERNMENT:

1. Rights to freedom of expression and information should be guaranteed and realized for all Chinese citizens

    i. As provided for in the PRC Constitution, the PRC government should take all necessary steps to ensure that the right to freedom of expression is protected, including **ratifying the ICCPR** and enacting necessary domestic legislation and other measures to effectively implement the treaty.

    ii. **State secrets charges should not be used as a means to silence dissent** and inappropriately curtail freedom of expression. The politicized use of state secrets charges to silence dissent and the dissemination of "sensitive" information need to be prohibited and monitored through legislative and agency guidelines and other measures.

    iii. Measures, both legislative and educational, should be undertaken to **end the PRC's culture of secrecy and cultivate open government.** A culture of tolerance of different views and transparency needs to be fostered to allow self-censorship to end and to enable an independent civil society to flourish.

    iv. **The CPC needs to be governed under the law and cease its interference in the court system.** The one-party system should not protect the CPC from being held accountable under Chinese law, nor should it allow for party influence in what should be an independent judicial system.

    v. **The Chinese government should take immediate steps to effectively address and end complicity in extrajudicial retribution** and the rise of thug violence against journalists, lawyers, rights activists and other civil society groups. All governments have an obligation to protect citizens from the illegal actions of non-state actors.

2. Legislative amendments and reforms should be made to the state secrets system

i. **The State Secrets Law must be revised to include a clear and concise definition of state secrets** that is in keeping with international legal standards. As provided for in the ICCPR and the Johannesburg Principles on National Security, Freedom of Expression and Access to Information, any restriction placed on freedom of expression must be narrow, specific and limited to information that would threaten the life of the nation if disclosed.

ii. Also in keeping with the Johannesburg Principles, **the State Secrets Law, the Criminal Law, and the State Security Law should be revised so that punishment is only levied for actual harm to a legitimate national security interest.** The current provisions allowing for the classification of information that could cause potential harm should be revised to ensure that the law only punishes actual harm, and that if information has already been made generally available, the public's right to know overrides any invoked justification for stopping further publication of the information.

iii. **An independent review mechanism for the classification of state secrets should be established.** Both institutions and bureaus, as well as individuals involved in state secrets legal proceedings, should have the right to seek independent review of the classification of the information involved.

iv. Revisions should be made to the State Secrets Law and other regulations to **eliminate retroactive classification of information**.

v. Revisions should be made to the State Secrets Law in accordance with international norms and standards to **eliminate the distinctions in the scope of state secrets, and the severity of criminal sanctions, between domestic and external disclosure of state secrets.**

Introduction and Section I Notes

1. This report will use "government" and "the State" interchangeably to refer to the Chinese governing processes at the national level. Use of "the Party" likewise refers to Communist Party of China (CPC) processes and directives at the national level. Both the civil government and the Party have offices at the provincial, city and other local levels, much like local offices of the national State Secrets Bureau (NAPSS). These will be identified specifically when necessary. Ruling elite refers to the top decision-making leadership of the CPC.

2. The state secrets system is founded on a historical culture of secrecy that stretches back beyond the 1949 establishment of the PRC to the early stages of the CPC, when it borrowed from the Soviet model and established guidelines for dissemination of information during the Jiangxi Soviet.

3. On October 18, 2006, the Central Committee of the CPC passed a resolution on the building of a "harmonious socialist society." See "China Publishes Resolution on Building Harmonious Society," *Xinhua News,* October 18, 2006, http://news.xinhuanet.com/english/2006-10/18/content_5219143.htm. For a full text of the resolution see "Resolution on Major Questions Regarding Building a Harmonious Socialist Society" (构建社会主义和谐社会若干重大问题决定), EastDay.com, October 18, 2006, http://news.eastday.com/eastday/node81741/node81762/node166523/u1a2385447.html.

4. Within the limits of the current legal publication system in the PRC, best efforts have been made to verify the authority of promulgated laws and regulations, including through bulletins, commentaries, and treatises available published or online. Many of the laws and regulations comprising the state secrets system are not readily accessible and are found mainly in classified publications, despite provisions in the Legislation Law that mandate distribution in publicly accessible documents in a timely manner. The Legislation Law of the People's Republic of China (中华人民共和国立法法), issued by the National People's Congress, promulgated March 15, 2000, effective July 1, 2000, Articles 52, 62, 70, 77.

5. The PRC is State Party to: Convention on the Elimination of All Forms of Discrimination Against Women (CEDAW), G.A. res. 34/180, 34 U.N. GAOR Supp. (No. 46) at 193, U.N. Doc. A/34/46, *entered into force* Sept. 3, 1981 (PRC signed July 17, 1980, ratified Nov. 4, 1980); International Convention on the Elimination of All Forms of Racial Discrimination (CERD), 660 U.N.T.S. 195, *entered into force* Jan. 4, 1969 (acceded Dec. 29, 1981); Convention Against Torture and Other Cruel, Inhuman or Degrading Treatment or Punishment (CAT), G.A. res. 39/46, annex, 39 U.N. GAOR Supp. (No. 51) at 197, U.N. Doc. A/39/51 (1984), *entered into force* June 26, 1987 (signed Dec. 12, 1986, ratified Oct. 4, 1988); Convention on the Rights of the Child (CRC), G.A. res. 44/25, annex, 44 U.N. GAOR Supp. (No. 49) at 167, U.N. Doc. A/44/49 (1989), *entered into force* Sept. 2, 1990 (signed Aug. 29, 1990, ratified March 2, 1992); International Covenant on Economic, Social and Cultural Rights (ICESCR), G.A. res. 2200A (XXI), 21 U.N. GAOR Supp. (No. 16) at 49, U.N. Doc. A/6316 (1966), 993 U.N.T.S. 3, *entered into force* Jan. 3, 1976. (signed Oct. 27, 1997, ratified March 27, 2001). In addition even though the PRC has yet to ratify the International Covenant on Civil and Political Rights (ICCPR), G.A. res. 2200A (XXI), 21 U.N. GAOR Supp. (No. 16) at 52, U.N. Doc. A/6316 (1966), 999 U.N.T.S. 171, *entered into force* Mar. 23, 1976, (PRC signed Oct. 5, 1998) as a signatory it is obligated

not to defeat the object and purpose of the treaty. China has also acceded to a total of 21 International Labour Organisation (ILO) conventions, which includes four of the eight core conventions: Equal Remuneration Convention (ILO No. 100), 165 U.N.T.S. 303, *entered into force* May 23, 1953 (PRC ratified 1990); Discrimination (Employment and Occupation) Convention (ILO No. 111), 362 U.N.T.S. 31, *entered into force* June 15, 1960 (ratified 2006); Minimum Age (Admission to Employment) Convention (ILO No. 138), 1973, 1015 U.N.T.S. 297 (1976), *entered into force* June 19, 1976 (ratified 1999); and Convention concerning the Prohibition and Immediate Action for the Elimination of the Worst Forms of Child Labour (ILO No. 182), 38 I.L.M. 1207 (1999), *entered into force* Nov. 19, 2000 (ratified 2002).

6. See, e.g., United Nations' Human Rights Committee, General Comment 10, Article 19 (Nineteenth session, 1983), "Compilation of General Comments and General Recommendations Adopted by Human Rights Treaty Bodies," U.N. Doc. HRI/GEN/1/Rev.6 at 132 (2003); U.N. Commission on Human Rights (CHR), "Report of the Special Rapporteur on Promotion and Protection of the Right to Freedom of Opinion and Expression," U.N. Doc. E/CN.4/1995/32 (1994) (Special Rapporteur, Abid Hussain), para 16.

7. See, e.g., Universal Declaration of Human Rights (UDHR), G.A. res. 217A (III), U.N. Doc A/810 at 71 (1948).

8. U.N. Commission on Human Rights, "Report of the Special Rapporteur on Promotion and Protection of the Right to Freedom of Opinion and Expression," op. cit., paras. 16 & 35. See also Joint Declaration: Adopted on 6 December 2004 by Ambeyi Ligabo, Special Rapporteur on the Right to Freedom of Opinion and Expression, Miklos Haraszti, the OSCE Representative on Freedom of the Media, and Eduardo Bertoni, the OAS Special Rapporteur on Freedom of Expression. UN Doc. E/CN.4/2006/55.

9. U.N. Commission on Human Rights, "Report of the Special Rapporteur on Promotion and Protection of the Right to Freedom of Opinion and Expression," op. cit., para. 14.

10. ICCPR, article 19(3); see also discussion in U.N. Commission on Human Rights, "Report of the Special Rapporteur on Promotion and Protection of the Right to Freedom of Opinion and Expression," op. cit., paras 48–53.

11. U.N. Commission on Human Rights, "Report of the Special Rapporteur on Promotion and Protection of the Right to Freedom of Opinion and Expression," op. cit., para. 48. See also "The Johannesburg Principles on National Security, Freedom of Expression and Access to Information," U.N. Doc. E/CN.4/1996/39 (1996), principle 6.

12. U.N. Commission on Human Rights, "Report of the Special Rapporteur on Promotion and Protection of the Right to Freedom of Opinion and Expression," op. cit., paras. 51 & 53; "The Johannesburg Principles on National Security, Freedom of Expression and Access to Information," U.N. Doc. E/CN.4/1996/39 (1996), principle 7. Principle 7 reads, in relevant part: (a) Subject to Principles 15 and 16, the peaceful exercise of the right to freedom of expression shall not be considered a threat to national security or subjected to any restrictions or penalties. Expression which shall not constitute a threat to national security includes, but is not limited to, expression that: (i) advocates non-violent change of government policy or the government itself; (ii) constitutes criticism of, or insult to, the nation, the state or its symbols, the government, its agencies, or public officials, or a foreign nation, state or its symbols, government, agencies or public officials; . . . (iv) is directed at communicating information about alleged violations of international human rights standards or international humanitarian law.

13. U.N. Commission on Human Rights, "Report of the Special Rapporteur on Promotion and Protection of the Right to Freedom of Opinion and Expression," op. cit., paras. 51 & 53.

14. "The Johannesburg Principles on National Security, Freedom of Expression and Access to Information," U.N. Doc. E/CN.4/1996/39 (1996), principle 11.

15. Ibid., principle 15.

16. Ibid., principle 19.

17. Ibid., principles 14 and 15.

18. See, e.g., Human Rights Committee, "General Comment No. 3: Implementation at the National Level" (Art. 2), July 27, 1981, para. 1; Committee on Economic, Social and Cultural Rights, "General Comment No. 3: The Nature of States Parties Obligations" (Art. 2, par. 1), December 14, 1990, para. 4.

19. Katsuhiko Shimizu, "Jailed Uyghur Student Has Todai on His Side," *The Asahi Shimbun*, August 30, 2006, http://www.asahi.com/english/Herald-asahi/TKY200608300110.html. Also see "No Word For Wife On Jailed Uyghur Writer's Fate," Radio Free Asia, June 19, 2006, http://www.rfa.org/english/news/politics/2006/06/19/uyghur_writer.

20. United Nations, "Report of the Special Rapporteur on Torture and other Cruel, Inhuman or Degrading Treatment or Punishment—Mission to China," U.N. Doc. E/CN.4/2006/6/Add.6.

21. Administrative Council, 87th Administrative Affairs Meeting, Central People's Government, Provisional Regulation on Protecting State Secrets (保守国家机密暂行条例). This regulation was signed into law by Zhou Enlai in June 1951.

22. Law on the Protection of State Secrets of the People's Republic of China (hereinafter, State Secrets Law) (中华人民共和国保守国家秘密法), issued by the Standing Committee of the National People's Congress, promulgated September 1, 1988 and effective on May 1, 1989, Art. 2. See Section II, page 81, for the full text of this law.

23. Measures for Implementing the Law on the Protection of State Secrets of the People's Republic of China (hereinafter, Implementation Measures) (中华人民共和国保守国家秘密法实施办法), issued by the National Administration for the Protection of State Secrets, promulgated and effective on May 25, 1990. See Section II, page 95, for the full text.

24. State Security Law of the People's Republic of China (hereinafter, State Security Law) (中华人民共和国国家安全法), issued by the Standing Committee of the National People's Congress, promulgated and effective on February 22, 1993. See Section II, page 118, for relevant provisions.

25. Criminal Law of the People's Republic of China (hereinafter, Criminal Law) (中华人民共和国刑法), issued by the National People's Congress, promulgated July 1, 1979, amended 1997, 1999, 2001, 2002, 2005. See Section II, page 120, for relevant provisions.

26. Criminal Procedure Law of the People's Republic of China (hereinafter, Criminal Procedure Law), (中华人民共和国刑事诉讼法), issued by the National People's Congress, promulgated and effective on January 1, 1997. See Section II, page 122, for relevant provisions.

27. Law of the People's Republic of China on Lawyers (中华人民共和国律师法), issued by the Standing Committee of the National People's Congress in 1996, amended in 2001, Art. 45.

28. Accounting Law of the People's Republic of China (中华人民共和国会计法), issued by the Standing Committee of the National People's Congress in 1985, amended in 1993 and 1999, Arts. 34 and 47.

29. Regulation on Telecommunications of the People's Republic of China (中华人民共和国电信条例), issued by the State Council in 2000, Art. 57.

30. State Secrets Law, Art. 1.

31. Ibid., Art. 2.

32. See State Secrets Law, Article 8, in Section II, page 84, for a full list of matters classified as state secrets. Communist Party of China (CPC) documents are indirectly brought into the scope of state secrets through a stipulation that "secrets of political parties" are to be protected if they are determined to affect the security and interests of the PRC.

33. Regulation on State Secrets and the Specific Scope of Each Level of Secrets in the Work of the People's Courts (hereafter, SPC Regulation) (人民法院工作中国家秘密及其密级具体范围的规定), issued jointly by the Supreme People's Court and the National Administration for the Protection of State Secrets, 1995, Art. 3(A)(1). See Section II, page 143, for the full text of this regulation.

34. Criminal Law, Art. 111.

35. The Supreme People's Court Interpretation of Certain Issues Regarding the Specific Application of the Law When Trying Cases of Stealing, Gathering, Procuring or Illegally Providing State Secrets Outside of the Country (hereinafter, SPC Interpretation of Certain Issues), issued by the Supreme People's Court of the People's Republic of China, 2001, Art. 1. See Section II, page 112, for the full text.

36. See Yu Zhigang (于志刚), ed., *Crimes of Endangering State Security* (危害国家安全罪). Beijing: Chinese People's Public Security University Publishing House, 1999, p. 337. The authors suggest that intelligence has not been stipulated as secret according to the state secrets classification system, but is information that, if disclosed overseas, would endanger the security and interests of the state. Thus even with information where the relation to state security is not apparent, if its disclosure could cause such endangerment, it should be considered intelligence under Article 111 of the Criminal Law.

37. National Administration for the Protection of State Secrets (国家保密局), *Manual of State Secrets Protection Knowledge* (保密知识读本), Beijing: Jincheng Publishing House, 1999, p. 244.

38. The State Secrets Law stipulates in Article 14 that when organs and units are determining the classification level of state secrets, they should also determine the length of time that the secrets should be protected. Article 15 stipulates that the classification levels of state secrets and the length of time of protection may change with circumstances, again with the decision being made by the same organ or unit that originally classified the secrets. Article 16 stipulates that state secrets shall be automatically declassified when the time period for protection has expired. NAPSS has issued additional regulations for determining the duration of confidentiality, which can be extended. Regulation on the

Time Limits of State Secrets (国家秘密保密期限的规定), issued by the National Administration for the Protection of State Secrets, 1990, Arts. 3, 4.

39. State Secrets Law, Arts. 17–24.

40. State Secrets Law, Art. 11; Implementation Measures, Art. 8.

41. SPC Regulation, Art. 3.

42. Regulation on State Secrets and the Specific Scope of Each Level of Secrets in Judicial Administration Work (hereinafter, MOJ Regulation) (司法行政工作中国家秘密及其密级具体范围的规定), issued by the Ministry of Justice and the National Administration for the Protection of State Secrets, 1995, Art. 2(A) 1 and 2(B) 1. See Section II, page 152, for the full text of this regulation.

43. Implementation Measures, Art. 4.

44. Although the Implementation Measures do not mention the requirement of a specific harm or distinguish between degrees of harm, it is stated in an official interpretation of the Implementation Measures that "the consequences of any of these eight crimes are all considered to harm the security and interests of the state." See *Legal Focus of the People's Republic of China* (中华人民共和国法律集注), Office of Law Drafting of the Standing Committee of the National People's Congress and the Training Center for Senior Level Notary Publics and Senior Level Lawyers, ed. (全国人大常委会法制工作刑法室及中国高级律师高级公证员培训中心编著), Beijing: Legal Publishing House, 1992, p. 1838.

45. Wang Shouxin (王守信), *Overview of the Management of State Secrets Protection Work* (保密工作管理概论), Beijing: Jincheng Publishing House, 1999, p. 70–71.

46. Work secrets are formulated according to each organ and unit's relevant measures and proper management. Ibid.

47. Regulation on State Secrets and the Specific Scope of Each Level of Secrets in Public Security Work (hereinafter, MPS Regulation), issued by the Ministry of Public Security and the National Administration for the Protection of State Secrets, 1995, Art. 3. Neibu matters "are not categorized as state secrets, but are matters to be managed internally, and [which] may not be disseminated without approval from the organ." See Section II, page 125, for the full text of this regulation.

48. Implementation Measures, Art. 37.

49. MPS Regulation, op. cit., Art. 3 (10). See *infra* case story: Zheng Enchong, page 28.

50. Constitution of the People's Republic of China (hereinafter, PRC Constitution), amended by the National People's Congress on March 14, 2004, Art. 53. See also Provisional Rules for State Personnel (国家公务员暂行条例), issued by the State Council on August 14, 1993, effective October 1, 1993, Arts. 6, 31.

51. State Secrets Law, Art. 10.

52. PRC Constitution, Art. 53. See also Provisional Rules for State Personnel, op. cit., Arts. 6, 31.

53. "Baseline of the Protection of State Secrets System Redefined" (中国保密制度重置底线政府信息公开进立法程序), *The Beijing News*, September 20, 2005, available at http://gov.people.com.cn/BIG5/46737/3709800.html.

54. State Secrets Law, Art. 5.

55. Ibid., Art. 6.

56. See "Selection of State Secrets Provisions Regulating Specific Activities" in Section II, page 168.

57. State Secrets Law, Art. 11.

58. Ibid.

59. State Secrets Law, Art. 6. The major exception is the scope and classification levels of state secrets related to national defense, which are stipulated by the Central Military Commission, Art. 11.

60. PRC Constitution, Art. 35.

61. Ibid. See also Provisional Rules for State Personnel (国家公务员暂行条例), issued by the State Council on August 14, 1993, effective October 1, 1993.

62. Implementation Measures, Arts. 27–34.

63. State Secrets Law, Art. 31.

64. State Secrets Law, Art. 32.

65. "Uyghur Dissident's Sons Detained, Beaten in Front of Children," Radio Free Asia, June 1, 2006, http://www.rfa.org/english/uyghur/2006/06/01/uyghur_kadeer/.

66. "Rebiya Kadeer's Son Sentenced to Seven Years; Another Fined; Another Feared Tortured," Uyghur Human Rights Project, November 27, 2006, http://uhrp.org/articles/351/1/Rebiya-Kadeers-son-sentenced-to-seven-years-another-fined-another-feared-tortured/rabiye.html.

67. Ibid.

68. "Son of Rebiya Kadeer Sentenced to Nine Years in Prison on Charges of 'Secessionism,'" Uyghur Human Rights Project, April 17, 2007, http://uhrp.org/articles/465/1/Son-of-Rebiya-Kadeer-sentenced-to-nine-years-in-prison-on-charges-of-quotsecessionismquot/index.html.

69. State Secrets Law, Art. 32.

70. Article 111 of the Criminal Law states: "Whoever steals, gathers, procures or illegally provides state secrets or intelligence for an organ, organization or individual outside the country shall be sentenced to fixed-term imprisonment of not less than five years but not more than 10 years. If the circumstances are deemed to be especially serious, he shall be sentenced to fixed-term imprisonment of not less than 10 years or life imprisonment. If the circumstances are deemed to be less serious, he shall be sentenced to fixed-term

imprisonment of not more than five years, forced labor, public surveillance or deprivation of political rights." See Section II, page 120.

71. SPC Interpretation of Certain Issues, Article 5, states: "If a person knows, or should know, that any matter not marked with a security classification has a bearing on state security and interests but still steals, gathers, procures or illegally provides such matters to anyone outside of the country, the determination and punishment for this crime shall be that of stealing, gathering, procuring or illegally providing state secrets to anyone outside of the country according to the provisions in Article 111 of the Criminal Law." See Section II, page 116.

72. Criminal Law, Art. 282. See Section II, pages 121–122.

73. Ibid.

74. Implementation Measures, Art. 35.

75. Criminal Law, Art. 282.

76. Ibid.

77. Criminal Law, Art. 111.

78. Criminal Law, Art. 113.

79. Ibid.

80. Criminal Law, Art. 398.

81. Ibid.

82. State Secrets Law, Art. 31.

83. Implementation Measures, Art. 32.

84. *Manual of State Secrets Protection Knowledge* (保密知识读本), op. cit., Chapter 8.

85. *Chinese Communist Party Rules on Disciplinary Action* (中国共产党纪律处分条例), Office of the Central Discipline Inspection Committee, ed. (中央纪委法规室编), Beijing: China Fangzheng Publishing House, 1997, Art. 109.

86. SPC Interpretation of Certain Issues, Art. 1.

87. State Security Law. See e.g., Arts. 20, 28–29.

88. State Security Law, Article 4, lists five types of crimes that are deemed to endanger state security. See Section II, page 118. Articles 102–113 of the Criminal Law are crimes of endangering state security.

89. See Appendices II: Cases Involving State Secrets, page 213.

90. Criminal Law, Art. 113.

91. Ibid.

92. SPC Interpretation of Certain Issues, Art. 2. See Section II, pages 114–115. Article 2 states that the following are crimes involving "especially serious circumstances" and warrant sentences of between ten years and life imprisonment, plus confiscation of property: 1) Stealing, gathering, procuring, or illegally providing top-secret level state secrets to anyone outside of the country; 2) Stealing, gathering, procuring, or illegally providing three or more highly-secret level state secrets to anyone outside of the country; 3) In any other way causing especially serious harm to state security and interests by stealing, gathering, procuring, or illegally providing state secrets or intelligence to anyone outside of the country.

93. SPC Interpretation of Certain Issues, Art. 2.

94. Different criminal proceedings demonstrate the differences in penalties given where "especially serious circumstances" are invoked, or not. In the criminal ruling against Shi Tao, the court determined that "the state secrets that defendant Shi Tao illegally provided outside of the country were verified by the State Secrecy Bureau as being top-secret level state secrets, and his actions should be held to be especially serious circumstances." Changsha Intermediate People's Court of Hunan Province, *Changsha Intermediate People's Court Criminal Verdict*, First Trial Docket No. 29, 2005. Zheng Enchong, on the other hand, was convicted of disclosing low-level information, including some neibu (internal) information that was not classified as a state secret, and the circumstances of his crime were deemed to be "relatively minor." Shanghai No. 2 Intermediate People's Court, *Shanghai No. 2 Intermediate People's Court Criminal Verdict*, Criminal Docket No. 136, 2003.

95. See "Empty Promises: Human Rights Protections and China's Criminal Procedure Law in Practice" (hereinafter, "Empty Promises"), Human Rights in China report, March 2001, for a study of the implementation of the CPL, concluding that in most cases examined these protections are widely ignored or violated. Available at http://www.hrichina.org/fs/view/downloadables/pdf/downloadable-resources/Empty_Promises_Text.pdf.

96. Criminal Procedure Law, Art. 45.

97. Criminal Procedure Law, Art. 96.

98. Criminal Procedure Law, Art. 152.

99. Joint Regulation Concerning Several Issues in the Implementation of the Criminal Procedure Law (hereinafter, Joint Regulation) (最高人民法院，最高人民检察院，公安部，国家安全部，司法部，全国人大常委会法制工作委员会关于刑事诉讼法实施中若干问题的规定), Art. 9. This regulation was jointly issued by the Supreme People's Court, the Supreme People's Procuratorate, the Ministry of Public Security, the Ministry of State Security, the Ministry of Justice, and the National People's Congress Standing Committee's Legal System Working Committee on January 19, 1998.

100. See, e.g., Johannesburg Principles.

101. State Secrets Law, Art. 8(7).

102. See *Empty Promises,* op. cit., Chapter 2.

103. See Appendices II: Cases Involving State Secrets, page 213.

104. "The Liaoyang Four Have Been Detained For Almost Seven Months—With No Formal Charges," China Labour Bulletin, http://www.china-labour.org.hk/public/contents/ news?revision%5fid=4853&item%5fid=4852.

105. Joint Regulation, Art. 9.

106. State Security Law, Art. 28.

107. For example, Article 11 of the Joint Regulation states that: "The Criminal Procedure Law, Article 96, stipulates that in cases involving state secrets, lawyers must get permission from the investigative organ in order to meet with criminal suspects being held in custody. In cases that do not involve state secrets, lawyers do not need to get permission in order to meet with criminal suspects. It is not allowed for such permission to be denied because a case is said to be a case that involves state secrets due to the fact that secrets must be protected during the investigative process. Lawyers asking to meet with criminal suspects must arrange meetings within 48 hours of their request. In cases of organizing, leading or participating in triad-type organizations; organizing, leading or participating in terrorist activities or organizations; smuggling; drug trafficking; corruption; or other major, complex cases involving two or more people, lawyers asking to meet with criminal suspects must arrange the meeting within five days of their request."

108. State Secrets Law, Art. 8. Also see MPS Regulation, Arts. 2(A)(6), 2(B)(7) and 2(C)(8).

109. See Appendices II: Cases Involving State Secrets, page 213.

110. See Human Rights in China, "Setback for the Rule of Law—Lawyers Under Attack in China," HRIC Trends Bulletin, August 28, 2006, http://hrichina.org/public/contents/ article?revision%5fid=30434&item%5fid=30425.

111. Pamela Pun, "First PRC Lawyer Jailed for Leaking State Secrets," Hong Kong iMail, May 15, 2001, available at http://www.fas.org/sgp/news/2001/05/hk051501.html.

112. See SPC Interpretation of Certain Issues, Art. 7, in Section II, page 116.

113. UN Convention Against Corruption, signed on December 20, 2003, ratified January 13, 2006.

114. UN Convention Against Corruption, Art. 13.

115. Zhang Chengfu, assistant dean of the Government Management Studies Institute at Chinese People's University said: "Eighty percent of the relevant (or useful, 有用) information in China is held by the government. If the majority of this information were not allowed to be disclosed to the public, it would seriously restrict our country's economic development.... The Law on the Protection of State Secrets has been in effect for nearly 10 years; in the provisions that stipulate how to determine security classification levels, the standards are vague, the procedures are not strictly followed, the scope is too broad, and the time limits are too long. Placing so many ordinary matters under the protection of state secrets increases the costs to society, prevents government information from becoming a resource that people can access, and is a huge waste of resources." "Our Country's First Announcement of the Declassification of State Secret Matters; The Number of Deaths by Natural Disasters Will No Longer Be a State Secret" (我国首次宣布 解密国家秘密事项 因灾死亡人数不再是国家秘密), China Youth Daily, September 13, 2005, available at http://zqb.cyol.com/content/2005-09/13/content_1175471.htm.

116. The 6th Global Forum on Reinventing Government, *The Seoul Declaration on Participatory and Transparent Governance*, May 27, 2005, Seoul, Republic of Korea.

117. The concept of good governance emerged in the late 1980s to address failures in development policies due to governance concerns, including failure to respect human rights. The concepts of good governance and human rights are mutually reinforcing, both being based on core principles of participation, accountability, transparency and State responsibility. See Office of the United Nations High Commissioner for Human Rights, *Frequently Asked Questions on a Human Rights-Based Approach to Development Cooperation*, HR/PUB/06/8, NY and Geneva 2006, http://www.ohchr.org/english/about/publications/docs/FAQ_en.pdf.

118. See, e.g. He Qinglian, *The Fog of Censorship: Media Control in China*. Human Rights in China: New York, Hong Kong and Brussels (forthcoming summer 2007).

119. See Appendices III: Incidents of Official Cover-Ups, page 236.

120. See Regulation on the Protection of State Secrets in News Publishing, (新闻出版保密规定), issued by the National Administration for the Protection of State Secrets, promulgated June 12, 1992 and effective on October 1, 1992. See Section II, page 160, for the full text of this regulation.

121. Peter Ford, "Ahead of Olympics, China Lifts Foreign Media Restrictions," *The Christian Science Monitor*, December 1, 2006.

122. See "China's Foreign News Rules Spell Trouble for an Open Olympics," HRIC Statement, September 11, 2006, http://www.hrichina.org/public/contents/press?revision%5fid=30672&item%5fid=30669.

123. "China Announces New Measures to Avoid Cover Up of Disasters," *Press Trust of India*, February 7, 2006.

124. "State Council's Legislative Affairs Office Introduces Draft Law on Emergency Response" (国务院法制办介绍《突发事件应对法(草案)》), China.com, July 3, 2006, http://news.china.com/zh_cn/domestic/945/20060703/13444571.html.

125. "Draft Law on Emergency Response Submitted to NPC for Review and Likely to be Made Public Next Year" (突发事件应对法已送人大审议 如无意外明年将出台), China.com, September 22, 2006, http://www.china.com.cn/law/txt/2006-09/22/content_7182459.htm.

126. For example, it was reported that "Dr. David Heymann of the World Health Organization told a US Senate committee that the worldwide epidemic could possibly have been controlled if the Chinese had asked for help earlier." Elisabeth Rosenthal, "Doctor Says China Lied About SARS in Beijing," *International Herald Tribune*, April 11, 2003.

127. See Section II, page 180, for selected provisions of the 1996 regulation. References to a 2001 regulation have not been confirmed, nor has the text been found. For a review of this culture of secrecy and its impact on the SARS epidemic, see Civic Exchange, Christine Loh ed., *At the Epicenter: Hong Kong and the SARS Outbreak*, Hong Kong University Press, Hong Kong, 2004, Chapters 9 & 10.

128. Ministry of Health, Joint United Nations Programme on HIV/AIDS and World Health Organization, *2005 Update on the HIV/AIDS Epidemic and Response in China*, January 2006, p. 1.

129. "Harassment Continues After Prison", China Aid Association, February 13, 2006, http://www.persecutedchurch.com/SOS/Current/SOS-06-02-13.html.

130. See Appendices III: Incidents of Official Cover-Ups, page 236.

131. MOJ Regulation, Art. 2.

132. Ibid.

133. Ibid. See also MPS Regulation, Art. 2.

134. Six Prohibitions on the People's Prison Police (监狱人民警察六条禁令), issued by the Ministry of Justice on February 14, 2006. Six Prohibitions on the People's Reeducation-Through-Labor Police (劳教人民警察六条禁令), issued by the Ministry of Justice on February 14, 2006.

135. According to the UN Working Group on Arbitrary Detention, "a commission vested with the power to take this decision in practice never or seldom meets, the person affected does not appear before it and is not heard, no public and adversarial procedure is conducted, no formal and reasoned decision on a placement is taken . . . the decision-making process completely lacks transparency." United Nations, "Report of the Working Group on Arbitrary Detention, Addendum: Mission to China," December 29, 2004, E/CN.4/2005/6/Add.4, available at http://daccessdds.un.org/doc/UNDOC/GEN/G05/102/74/PDF/G0510274.pdf?OpenElement.

136. United Nations, "Report of the Special Rapporteur on Torture and other Cruel, Inhuman or Degrading Treatment or Punishment—Mission to China," op. cit.

137. International Covenant on Civil and Political Rights (ICCPR), Arts. 4, 7 and Convention Against Torture (CAT) Art. 2; See also Universal Declaration of Human Rights (UDHR), Art. 5.

138. Criminal Law, Arts. 247, 248.

139. In Sichuan Province, as of May 1, 2005, confessions extracted through torture could not be used as evidence. See Several Opinions Regarding the Standardization of Criminal Evidence Work (关于规范刑事证据工作的若干意见), jointly issued by the Sichuan Higher People's Court, the Sichuan People's Procuratorate, and the Sichuan Office of Public Security, effective on May 1, 2005. Also see "Police Testify as to Whether or Not Torture Was Used to Extract Confessions: Sichuan Stipulates Two Situations Under Which Confessions May Be Retracted" (是否刑讯逼供 警察出庭证证：四川规定两种情况下翻供成立), *Legal Daily*, June 7, 2005, http://www.legaldaily.com.cn/xwzx/2005-06/07/content_150861.htm. Confessions extracted under torture are also inadmissible in certain cases of administrative punishment for violations of public order, where the maximum length of detention is 15 days. Law on Punishing Public Order Management Crimes in the PRC (治安管理处罚法), 2006. Examples of public order offenses include solicitation for prostitution (Arts. 67–69), begging (Arts. 40, 41), organizing protests (Arts. 5, 55) and separatism (Art. 47).

140. In 2003, there were a total of 730,355 people convicted under the Criminal Law out of a total of 747,096 individuals prosecuted, which amounts to a conviction rate of 97.8 percent. *Law Yearbook of China 2004* (中国法律年鉴) Beijing: China Law Press, 2004, p. 1054.

141. "Deputy Procurator-General Urges Protection of Suspects' Rights," Xinhua News, November 19, 2006, http://news3.xinhuanet.com/english/2006-11/20/content_5350883.htm.

142. See e.g. MPS Regulation, Art. 2 (B)(7), Art. 2 (C)(7).

143. Article 43 of the Criminal Procedure Law states that the use of torture to coerce statements is strictly prohibited, while Article 45 provides that the gathering of evidence by threats, enticement, deceit or unlawful methods is strictly prohibited. However, evidence obtained by torture or coercion is still admissible in courts.

144. "Authorities Indicate That Compensation May Be Available in the Wrongful Execution Case of Nie Shubin" (聂树斌死刑案官方首次表态 律师可能提出国家赔偿), *People's Daily*, March 18, 2005, http://legal.people.com.cn/GB/42733/3252380.html.

145. United Nations, "Report of the Special Rapporteur on Torture and Other Cruel, Inhuman or Degrading Treatment or Punishment—Mission to China," op. cit., para. 16 and 17 and recommendations. In his report, Dr. Nowak reports that of the 314 cases reported since 2000, the highest percentage (27%) of incidents took place in pre-trial detention centers, with the next highest percent (25%) taking place in reeducation-through-labor camps.

146. "China Denies U.N. Claim of Widespread Torture," MSNBC News Services, December 8, 2005, http://www.msnbc.msn.com/id/10347827.

147. In fact, statistics about death penalty are protected as "top secrets" at the national level. The same statistics at the level of province, autonomous region and directly-administered municipality are classified as "highly secret" and those at the intermediate court level are classified as "secrets." SPC Regulation, Art. 3 (A)(3), Art. 3 (B)(3), Art. 3 (C)(3).

148. "China Executes 10,000 People a Year: NPC Delegate," Agence France Presse, March 15, 2004.

149. See e.g. MOJ Regulation, Article 2 (B)(1), Article 2 (C)(3); SPC Regulation, Article 3 (B)(3), Article 3 (C)(3–5), and Regulation on State Secrets and the Specific Scope of Each Level of Secrets in the Work of the People's Courts (hereinafter, SPP Regulation) (人民法院工作中国家秘密及其密级具体范围的规定), issued by the Supreme People's Court and the National Administration for the Protection of State Secrets in July 1995, Art. 3 (A)(3).

150. Ibid.

151. "'Kinder' Policy Targets Executions," *South China Morning Post*, March 10, 2004. Luo Gan was reported as saying, "If it's possible to execute fewer people, then execute fewer people. If it's possible not to execute people, then don't execute people."

152. The figure of 1,770 known executions that took place in China in 2005 is from Amnesty International. Mark Magnier, "China's High Court to Review Death Sentences," *L.A. Times*, November 1, 2006, http://www.latimes.com/news/nationworld/world/la-fg-death1nov01,1,3315103.story?coll=la-headlines-world. Many believe that the actual number could be as high as 10,000 a year, for Amnesty International reported that, "in March 2004 a delegate at the National People's Congress said that 'nearly 10,000' people are executed per year in China. "Amnesty: Record Rise in Executions," CNN, April 5, 2005, http://edition.cnn.com/2005/POLITICS/04/05/amnesty.death.

153. Edward Cody, "China Puts Journalist on Trial; Writer Had Supported Official Who Denounced Party Members' Graft," *Washington Post,* January 20, 2006.

154. Ibid.

155. Philip P. Pan, "Chinese Whistle-Blower Gets Life Sentence in Bribery Case; Local Party Official Gained Prominence with Letter on Internet," *Washington Post,* November 11, 2005.

156. Cody, op. cit. The *Washington Post* reported that according to Li, all of his interrogations were focused exclusively on articles Li wrote in support of Huang.

157. United Nations' Human Rights Committee, "General Comment 6, The Right to Life," para. 6, http://www.ohchr.org/english/bodies/hrc/comments.htm.

158. ICCPR, Art. 6 (1). See also UDHR Art. 3.

159. United Nations, "Special Rapporteur on Extrajudicial, Summary or Arbitrary Execu-tions, Annual Report 2006," UN Doc. E/CN.4/2006/53, March 8, 2006, para. 3.

160. United Nations, "Report of the Special Rapporteur on Torture and Other Cruel, Inhu-man or Degrading Treatment or Punishment—Mission to China," op. cit., para. 57–58.

161. MPS Regulation, Art. 2 (A)(7), see Section II, page 128.

162. Regulation on State Secrets and the Specific Scope of Each Level of Secrets in Civil Affairs Work (民政工作中国家秘密及其密级具体范围的规定), issued by the Ministry of Civil Affairs and the National Administration for the Protection of State Secrets in 1995, Art. 3.2.1, see Section II, page 179.

163. In the Appellate Ruling on Li Zhi, the Sichuan State Security Bureau confirmed that the China Democracy Party (CDP) is a hostile organization. Li was convicted of member-ship in the CDP. *Sichuan Higher People's Court Criminal Ruling,* (四川省高级人民法院刑事裁定书(2004)川刑终字第43号), No. 43 (2004), February 26, 2004.

164. MPS Regulation, Art. 2 (A)(7), see Section II, p. 128.

165. "Weiquan Online," *China Rights Forum* 3 (2006): 17–20.

166. *Shenzhen Daily* reported on December 8, 2005 that Qiao Songju was "suspected of extort-ing 45,500 *yuan* (US$5,600) and swindling 19,000 *yuan* (US$2,345) from poultry research institutes and companies that produced bird flu vaccines, by threatening reports to rele-vant organs." "Blackmailer Held," *Shenzhen Daily,* December 8, 2005, available at http://my.tdctrade.com/airnewse/index.asp?id=13837&w_sid=99&w_pid=196&w_nid=1757&w_cid=489825&w_idt=2005-12-13.

167. "Bird Flu Whistle-blower Gets Jail Term for Graft," *South China Morning Post,* July 10, 2006.

168. See Human Rights in China, "Implementation of the Convention on the Elimination of All Forms of Discrimination Against Women in the People's Republic of China: A Parallel NGO Report by Human Rights in China," June 26, 2006, http://hrichina.org/public/PDFs/HRIC-CEDAW-REPORT.6.26.2006.pdf.

169. Guangzhou Municipal Regulation on Open Government Information (广州市政府信息公开规定), November 6, 2002, effective January 1, 2003, Decree no. 8 of the Guangzhou Municipal People's Government. Article 2 defines government information as "information made, obtained, or possessed in the course of managing or providing public services by all levels of people's government."

170. Li Yajie and Zhang Qin, "Currently Across China There Are 31 Jurisdictions with Open Government Information Initiatives" (目前全国31个省［自治区、直辖市］政府建立政务公开管理制度), Xinhua News, December 10, 2006, http://news.xinhuanet.com/lianzheng/2006-12/10/content_5466668.htm.

171. The Measures of Shenzhen Municipality for Online Open Government Information (深圳市政府信息网上公开办法), February 25, 2004, effective April 1, 2004, Decree no. 130 of the Shenzhen Municipal People's Government.

172. Shanghai Municipal Regulation on Open Government Information (上海市政府信息公开规定), January 20, 2004, effective May 1, 2004, Decree no. 19 of the Shanghai Municipal People's Government. Horsley, Jamie P. "Shanghai Advances the Cause of Open Government Information in China." *The China Law Center*, April 15, 2004, http://www.law.yale.edu/documents/pdf/Shanghai_Advances.pdf.

173. Horsley, "Shanghai Advances the Cause of Open Government Information in China," op. cit.

174. Ibid.

175. "Citizens Can Sue Local Government for Refusal to Disclose Information" (拒绝公开信息市民可打行政官司), *Legal Daily,* December 3, 2006.

176. Ibid.

177. Chengdu Municipal Measures for Disclosing Government Information in Response to Requests by Application (成都市政务公开依申请公开办法), promulgated and effective November 30, 2006.

178. "Administrative Bodies Cannot Charge Fees for Disclosing Government Information" (行政机关提供政务信息不得收费), *Legal Daily,* December 5, 2006.

179. "Official: Regulations to Balance Public Right to Know Against State Secrets," Xinhua News, December 12, 2006, http://news.xinhuanet.com/english/2006-12/12/content_5474470.htm.

180. "State Council Passes Draft Open Government Information Disclosure Regulation" (国务院原则通过政府信息公开条例(草案)), *Legal Daily,* January 17, 2007.

181. Regulation on Open Government Information of the People's Republic of China (hereinafter, National OGI Regulation) (中华人民共和国政府信息公开条例), January 17, 2007, effective May 1, 2008, Decree no. 492 of the State Council, available at http://www.gov.cn/zwgk/2007-04/24/content_592937.htm. "China Issues Landmark Decree to Encourage Gov't Transparency," Xinhua News, April 24, 2007, http://news.xinhuanet.com/english/2007-04/24/content_6017635.htm.

182. Information Office of the State Council of the People's Republic of China, *China's 'White Paper' on Progress in China's Human Rights Cause in 2003*, March 30, 2004, available at http://english.peopledaily.com.cn/whitepaper/hr2004/hr2004.html.

183. "Citizens' freedom of information, of speech and of the press, as prescribed by law, has been further protected", Chapter 2. Ibid.

184. Horsley, "Shanghai Advances the Cause of Open Government Information in China," op. cit.

185. National OGI Regulation, Art. 4.

186. National OGI Regulation, Art. 1.

187. National OGI Regulation, Art. 14.

188. See Human Rights in China, "Implementation of the Convention on the Elimination of All Forms of Discrimination Against Women in the People's Republic of China: A Parallel NGO Report by Human Rights in China, " op. cit.

189. National OGI Regulation, Art. 12.

190. National OGI Regulation, Arts. 34–5.

191. National OGI Regulation, Art. 8.

192. "China Amends State Secrets Law, Media Considers it a Standard for Drafting Law on Public Disclosure of Information" (中国修改保密法 媒体析称为制定信息公开法准备), China News.com, September 26, 2005, http://www.chinanews.com.cn/news/2005/2005-09-26/8/631072.shtml.

193. Jing Tao (景涛), "Guangzhou: To Guarantee That Information is Made Public, More Than 100,000 Secrets Get Declassified" (广州: 清理解密十万馀项 为信息公开提供保障), *(Protection of State Secrets Work)*, May 2003, p. 6–7.

194. "When the time limit for a state secret matters expires, it should be automatically declassified: If there is a need to extend the time limit, the decision to extend should be made by the unit that made the initial classification or a unit overseeing that unit." State Secrets Law, Art. 16.

195. Jing Tao (景涛), op. cit.

196. Xiao Fang (萧坊), "Amending State Secrets Law Is a Preparation for Drafting Law on Public Disclosure of Information" (修改保密法，为制定信息公开法作准备), *Procuratorial Daily*, September 26, 2005, http://www.jcrb.com/n1/jcrb843/ca416853.htm.

197. "The 4th Conference of the Central Commission for the Protection of State Secrets Opens in Beijing" (中共中央保密委员会第四次会议在北京召开), *(Protection of State Secrets Work)*, January 2006, p. 3.

198. "Revisions to the State Secrets Law Soon to be Submitted to the State Council" (保密法修订草案稿将尽快上报国务院), *Legal Daily*, December 5, 2006.

199. "Baseline of the Protection of State Secrets System Redefined (中国保密制度重置底线 政府信息公开进立法程序), *The Beijing News*, September 20, 2005, available at http://gov.people.com.cn/BIG5/46737/3709800.html.

200. "Our Country Pushes Ahead with Making Civil Affairs Public; the Baseline is Reset for the System of Protecting State Secrets" (我国大力推行政务公开 保密制度重置底线), *Beijing News*, September 20, 2006, available at http://news.sina.com.cn/c/p/2005-09-20/0322781 1050.shtml.

201. "Regulation on Disclosure of Government Information to Be Enacted Soon" (政府信息 公开法规早该出台), Xinhua News, September 14, 2005, http://news.xinhuanet.com/ comments/2005-09/14/content_3484447.htm.

202. "National Administration for the Protection of State Secrets Corrects Direction; Expert Says, 'Our Country Can't Have Too Many Secrets'" (国家保密局调整方向，专家称：国家不 能有太多秘密), *Oriental Outlook*, September 20, 2005, available at http://cn.news.yahoo. com/050920/1005/2f3eh.html.

203. "Our Country Pushes Ahead with Making Civil Affairs Public; the Baseline is Reset for the System of Protecting State Secrets" (我国大力推行政务公开 保密制度重置底线)，op. cit.

204. See Section II, page 179, for relevant excerpts of this regulation.

205. Chan Siu-sin, "Lifting of Secrecy Veil Sheds Light on Worst Dam Tragedy," *South China Morning Post*, October 2, 2005, available at: http://www.probeinternational.org/tgp/index. cfm?DSP=content&ContentID=13830.

206. Ibid.

207. "Our Country Pushes Ahead with Making Civil Affairs Public; the Baseline is Reset for the System of Protecting State Secrets" (我国大力推行政务公开 保密制度重置底线)， op. cit.

208. "State Council's Law Drafting Office Introduces 'Draft Law on Handling Emergency Response Work'" (国务院法制办介绍《突发事件应对法(草案)》), China.com, July 3, 2006, http://news.china.com/zh_cn/domestic/945/20060703/13444571.html.

209. "China Promotes Recording, Videotaping of Interrogations," Xinhua News, May 16, 2006, http://news.xinhuanet.com/english/2006-05/16/content_4554452.htm.

210. Notice Regarding Further Improving Open Court Session Work in Second Instance Death Penalty Cases (最高人民法院关于进一步做好死刑第二审案件开庭审理工作的通知), issued by the Supreme People's Court, December 7, 2005. According to the Criminal Procedure Law, in reviewing appeals, after a review of the paper file it is not required that courts hold a hearing on the appeal as long as the facts and evidence are clear.

211. "China Amends Law to Limit Death Sentences," *China View*, October 31, 2006, available at http://news.xinhuanet.com/english/2006-10/31/content_5272422.htm.

212. "China's Audit Results Will be Made Public Until 2010 Unless They Contain State Secrets" (到2010年中国审计结果除涉国家机密等将全部公开), *Xinhua News,* September 22, 2006, http://news.xinhuanet.com/lianzheng/2006-09/22/content_5124374.htm.

213. "Regulation on Disclosure of Government Information to Be Enacted Soon" (政府信息公开法规早该出台)," op. cit.

214. Dong Zhihui（董智慧）, "The Need to Look at Amending the State Secrets Law from the Basis of the Evolution of Legislation" (从立法基础的演变看修《保密法》的必要性), *(Protection of State Secrets Work),* July 2003, p. 15.

State Secrets Laws and Regulations of the PRC

Editors' Introduction

Up until now—and indeed for the entire history of the Chinese Communist Party—the system of administration used by the Chinese government to manage and control the many matters that it deems to be "state secrets" has been a carefully guarded secret of its own. The laws and regulations that comprise the state secrets system are found mainly in classified publications, only some of which become publicly available.

In this section, we present a comprehensive and wide-ranging set of the main laws and regulations concerning state secrets. **Part A,** Main Statues, Regulations and Supreme Court Interpretation Governing the State Secrecy System in China, contains the two most relevant national laws on this subject, the Law on the Protection of State Secrets (issued in 1988 by the Standing Committee of the National People's Congress) and the Measures for Implementing the Law on the Protection of State Secrets (issued in 1990 by the National Administration for the Protection of State Secrets, or NAPSS), both of which are translated here in full. The third item is the Supreme People's Court's Interpretation of Certain Issues Regarding the Specific Application of the Law When Trying Cases of Stealing, Gathering, Procuring or Illegally Providing State Secrets or Intelligence Outside of the Country, also translated in full.

Part B provides relevant excerpts from several of the key national laws that contain provisions on state secrets crimes: the Criminal Law, the Criminal Procedure Law and the State Security Law.

In **Part C,** we present the four regulations (issued jointly by the NAPSS and the relevant ministry) that specifically set forth the matters classified as state secrets in the work of the public security organs, the people's courts, the procuratorates, and in the administration of prisons and labor camps.

The Regulation on the Protection of State Secrets in News Publishing in **Part D** provides a legal basis for understanding state secrets in media work in China.

Finally, in **Part E,** we offer excerpts from a selection of regulations—issued jointly by the NAPSS and a variety of government bodies and ministries—mandating which matters are to remain state secrets in such diverse areas as environmental protection, family planning, ethnic affairs, and social science research.

The numerous laws and regulations comprising the state secrets system are not readily available to the public. Due to the lack of a comprehensive system of access, it is difficult to determine if these laws have been updated or even, as noted in this report, if they have been rescinded. Within these limits, HRIC has made best efforts to identify the most current versions of the laws and regulations. In compiling this compendium, primary and secondary legal sources were consulted, including bulletins, commentaries and treatises published or available online.

This is the first time that such an extensive compilation of laws and regulations on state secrets has ever been published in English, and the first time that many of the individual documents have been made available to English readers. The importance of making these laws and regulations more generally available is to assist ordinary citizens, reporters, human rights workers and others to understand the state secrets system—not only so that they might avoid disclosing or possessing state secrets themselves, but perhaps more importantly, to begin the process of transparency that is essential to fair governance and judicial openness, and to reveal the arbitrariness of the system.

A.

Main Statutes, Regulations, and Supreme Court Interpretation Governing the State Secrecy System in China

1. LAW ON THE PROTECTION OF STATE SECRETS OF THE PEOPLE'S REPUBLIC OF CHINA

Editors' Note:

Promulgated in 1988, the Law on the Protection of State Secrets lays out the scope of matters that are designated as state secrets, as well as the responsibilities of each level of state secrets organ in classifying and handling information. Article 2, the wording of which is repeated in numerous other documents related to state secrets, sets forth the broad definition of what constitutes a state secret: all matters that are "related to state security and national interests and, as specified by legal procedure, are entrusted to a limited number of people for a given period of time."

Article 8, the key article in this law, lists seven categories of matters that are classified as state secrets: policies on national affairs and national defense, diplomatic affairs, matters involving national economic and social development, national scientific and technology matters, and investigations of criminal offenses. The seventh item is a "catch-all" phrase that encompasses "all other matters classified as state secrets by the national State Secrets Bureau," thus giving that body (the NAPSS) unlimited and unlegislated power to classify as a state secret virtually any information that it deems could harm the "security and interests of the state."

The Chinese text of the following law is available at: http://www.gov.cn/banshi/2005-08/21/content_25096.htm.

中华人民共和国保守国家秘密法

Law on the Protection of State Secrets of the People's Republic of China

颁布日期 ： 1988年9月5日
实施日期 ： 1989年5月1日
颁布单位 ： 全国人大常委会

Promulgation Date: September 5, 1988
Effective Date: May 1, 1989
Promulgation Body: The Standing Committee of the National People's Congress

第一章 总则

Chapter One: General Provisions

Purpose

第一条
为保守国家秘密，维护国家的安全和利益，保障改革开放和社会主义建设事业的顺利进行，制定本法。

Article 1

This law is formulated for the purpose of protecting state secrets, safeguarding state security and national interests and ensuring the smooth progress of reform, of opening to the outside world, and of socialist construction.

Definition of state secrets

第二条
国家秘密是关系国家的安全和利益，依照法定程序确定，在一定时间内只限一定范围的人员知悉的事项。

Article 2

State secrets are matters that are related to state security and national interests and, as specified by legal procedure, are entrusted to a limited number of people for a given period of time.

Obligation to protect state secrets

第三条
一切国家机关、武装力量、政党、社会团体、企业事业单位和公民都有保守国家秘密的义务。

Article 3

All state organs, armed forces, political parties, public organizations, enterprises, institutions and citizens have an obligation to protect state secrets.

Principle of active prevention, emphasizing priorities

第四条
保守国家秘密的工作，实行积极防范、突出重点、既确保国家秘密又便利各项工作的方针。

Article 4

The work of protecting state secrets shall be carried out in line with the principle of active prevention, emphasizing priorities, and ensuring the safety of state secrets while at the same time facilitating work in all other fields.

第五条

国家保密工作部门主管全国保守国家秘密的工作。县级以上地方各级保密工作部门在其职权范围内，主管本行政区域保守国家秘密的工作。

中央国家机关在其职权范围内，主管或者指导本系统保守国家秘密的工作。

第六条

县级以上国家机关和涉及国家秘密的单位，根据实际情况设置保密工作机构或者指定人员，管理本机关和本单位保守国家秘密的日常工作。

第七条

在保守、保护国家秘密以及改进保密技术、措施等方面成绩显著的单位或者个人，应当给予奖励。

Article 5

The national State Secrets Bureau shall be responsible for protecting state secrets throughout the country. The local state secrets bureaus at or above the county level shall, within the scope of their functions and powers, be responsible for protecting state secrets in the administrative areas under their jurisdiction.

The central state organs shall, within the scope of their functions and powers, be responsible for and guide the work of protecting state secrets in their own organs and in the departments subordinate to them.

Article 6

State organs at or above the county level and units whose work involves state secrets shall, in accordance with their actual conditions, set up bodies or designate personnel to administer the day-to-day work of protecting state secrets within their own organs or units.

Article 7

Units or individuals that have rendered meritorious service in protecting and safeguarding state secrets and improving techniques and measures in this field should be rewarded.

National State Secrets Bureau

State organs at or above the county level

Rewards

第二章 国家秘密的范围和密级

Chapter Two: The Scope and Classification of State Secrets

Scope of state secrets

第八条
国家秘密包括符合本法第二条规定的下列秘密事项：

Article 8

In accordance with the provisions of Article 2 of this law, state secrets shall include the following:

（一）国家事务的重大决策中的秘密事项；

（二）国防建设和武装力量活动中的秘密事项；

（三）外交和外事活动中的秘密事项以及对外承担保密义务的事项；

（四）国民经济和社会发展中的秘密事项；

（五）科学技术中的秘密事项；

（六）维护国家安全活动和追查刑事犯罪中的秘密事项；

（七）其他经国家保密工作部门确定应当保守的国家秘密事项。

(1) secret matters concerning major policy decisions on state affairs;

(2) secret matters in the building of national defense and in the activities of the armed forces;

(3) secret matters in diplomatic activities and in activities related to foreign countries, as well as secrets to be maintained as commitments to foreign countries;

(4) secret matters in national economic and social development;

(5) secret matters concerning science and technology;

(6) secret matters concerning activities for safeguarding state security and the investigation of criminal offenses; and

(7) other matters that are classified as state secrets by the national State Secrets Bureau.

不符合本法第二条规定的，不属于国家秘密。

政党的秘密事项中符合本法第二条规定的，属于国家秘密。

Matters that do not conform with the provisions of Article 2 of this law shall not be considered state secrets.

Secrets of political parties that conform with the provisions of Article 2 of this law shall be considered state secrets.

第九条
国家秘密的密级分为"绝密"、"机密"、"秘密"三级。

"绝密"是最重要的国家秘密，泄露会使国家的安全和利益遭受特别严重的损害；"机密"是重要的国家秘密，泄露会使国家的安全和利益遭受严重的损害；"秘密"是一般的国家秘密，泄露会使国家的安全和利益遭受损害。

Article 9

State secrets are classified into three categories: top secret, highly secret and secret.

Top secret information refers to vital state secrets, the disclosure of which will cause extremely serious harm to state security and national interests; highly secret information refers to important state secrets, the disclosure of which will cause serious harm to state security and national interests; and secret information refers to ordinary state secrets, the disclosure of which will cause harm to state security and national interests.

Classification categories

第十条
国家秘密及其密级的具体范围，由国家保密工作部门分别会同外交、公安、国家安全和其他中央有关机关规定。

国防方面的国家秘密及其密级的具体范围，由中央军事委员会规定。

关于国家秘密及其密级的具体范围的规定，应当在有关范围内公布。

Article 10

The specific scope of state secrets and their classification levels shall be stipulated by the national State Secrets Bureau together with the ministries of Foreign Affairs, Public Security and State Security and other relevant central organs.

The specific scope of state secrets related to national defense, and their classification levels, shall be stipulated by the Central Military Commission.

Provisions on the specific scope and classification levels of state secrets shall be made known within relevant quarters.

Central responsibility for stipulating scope and classification levels

第十一条
各级国家机关、单位对所产生的国家秘密事项，应当按照国家秘密及其密级具体范围的规定确定密级。

对是否属于国家秘密和属于何种密级不明确的事项，由国家保密工作部门，省、自治区、直辖市的保密工作部

Article 11

State organs and units at various levels shall, in accordance with the provisions on the specific scope and classification levels of state secrets, determine the classification level of any state secret that arises in said organs and units.

If it is unclear whether or not a certain matter is a state secret or which classification level a matter should belong to,

Responsibility of state organs and units

Unclear scope or classification

门，省、自治区政府所在地的市和经国务院批准的较大的市的保密工作部门或者国家保密工作部门审定的机关确定。在确定密级前，产生该事项的机关、单位应当按照拟定的密级，先行采取保密措施。

the question shall be determined by either the national State Secrets Bureau; the state secrets bureaus at the level of province, autonomous region or directly-administered municipality; the state secrets bureau of a city where the government of a province or an autonomous region is located; the state secrets bureau of a larger city approved by the State Council; or an organ examined and approved by the national State Secrets Bureau. Pending the classification of the secret, the state organ or unit where the matter has arisen shall initially take security measures in accordance with the classification level proposed.

Marking classified materials

第十二条

属于国家秘密的文件、资料，应当依照本法第九条、第十条、第十一条的规定标明密级。不属于国家秘密的，不应标为国家秘密文件、资料。

Article 12

In accordance with the provisions in Articles 9, 10 and 11 of this law, documents and other materials that are determined to contain state secrets shall be marked with their classification level. Documents and other materials that are not determined to be state secrets shall not be marked as such.

Determination when differences arise regarding definition/classification

第十三条

对是否属于国家秘密和属于何种密级有争议的，由国家保密工作部门或者省、自治区、直辖市的保密工作部门确定。

Article 13

When differences arise as to whether or not a matter is a state secret, or regarding which classification level it belongs to, the question shall be determined by the national State Secrets Bureau or the state secrets bureaus at the level of province, autonomous region or directly-administered municipality.

第十四条

机关、单位对国家秘密事项确定密级时，应当根据情况确定保密期限。确定保密期限的具体办法由国家保密工作部门规定。

第十五条

国家秘密事项的密级和保密期限，应当根据情况变化及时变更。密级和保密期限的变更，由原确定密级和保密期限的机关、单位决定，也可以由其上级机关决定。

第十六条

国家秘密事项的保密期限届满的，自行解密；保密期限需要延长的，由原确定密级和保密期限的机关、单位或者其上级机关决定。

国家秘密事项在保密期限内不需要继续保密的，原确定密级和保密期限的机关、单位或者其上级机关应当及时解密。

Article 14

When determining the classification level of state secrets, state organs and units shall, according to the circumstances, also determine the length of time that the secrets should be protected. Specific measures for determining the time period shall be formulated by the national State Secrets Bureau.

Length of time for secrets protection

Article 15

The classification levels of state secrets and the length of time that they should be protected should be altered in accordance with changing circumstances. Such alterations shall be decided on by the state organs or units that originally determined the classification level of the secrets and the time period for protecting them, or by a higher-level department.

Alteration of classification levels and length of time for protection

Article 16

A state secret shall be automatically declassified when the time period for protecting it has expired; in cases where it is necessary to extend the time period, the matter shall be decided on by the state organ or unit that originally determined the classification level of the secret and the time period for protecting it, or by a higher-level department.

If the time period for protecting a state secret does not need to be extended, it should be declassified without delay by the state organ or unit that originally determined its classification level and the time period for protecting it, or by a higher-level department.

Automatic declassification and time extension

第三章 保密制度

Chapter Three: The System for Protecting State Secrets

Security measures for classified documents, materials and objects

第十七条
属于国家秘密的文件、资料和其他物品的制作、收发、传递、使用、复制、摘抄、保存和销毁，由国家保密工作部门制定保密办法。

Article 17

The national State Secrets Bureau shall formulate security measures regarding the making, receiving, dispatching, transmitting, use, copying, excerpting, preservation and destruction of documents and other materials and objects that are state secrets.

采用电子信息等技术存取、处理、传递国家秘密的办法，由国家保密工作部门会同中央有关机关规定。

Measures for electronically storing, processing and transmitting state secrets by this and other technical means shall be formulated by the national State Secrets Bureau together with the relevant central authorities.

Security measures for top-secret documents, materials and objects

第十八条
对绝密级的国家秘密文件、资料和其他物品，必须采取以下保密措施：

Article 18

Documents and other materials and objects that are classified as top-secret state secrets must be protected by the following security measures:

（一）非经原确定密级的机关、单位或者其上级机关批准，不得复制和摘抄；

(1) They shall not be copied or excerpted without prior approval from the state organ or unit that originally determined their classification level, or by a higher-level department.

（二）收发、传递和外出携带，由指定人员担任，并采取必要的安全措施；

(2) They shall be dispatched, received, delivered and carried only by personnel that are specially designated to take on these responsibilities, and additional security measures shall be adopted as needed; and

（三）在设备完善的保险装置中保存。

(3) They shall be kept in perfectly equipped safes.

经批准复制、摘抄的绝密级的国家秘密文件、资料和其他物品，依照前款规定采取保密措施。

Once approval has been granted for the copying or excerpting of documents and other materials or objects classified as top-secret state secrets, security measures shall be adopted in accordance with the provisions in the preceding paragraphs.

第十九条

属于国家秘密的设备或者产品的研制、生产、运输、使用、保存、维修和销毁，由国家保密工作部门会同中央有关机关制定保密办法。

Article 19

Security measures shall be formulated by the national State Secrets Bureau, together with the relevant central authorities, for the manufacture, production, transportation, use, storage, maintenance and destruction of equipment or goods classified as state secrets.

Security measures for classified equipment or goods

第二十条

报刊、书籍、地图、图文资料、声像制品的出版和发行以及广播节目、电视节目、电影的制作和播放，应当遵守有关保密规定，不得泄露国家秘密。

Article 20

In the publication and distribution of newspapers, periodicals, books, maps, illustrated materials and audio-visual products, and in the production and broadcast of radio and television programs and films, the relevant security regulations shall be complied with and no state secrets shall be disclosed.

Publication, distribution and broadcast

第二十一条

在对外交往与合作中需要提供国家秘密事项的，应当按照规定的程序事先经过批准。

Article 21

When state secrets must be provided in order to maintain relations and cooperation with foreign countries, prior approval must be obtained in accordance with the prescribed procedures.

第二十二条

具有属于国家秘密内容的会议和其他活动，主办单位应当采取保密措施，并对参加人员进行保密教育，规定具体要求。

Article 22

With regard to meetings and other activities that involve state secrets, the host unit shall adopt the appropriate security measures, provide the participants with education on how to protect state secrets, and set the specific requirements for doing so.

Meetings and other activities

Forbidden military zones and places not open to the public

第二十三条
军事禁区和属于国家秘密不对外开放的其他场所、部位，应当采取保密措施，除依照国家有关规定经过批准外，不得擅自决定对外开放或者扩大开放范围。

Article 23

Forbidden military zones and other places that involve state secrets and are not open to the public shall be protected by security measures; no one may decide to open them to the public or enlarge the area that is open to the public without prior approval obtained in accordance with the relevant state regulations.

Private contacts or correspondence

第二十四条
不准在私人交往和通信中泄露国家秘密。

Article 24

No state secrets shall be disclosed in private contacts or correspondence.

Carrying documents and other materials and objects

携带属于国家秘密的文件、资料和其他物品外出不得违反有关保密规定。

When carrying documents and other material and objects classified as state secrets outside of one's unit, the relevant security regulations shall be obeyed.

不准在公共场所谈论国家秘密。

No state secrets shall be discussed in public places.

Transmission of state secrets

第二十五条
在有线、无线通信中传递国家秘密的，必须采取保密措施。

Article 25

Transmission of state secrets through wired or wireless communications shall be protected by security measures.

不准使用明码或者未经中央有关机关审查批准的密码传递国家秘密。

No state secrets shall be transmitted either by plain code or by a secret code that has not been examined and ap-proved by the relevant central authorities.

不准通过普通邮政传递属于国家秘密的文件、资料和其他物品。

No documents or other materials and objects classified as state secrets shall be transmitted by ordinary mail.

Transmission out of the country

第二十六条
未经有关主管部门批准，禁止将属于国家秘密的文件、资料和其他物品携带、传递、寄运至境外。

Article 26

Without prior approval by a higher-level department, no document or any other material or object classified as a state secret shall be carried, transmitted, posted or transported out of the country.

第二十七条
国家秘密应当根据需要，限于一定范围的人员接触。绝密级的国家秘密，经过批准的人员才能接触。

Article 27

State secrets shall, depending on the circumstances, be accessible only to a limited number of people. Top-secret state secrets shall be accessible only to personnel who have obtained prior approval.

Limited access to state secrets

第二十八条
任用经管国家秘密事项的专职人员，应当按照国家保密工作部门和人事主管部门的规定予以审查批准。

Article 28

Personnel to be placed in charge of state secrets shall be examined and approved in accordance with the regulations of the national State Secrets Bureau and the relevant personnel department.

Personnel in charge of state secrets

经管国家秘密事项的专职人员出境，应当经过批准任命的机关批准；国务院有关主管机关认为出境后将对国家安全造成危害或者对国家利益造成重大损失的，不得批准出境。

Exit from the country by personnel placed in charge of state secrets must be approved by the same organ that originally approved their appointment. If the State Council's department in charge of such matters determines that exiting the country will endanger state security or cause serious damage to national interests, no approval shall be granted for said exit.

Exit from the country

第二十九条
机关、单位应当对工作人员进行保密教育，定期检查保密工作。

Article 29

State organs and units shall provide education to their personnel on how to protect state secrets and shall check up on protection of state secrets work at regular intervals.

Personnel education

第三十条
国家工作人员或者其他公民发现国家秘密已经泄露或者可能泄露时，应当立即采取补救措施并及时报告有关机关、单位；有关机关、单位接到报告后，应当立即作出处理。

Article 30

If state employees and other citizens should find that state secrets have been disclosed or are in danger of being disclosed, they should immediately take measures to remedy the situation and promptly report the matter to the state organs and units concerned, which shall, upon receiving such reports, deal with the matter without delay.

Remedial action and reporting

第四章 法律责任

Chapter Four: Legal Responsibility

Criminal liability

第三十一条

违反本法规定，故意或者过失泄露国家秘密，情节严重的，依照刑法第一百八十六条的规定追究刑事责任。

Article 31

If any individual violates the provisions of this law and discloses state secrets intentionally or through negligence under circumstances that are deemed to be serious, he or she shall be held criminally responsible in accordance with the provisions of Article 186 of the [1979] Criminal Law*.

[*Ed. Note: Article 186 of the 1979 Criminal Law corresponds to Article 398 of the 1997 Criminal Law, the text of which is included below under "Selected Provisions of Major Laws Involving State Secrets."]

Administrative sanctions

违反本法规定，泄露国家秘密，不够刑事处罚的，可以酌情给予行政处分。

If any individual violates the provisions of this law and discloses state secrets under circumstances that are deemed not serious enough for criminal punishment, he or she may be given administrative sanctions in accordance with the specific circumstances of each case.

Criminal liability for providing state secrets/intelligence outside of the country

第三十二条

为境外的机构、组织、人员窃取、刺探、收买、非法提供国家秘密的，依法追究刑事责任。

Article 32

Any individual who steals, gathers, procures or illegally provides state secrets or intelligence outside of the country shall be held criminally responsible in accordance with the law.

第五章 附则

Chapter Five: Additional Provisions

第三十三条

国家保密工作部门根据本法制定实施办法，报国务院批准后施行。

Article 33

The national State Secrets Bureau shall, in accordance with this law, formulate measures for its implementation. These measures shall take effect once approval has been granted by the State Council.

Implementation

第三十四条

中央军事委员会根据本法制定中国人民解放军保密条例。

Article 34

The Central Military Commission shall, in accordance with this law, formulate the regulations of the Chinese People's Liberation Army on the protection of state secrets.

Central Military Commission regulations

第三十五条

本法自１９８９年５月１日起施行。１９５１年６月公布的《保守国家机密暂行条例》同时废止。

Article 35

This law shall take effect as of May 1, 1989. The Provisional Regulation on Protecting State Secrets, promulgated in June 1951, shall be rescinded as of the same date.

Effective date

2. MEASURES FOR IMPLEMENTING THE LAW ON THE PROTECTION OF STATE SECRETS OF THE PEOPLE'S REPUBLIC OF CHINA

Editors' Note:

Measures for Implementing the Law on the Protection of State Secrets, issued in 1990 by the National Administration for the Protection of State Secrets, provides for retroactive classification of information not already enumerated or classified as a state secret, if disclosure of information *could* result in any one of the "eight consequences" deemed to cause harm to the security and interests of the state. Those include "affecting national unity, ethnic unity or social stability," "hindering defense work," and "endangering the ability of the state to defend its power." This last clause has been invoked to prosecute charges of "endangering state security," which have been used to gain convictions for a wide range of non-violent political acts.

These measures also specify which security classification (top secret, highly secret and secret) is determined by which level of state secrets bureau throughout the country, with top-secret matters classified at the national level and so forth downward through the administrative levels (Article 10). This document also details the situations under which individuals may either be rewarded for protecting secrets (such as reporting potential or actual leaks to the authorities) or punished for disclosing them.

The Chinese text of the following measures is available at: http://www.stats.gov.cn/tjgl/swdcglgg/xgfg/t20041118_402209111.htm.

中华人民共和国保守国家秘密法实施办法

Measures for Implementing the Law on the Protection of State Secrets of the People's Republic of China

颁布日期 ： 1990年5月25日
实施日期：1990年5月25日
颁布单位 ： 国家保密局（第1号）

Promulgation Date: May 25, 1990
Effective Date: May 25, 1990
Promulgation Body: National Administration for the Protection of State Secrets (Document No. 1)

第一章 总 则

Chapter One: General Provisions

第一条
根据《中华人民共和国保守国家秘密法》（以下简称保密法）的规定，制定本办法。

Article 1

These measures have been formulated in accordance with the Law on the Protection of State Secrets of the People's Republic of China (hereafter referred to as the State Secrets Law).

Promulgating authority

第二条
国家保密工作部门是国务院的职能机构，根据《保密法》和本办法主管全国的保密工作。

Article 2

The national State Secrets Bureau is a functioning organ of the State Council and, in accordance with the State Secrets Law and these measures, is in charge of all protection of state secrets work performed throughout the country.

National State Secrets Bureau

县以上地方各级政府的保密工作部门，在上级保密工作部门的指导下，依照保密法律、法规和规章管理本行政区域的保密工作。

State secrets bureaus in all local governments at the county level or above, under the direction of a higher-level state secrets bureau, shall administer work that comes under the domain of protecting state secrets in accordance with the laws, rules and regulations on protection of state secrets work.

State secrets bureaus at or above the county level

第三条
中央国家机关在其职权范围内主管或者指导本系统的保密工作，组织和监督下级业务部门执行保密法律、法规和规章，可以根据实际情况单独或者会同有关部门制定主管业务方面的保密规章。

Article 3

Organs of the central government shall, within the limits of their authority, either be in charge themselves, or direct another body to be in charge of, protection of state secrets work; shall organize and supervise lower-level pro-

Organs of the central government

fessional departments in the implementation of laws, regulations and rules for protecting state secrets, and may, in accordance with the actual circumstances, by itself or in cooperation with the relevant department, formulate rules and regulations on the protection of state secrets to be used within that professional field.

Consequences of disclosure and classification

第四条

某一事项泄露后会造成下列后果之一的，应当列入国家秘密及其密级的具体范围（以下简称保密范围）：

（一）危害国家政权的巩固和防御能力；

（二）影响国家统一、民族团结和社会安定；

（三）损害国家在对外活动中的政治、经济利益；

（四）影响国家领导人、外国要员的安全；

（五）妨害国家重要的安全保卫工作；

（六）使保护国家秘密的措施可行性降低或者失效；

（七）削弱国家的经济、科技实力；

（八）使国家机关依法行使职权失去保障。

Article 4

If any matter, once disclosed, could result in any of the following, it should be considered to fall within the scope of state secrets and their security classifications (hereafter referred to as the "scope of state secrets protection"):

(1) Endangering the ability of the state to consolidate and defend its power.

(2) Affecting national unity, ethnic unity or social stability.

(3) Harming the political or economic interests of the state in its dealings with foreign countries.

(4) Affecting the security of state leaders or top foreign officials.

(5) Hindering important security or defense work of the state.

(6) Causing a decrease in the feasibility, or a loss of effectiveness to, the measures used to safeguard state secrets.

(7) Weakening the economic or technological strength of the nation.

(8) Causing state organs to lose the ability to exercise their authority according to law.

第五条

保密范围应当根据情况变化适时修订，修订的程序依照《保密法》第十条的规定办理。

Article 5

The scope of secrets to be protected should be amended according to changing circumstances and in a timely manner. The procedure for making such amendments shall be handled in accordance with the provisions in Article 10 of the State Secrets Law.

Amendment of scope of secrets

第六条

涉及国家秘密的机关、单位，应当进行经常性的保密教育和检查，落实各项保密措施，使所属人员知悉与其工作有关的保密范围和各项保密制度。

Article 6

All organs and units whose work involves state secrets shall carry out regular education on, and inspections of, protection of state secrets work, and they shall implement various measures related to such work so that their personnel may learn the scope of secrets to be protected in their work and the various systems related to protecting state secrets.

Implementation by organs and units

第二章 确定密级、变更密级和解密

Chapter Two:
Determining Security Classifications, Changing Classification Levels and Declassification

第七条

各机关、单位依照规定确定密级、变更密级和解密，应当接受其上级机关和有关保密工作部门的指导和监督。

Article 7

All organs and units shall determine security classifications, change security classifications and declassify matters according to regulations and shall receive guidance and supervision from a higher-level organ or a relevant state secrets bureau.

Guidance and supervision

第八条

各机关、单位对所产生的国家秘密事项，应当依照保密范围的规定及时确定密级，最迟不得超过十日。

Article 8

The security classification of any state secret matter that arises within an organ or unit shall be determined in a timely manner, not to exceed a period of 10 days, in accordance with the regulations on the scope of state secrets protection.

Determination in a timely manner

Amendment of classification

第九条

密级确定以后，确定密级的机关、单位发现不符合保密范围规定的，应当及时纠正；上级机关或者有关保密工作部门发现不符合保密范围规定的，应当及时通知确定密级的机关、单位纠正。

Article 9

After the security classification has been determined, if the organ or unit that made the determination finds that the classification level does not correspond to the level stipulated for its scope of state secrets protection, it shall amend the determination in a timely manner. If a higher-level organ or a relevant state secrets bureau finds that the classification level does not correspond to the level stipulated for the scope of state secrets protection for that matter, it shall immediately notify the organ or unit that made the determination and request that the determination be amended.

Determination when classification is unclear

第十条

对是否属于国家秘密和属于何种密级不明确的事项，依照下列规定确定：

Article 10

If it is unclear whether or not a certain matter is a state secret or which classification level a matter should belong to, the following provisions shall be used to make the determination:

- **Top-secret level**

（一）绝密级由国家保密工作部门确定；

(1) Top-secret level matters shall be determined by the national State Secrets Bureau.

- **Highly-secret level**

（二）机密级由省、自治区、直辖市的或者其上级的保密工作部门确定；

(2) Highly-secret level matters shall be determined by the state secrets bureau of a province, autonomous region or directly-administered municipality, or by another higher-level state secrets bureau.

- **Secret level**

（三）秘密级由省、自治区政府所在地的市和国务院批准的较大的市的或者其上级的保密工作部门确定。

(3) Secret level matters shall be determined by the state secrets bureau of a city in which the government of a province or an autonomous region is located, by the state secrets bureau of a larger city approved by the State Council, or by another higher-level state secrets bureau.

其他机关经国家保密工作部门审定，可以在其主管业务方面行使前款规定的确定密级权。

Other organs approved by the national State Secrets Bureau may also exercise their authority to determine the security classification of matters that are within their area of expertise.

第十一条

对是否属于国家秘密和属于何种密级不明确的事项，产生该事项的机关、单位无相应确定密级权的，应当及时拟定密级，并在拟定密级后的十日内依照下列规定申请确定密级：

（一）属于主管业务方面的事项，逐级报至国家保密工作部门审定的有权确定该事项密级的上级机关；

（二）其他方面的事项，逐级报至有权确定该事项密级的保密工作部门。

接到申请的机关或者保密工作部门，应当在三十日内作出批复。

Article 11

Classification if organ/unit does not have relevant authority

If it is unclear whether or not a certain matter is a state secret or which classification level a matter should belong to, and if the organ or unit in which the matter arose does not have the relevant authority to determine its security classification, the organ or unit in which the matter arose shall make an initial determination. Once an initial determination has been made, the organ or unit shall submit an application for approval of the security classification within 10 days according to the following provisions:

(1) Matters that are within that organ or unit's area of expertise should be sent to a higher-level organ that has been approved by the national State Secrets Bureau and that has the authority to determine the security classification of that matter.

(2) Other matters should be sent to the state secrets bureau that has the authority to determine the security classification of that matter.

The organ or state secrets bureau shall issue a reply within 30 days of receipt of the application.

Reporting by state secrets bureaus and other organs

第十二条
依照本办法第十条、第十一条的规定行使确定密级权的保密工作部门和其他机关，应当将其行使确定密级权的情况报至规定保密范围的部门。

Article 12

In exercising their authority to determine security classifications according to the provisions in Article 10 and Article 11 of these measures, state secrets bureaus and other organs shall report the details of the matter they are determining to the department that stipulates the scope of state secrets protection for that matter.

Responsibility for marking classified documents, information or other materials

第十三条
属于国家秘密的文件、资料和其他物品，由确定密级的机关、单位标明密级；依照本办法第十条、第十一条的规定确定密级的，由提出申请的机关、单位标明密级。

Article 13

Documents, information or other materials that are state secrets shall be marked with their security classification by the organ or unit that determined the classification level. If their security classification was determined according to Article 10 and/or Article 11 of these measures, the organ or unit that applied for approval shall mark them with their security classification level.

属于国家秘密的事项不能标明密级的，由产生该事项的机关、单位负责通知接触范围内的人员。

If it is not possible to mark a state secret matter with a security classification, the organ or unit responsible for producing the matter should notify all personnel who could come into contact with that matter.

Change of initial determination if:

第十四条
国家秘密事项的密级，应当根据下列情形之一，由确定密级的机关、单位及时变更：

Article 14

If either of the following situations should arise, the security classification level of a state secret matter shall be promptly changed by the organ or unit that made the initial determination:

- **definite change in level of harm**

（一）该事项泄露后对国家的安全和利益的损害损害程度已发生明显变化的；

(1) The level of harm that could be caused to state security and interests if the secret were disclosed has undergone a definite change; or

（二）因为工作需要，原接触范围需作很大改变的。

情况紧急时，可以由上级机关直接变更密级。

第十五条

对保密期限内的国家秘密事项，根据情况变化，有下列情形之一，由确定密级的机关、单位及时解密：

（一）该事项公开后无损于国家的安全和利益的；

（二）从全局衡量公开后对国家更为有利的。

情况紧急时，可以由上级机关直接解密。

第十六条

对于上级机关或者有关保密工作部门要求继续保密的事项，在所要求的期限内不得解密。

第十七条

各机关、单位确定密级、变更密级或者决定解密，应当由承办人员提出具体意见交本机关、单位的主管领导人审核批准；工作量较大的机关、单位可以由主管领导人授权本机关、单位的保密工作机构或者指定负责人员办理批准前的审核工作。

(2) For work reasons, the original scope of the matter must be changed.

If the situation is urgent, a higher-level organ may directly change a security classification.

Article 15

If either of the following situations should arise, state secret matters that are still within the time period for remaining classified shall be promptly declassified, according to changing circumstances, by the organ or unit that made the initial determination:

(1) If making the matter public would cause no harm to state security or interests; or

(2) If it is judged that, in light of the overall situation, making the matter public would benefit the country.

If the situation is urgent, a higher-level organ may directly declassify the matter.

Article 16

If a higher-level organ or a relevant state secrets bureau requests that a matter remain classified, then the matter should not be declassified during the time period requested.

Article 17

Whenever any organ or unit determines or changes a security classification, or decides to declassify a state secret, it shall pass on the specific opinion given by the person who initiated the matter to the leader in charge of that organ or unit for examination

- ***work reasons***

Declassification within remaining classified time period if:

- ***no harm or***

- ***benefit to country***

No declassification

and approval. If the work load of that organ or unit is too great, the leader in charge of that organ or unit may authorize its protection of state secrets office, or may appoint another person, to handle the work of examining the matter before it is approved.

Written record

前款规定的执行情况应当有文字记载。

The circumstances of the acts mentioned in the preceding paragraph shall be recorded in writing.

Notification of changed classification or declassification

第十八条

国家秘密事项变更密级或者解密后，应当及时通知有关的机关、单位；因保密期限届满而解密的事项除外。

Article 18

After the security classification of a state secret matter has been changed or the matter has been declassified, the relevant organ or unit shall be promptly notified; however, matters that have been declassified upon the expiration of the time limit for them to remain classified shall be exempt from this requirement.

Marking changed/declassified documents, information or other materials

国家秘密事项变更密级或者解密后，应当及时在有关文件、资料和其他物品上标明；不能标明的，应当及时将变更密级或者解密的决定通知接触范围内的人员。

After the security classification of a state secret matter has been changed or the matter has been declassified, the change shall be promptly marked on the relevant documents, information or other materials. If it is not possible to do so, personnel within the relevant field should be notified in advance of the decision to change the security classification or to declassify the matter.

Organ/unit closed down or merged

第十九条

确定密级的机关、单位被撤销或者合并，有关变更密级和解密的工作由承担其原职能的机关、单位负责；无相应的承担机关、单位的，由有关的上级机关或者保密工作部门指定的机关负责。

Article 19

If the organ or unit that determined a particular security classification is closed down or has been merged with another organ or unit, the work of changing that particular security classification or declassifying that matter is the responsibility of the organ or unit that formerly performed the functions of that organ or unit. If there is no corresponding organ or unit that formerly performed those functions, an organ appointed by a higher-level organ or state secrets bureau shall be responsible for performing such work.

第三章 保密制度

Chapter Three: The System for Protecting State Secrets

第二十条

接触国家秘密事项的人员或者机关、单位的范围，由确定密级的机关、单位限定。接触范围内的机关、单位，由其主管领导人限定本机关、单位的具体接触范围。

工作需要时，上级机关、单位可以改变下级机关、单位限定的国家秘密的接触范围。

Article 20

The organ or unit that determines the security classification of a state secret matter shall determine which individuals, organs or units may have access to that matter. The leaders in charge of the organs or units that have access to state secret matters shall determine the specific range of access allowed within that organ or unit.

When necessary, a higher-level organ or unit may change the range of access granted by a lower-level organ or unit.

Access

第二十一条

复制属于国家秘密的文件、资料和其他物品，或者摘录、引用、汇编其属于国家秘密的内容，不得擅自改变原件的密级。

Article 21

When copying or duplicating documents, information or other materials that contain state secrets, or when excerpting, quoting, or compiling information that contains state secrets, changing the security classification of such matters without authorization is not permitted.

No change of classification without authority

第二十二条

在对外交往与合作中，对方以正当理由和途径要求提供国家秘密时，应当根据平等互利的原则，按照国家主管部门的规定呈报有相应权限的机关批准，并通过一定形式要求对方承担保密义务。

Article 22

In working and cooperating with foreign countries, if the other party makes a request for a state secret, providing there is a suitable reason and the request is made via the appropriate channels, the request may be granted on the basis of equality and mutual benefit. According to the regulations of the relevant state department, a report must

Requests by foreign countries

be submitted to the organ with the corresponding jurisdiction and approval must be granted. In addition, the other party must be asked, in a specified manner, to take on the responsibility of protecting that state secret.

对外提供国家秘密涉及多部门的，可以由有关的保密工作部门进行组织、协调工作。

If a state secret that is provided to a foreign country involves multiple departments, the relevant state secrets bureau may do the work of organizing and coordinating these procedures.

对外提供涉及经济、科技和社会发展方面的国家秘密，批准机关应当向同级政府的保密工作部门通报有关情况。

If a state secret that is provided to a foreign country involves the economy, science and technology, or social development, the organ that gave the approval shall inform the state secrets bureau at the appropriate governmental level of the situation.

Measures for meetings

第二十三条
具有属于国家秘密内容的会议，主办单位应当采取下列保密措施：

Article 23
Whenever meetings are held that involve state secrets, the host unit shall adopt the following measures to protect state secrets:

- *location*

（一）选择具备保密条件的会议场所；

(1) It shall select a meeting location that has suitable facilities for protecting state secrets.

- *participants*

（二）根据工作需要，限定参加会议人员的范围，对参加涉及绝密级事项会议的人员予以指定；

(2) It shall limit the scope of participants to only those required for the work at hand, and it shall be responsible for appointing the participants at meetings involving top-secret matters.

- *equipment and documents*

（三）依照保密规定使用会议设备和管理会议文件、资料；

(3) It shall follow the regulations on the protection of state secrets in using equipment and managing documents and information during meetings.

- *passing on contents*

（四）确定会议内容是否传达及传达范围。

(4) It shall determine whether or not the contents of the meeting

should be passed on to others,
and if so, to whom.

第二十四条

涉及国家秘密的重要活动，主办单位可以制定专项保密方案并组织实施；必要时，有关保密工作部门应当会同主办单位工作。

Article 24

When important events are held that involve state secrets, the host unit may formulate special plans for the protection of state secrets and may organize and implement such plans. If necessary, the relevant state secrets bureau shall assist the host unit in this work.

Important events

第二十五条

属于国家秘密不对外开放的场所、部位的保密措施，由有关机关、单位制定或者与保密工作部门的共同商定。

Article 25

Measures to protect state secrets at locations or sites that are not open to outsiders shall be formulated by the relevant organ or unit, or decided upon in discussion with a state secrets bureau.

Locations/sites not open to the public

第二十六条

发生泄密事件的机关、单位，应当迅速查明被泄露的国家秘密的内容和密级、造成或者可能造成危害的范围和严重程度、事件的主要情节和有关责任者，及时采取补救措施，并报告有关保密工作部门和上级机关。

Article 26

In the event that a state secret is disclosed, the organ or unit in which the disclosure occurred shall immediately launch an investigation to determine the contents and security classification of the state secret that was disclosed, the extent of the damage that has been or could be caused, the main details of the incident, the severity of the punishment, and the names of those responsible for the incident. It should then take appropriate measures to remedy the situation and report the incident to a state secrets bureau and a higher-level organ.

Investigation, remedy and reporting if disclosure occurs

第四章 奖 惩

Chapter Four:
Rewards and Punishments

Rewards

第二十七条
凡有下列表现之一的个人或者集体，由其所在机关、单位、上级机关或者当地政府依照规定给予奖励：

Article 27
Individuals or groups that do any of the following shall be rewarded by the organ or unit where they work, a higher-level organ, or the local government, according to the relevant body's regulations:

（一）在危急情况下，保护国家秘密安全的；

(1) Safeguard state secrets under dangerous circumstances.

（二）对泄露或者非法获取国家秘密和行为及时检举的；

(2) Immediately report any acts involving the disclosure or illegal procurement of state secrets.

（三）发现他人泄露或者可能泄露国家秘密，立即采取补救措施，避免或者减轻损害后果的；

(3) Upon discovering that a state secret has been or could be disclosed, take immediate action to remedy the situation and thereby prevent or reduce any harmful results.

（四）在涉及国家秘密的专项活动中，严守国家秘密，对维护国家的安全和利益作出重要贡献的；

(4) Safeguard state secrets and make a major contribution to the protection of state security and interests during any special events that involve state secrets.

（五）在国家保密技术的开发、研究中取得重大成果或者显著成绩的；

(5) Obtain significant results or make outstanding achievements in the development or research of new technology used to protect state secrets.

（六）一贯严守国家秘密或者长期从事保密工作的管理，事迹突出的；

(6) Have consistently safeguarded state secrets or have been engaged in the work of managing state secrets over a long period of time and have made outstanding contributions.

（七）长期经管国家秘密的专职人
员，一贯忠于职守，确保国
家秘密安全的。

(7) Have worked as special state secrets personnel over a long period of time or have consistently and loyally safeguarded and guaranteed the security of state secrets.

第二十八条

对于为保守国家秘密作出突出贡献的
个人或者集体，各级保密工作部门和
其他有关的保密工作机构，应当向有
关机关、单位或者政府提出奖励的建
议；需要时，也可以直接给予奖励。

Article 28

For any individuals or groups that make outstanding contributions to the protection of state secrets, all levels of state secrets bureaus and other relevant state secrets organs shall make suggestions to the relevant organ, unit or government on the rewards to be granted. If needed, said departments and organs may grant the reward directly.

Rewards for outstanding contributions by individuals/groups

第二十九条

凡泄露国家秘密尚不够刑事处罚的，
有关机关、单位应当依照规定并根据
被泄露事项的密级和行为的具体情节
，给予行政处分。

Article 29

If the disclosure of a state secret is not serious enough to warrant criminal punishment, the relevant organ or unit shall apply administrative sanctions according to regulations and in accord with the specific circumstances of the act itself and the security classification of the state secret matter involved.

Administrative sanctions

第三十条

对泄露国家秘密尚不够刑事处罚，有
下列情节之一的，应当从重给予行政
处分：

（一）泄露国家秘密已造成损害后
果的；

（二）以谋取私利为目的的泄露国
家秘密的；

Article 30

If the disclosure of a state secret is not serious enough to warrant criminal punishment but one of the following circumstances apply, more severe administrative sanctions shall be imposed:

(1) Disclosure of the state secret has already resulted in harmful consequences.

(2) Disclosure of the state secret was done for the purpose of gaining profit for oneself.

More severe administrative sanctions if enumerated circumstances present

（三）泄露国家秘密危害不大但次数较多的或者数量较大的；

(3) Disclosure of the state secret did not result in a great amount of harm but there were either numerous incidences of disclosure or numerous secrets were disclosed.

（四）利用职权强制他人违反保密规定的。

(4) An individual used the authority and power of his or her position to force another person to break the regulations on the protection of state secrets.

Severe administrative sanctions if already punished/exempt from prosecution

第三十一条
泄露国家秘密已经人民法院判处刑罚的以及被依法免予起诉或者免予刑事处罚的，应当从重给予行政处分。

Article 31

If a verdict has been reached by a people's court on the disclosure of a state secret and the defendant was exempted from prosecution or punishment according to law, severe administrative sanctions shall be imposed.

Lenient administrative sanctions or exemption from punishment

第三十二条
泄露秘密级国家秘密，情节轻微的，可以酌情免予或者从轻给予行政处分；泄露机密级国家秘密，情节轻微的，可以酌情从轻给予行政处分，也可以免予行政处分；泄露绝密级国家秘密，情节特别轻微的，可以酌情从轻给予行政处分。

Article 32

If a secret-level state secret is disclosed under circumstances deemed to be minor, the perpetrator may be duly exempt from punishment or lenient administrative sanctions may be imposed. If a highly-secret level state secret is disclosed under circumstances deemed to be minor, the perpetrator may also be duly exempt from punishment or lenient administrative sanctions may be imposed. If a top-secret level state secret is disclosed under circumstances deemed to be very minor, lenient administrative sanctions may be imposed.

Request for administrative sanctions/punishment

第三十三条
各级保密工作部门和其他有关的保密工作机构，可以要求有关机关、单位对泄密责任者给予行政处分或者处罚；对行政处分或者处罚决定持有异议时，可以要求对作出的行政处分或者处罚进行复议。

Article 33

Any level of state secrets bureau, or any other organ related to the work of state secrets protection, may request the relevant organ or unit to impose administrative sanctions or punishments on those responsible for disclosing state secrets. If there is a dispute regarding the decision to impose an administrative sanction or punishment, a request may be made to the organ carrying out the sanction or punishment to reconsider its decision.

第三十四条

因泄露国家秘密所获取的非法收入，应当予以没收并上交国库。

Article 34

If any illegal funds are obtained through the disclosure of a state secret, such funds shall be confiscated and handed over to government coffers.

Confiscation of illegal funds

第五章 附 则

Chapter Five: Additional Provisions

第三十五条

《保密法》和本办法规定中的"泄露国家秘密"是指违反保密法律、法规和规章的下列行为之一：

（一）使国家秘密被不应知悉者知悉的；

（二）使国家秘密超出了限定的接触范围，而不能证明未被不应知悉者知悉的。

Article 35

The phrase "disclosing state secrets" as stipulated in the State Secrets Law and in these measures refers to any of the following acts that are in violation of the laws, rules and regulations pertaining to the protection of state secrets:

(1) Allowing a state secret to be known by any individual that is not allowed to know such information.

(2) Allowing a state secret to go beyond the specified group of individuals allowed access to that secret, and to not be able to prove that such a disclosure of information did not take place.

Disclosing state secrets

第三十六条

《保密法》和本办法规定中的"是否属于国家秘密和属于何种密级不明确的事项"，是指在有关的保密范围中未作明确规定，而符合本办法第四条规定的事项。

Article 36

The phrase "if it is unclear whether or not a certain matter is a state secret or which classification level a matter should belong to," as stipulated in the State Secrets Law and in these measures, refers to matters whose scope of state secrets protection has not yet been

If it is unclear whether or not a matter is a state secret or which classification level it should belong to

clearly stipulated and which correspond to any of the items listed under Article 4 of these measures.

No application to other secret matters or internal (neibu) matters

第三十七条
不属于国家秘密的其他秘密或者机关、单位的内部事项，不适用《保密法》和本办法。

Article 37

The State Secrets Law and these measures do not apply to other secret matters, or to the internal (*neibu*) matters of an organ or unit, that are not state secrets.

Documents, information or materials that were classified as state secrets before the State Secrets Law

第三十八条
《保密法》施行前所确定的各项国家秘密文件、资料和其他物品，应当依照《保密法》和本办法进行清理，重新确定密级和保密期者解密。

Article 38

Any documents, information or materials that were classified as state secrets before the State Secrets Law came into effect must be checked and verified in accordance with the State Secrets Law and these measures, and the matters must either be given new security classifications and new time periods for remaining protected as secrets, or be declassified.

尚未进行清理的，仍应当按照原定密级管理；发生、发现泄露行为时，应当依照《保密法》和本办法的有关规定，对所涉及的事项是否属于国家秘密和属于何种密级重新加以确认。

Matters that have not yet undergone the checking and approval process shall be handled according to their original security classification, and if an act of disclosing such a state secret occurs or is discovered, a new determination shall be made, in accordance with the State Secrets Law and these measures, as to whether or not the matter concerned is a state secret and if so, which security classification it should be given.

Implementation by central state organs and local governments

第三十九条
中央国家机关和各省、自治区、直辖市政府，可以根据本系统、本地区的实际情况，根据《保密法》和本办法制定实施细则。

Article 39

State organs belonging to the central government and all local governments at the level of province, autonomous region or directly-administered municipality shall formulate detailed principles for implementing the State Secrets Law and these measures according to the actual conditions of their system or region.

第四十条
本办法由国家保密工作部门负责。

Article 40
These measures are the responsibility of the national State Secrets Bureau.

Responsibility for measures

第四十一条
本办法自发布之日起施行。

Article 41
These measures shall take effect as of the day they are issued.

Effective date

3. THE SUPREME PEOPLE'S COURT INTERPRETATION OF CERTAIN ISSUES REGARDING THE SPECIFIC APPLICATION OF THE LAW WHEN TRYING CASES OF STEALING, GATHERING, PROCURING OR ILLEGALLY PROVIDING STATE SECRETS OR INTELLIGENCE OUTSIDE OF THE COUNTRY

Editors' Note:

The Supreme People's Court's Interpretation of Certain Issues Regarding the Specific Application of the Law When Trying Cases of Stealing, Gathering, Procuring or Illegally Providing State Secrets or Intelligence Outside of the Country lays out the punishments for this particular set of crimes based on the "seriousness" of the circumstances of the crime (e.g. providing top-secret state secrets is more serious than lower-level secrets), with the death penalty being mandated where the crime is considered to have been committed under "especially deplorable circumstances." Such vague wording leaves a great deal of latitude for the courts and procuratorates to determine the "seriousness" of any given crime.

A key article is Article 6, which extends the scope of punishment for this crime to any act of sending materials over the Internet that might contain state secrets or intelligence, a crime that has been used to punish many dissidents and writers in recent years.

The Chinese text of the following interpretation is available at: http://www.court. gov.cn/lawdata/explain/penal/200303210002.htm.

最高人民法院关于审理为境外窃取、刺探、收买、非法提供国家秘密、情报案件具体应用法律若干问题的解释

The Supreme People's Court's Interpretation of Certain Issues Regarding the Specific Application of the Law When Trying Cases of Stealing, Gathering, Procuring or Illegally Providing State Secrets or Intelligence Outside of the Country

文件号：法释〔2001〕4号
颁布部门：最高人民法院
颁布日期：2001年1月17日
实施日期：2001年1月22日

Document No.: Legal Interpretation No. 4 (2001)
Promulgation Body: The Supreme People's Court
Promulgation Date: January 17, 2001
Effective Date: January 22, 2001

为依法惩治为境外的机构、组织、人员窃取、刺探、收买、非法提供国家秘密、情报犯罪活动，维护国家安全和利益，根据刑法有关规定，现就审理这类案件具体应用法律的若干问题解释如下：

Purpose

In order to punish, according to law, the criminal activities of stealing, gathering, procuring or illegally providing state secrets or intelligence to bodies, organizations or individuals outside of the country, and to safeguard the security and interests of the state, the following interpretation of certain issues regarding the specific application of the law when hearing such cases is hereby given, based on the relevant provisions of the Criminal Law:

第一条

刑法第一百一十一条规定的"国家秘密"，是指《中华人民共和国保守国家秘密法》第二条、第八条以及《中华人民共和国保守国家秘密法实施办法》第四条确定的事项。

Article 1

The term "state secrets" as stipulated in Article 111 of the Criminal Law refers to those matters specified in Article 2 and Article 8 of the Law on the Protection of State Secrets of the People's Republic of China and in Article 4 of the Measures for Implementing the Law on the Protection of State Secrets of the People's Republic of China.

"State secrets"

刑法第一百一十一条规定的"情报"，是指关系国家安全和利益、尚未公开或者依照有关规定不应公开的事项。

The term "intelligence" as stipulated in Article 111 of the Criminal Law refers to those matters that concern state security and interests which have either not yet been made public, or should not be made public, according to relevant regulations.

"Intelligence"

Intelligence to bodies/organizations/individuals outside of country	对为境外机构、组织、人员窃取、刺探、收买、非法提供国家秘密之外的情报的行为，以为境外窃取、刺探、收买、非法提供情报罪定罪处罚。	Acts of stealing, gathering, procuring or illegally providing intelligence that is not a state secret to bodies, organizations or individuals outside of the country shall be determined to be, and punished as, the crime of stealing, gathering, procuring or illegally providing intelligence to anyone outside of the country.
State secrets/intelligence to anyone outside of country under "especially serious circumstances"	**第二条** 为境外窃取、刺探、收买、非法提供国家秘密或者情报，具有下列情形之一的，属于"情节特别严重"，处十年以上有期徒刑、无期徒刑，可以并处没收财产：	**Article 2** If an act of stealing, gathering, procuring or illegally providing state secrets or intelligence to anyone outside of the country is committed under any of the following circumstances, it shall be considered a crime committed under "especially serious circumstances" and a sentence of between ten years' imprisonment and life imprisonment may be imposed and the defendant's property and belongings may be confiscated:
• ***top-level***	（一）为境外窃取、刺探、收买、非法提供绝密级国家秘密的；	(1) Stealing, gathering, procuring or illegally providing top-secret level state secrets to anyone outside of the country;
• ***three or more highly-secret***	（二）为境外窃取、刺探、收买、非法提供三项以上机密级国家秘密的；	(2) Stealing, gathering, procuring or illegally providing three or more highly-secret level state secrets to anyone outside of the country;
• ***state secrets/intelligence and especially serious harm***	（三）为境外窃取、刺探、收买、非法提供国家秘密或者情报，对国家安全和利益造成其他特别严重损害的。	(3) Stealing, gathering, procuring or illegally providing state secrets or intelligence to anyone outside of the country, the results of which cause especially serious harm to state security and interests.
Especially deplorable circumstances and death penalty	实施前款行为，对国家和人民危害特别严重、情节特别恶劣的，可以判处死刑，并处没收财产。	If, in carrying out the acts mentioned in the above items, especially serious harm is caused to the state or the people, and if such acts are committed under especially deplorable circumstances, the death penalty may be

imposed and the defendant's property and belongings may be confiscated.

第三条	**Article 3**	*State secrets/intelligence to anyone outside of country under the following circumstances*
为境外窃取、刺探、收买、非法提供国家秘密或者情报，具有下列情形之一的，处五年以上十年以下有期徒刑，可以并处没收财产：	If an act of stealing, gathering, procuring or illegally providing state secrets or intelligence to anyone outside of the country is committed under any of the following circumstances, a sentence of between five and 10 years' imprisonment may be imposed and the defendant's property and belongings may be confiscated:	
（一）为境外窃取、刺探、收买、非法提供机密级国家秘密的；	(1) Stealing, gathering, procuring or illegally providing highly-secret level state secrets to anyone outside of the country;	• *highly-secret*
（二）为境外窃取、刺探、收买、非法提供三项以上秘密级国家秘密的；	(2) Stealing, gathering, procuring or illegally providing three or more secret-level state secrets to anyone outside of the country; and	• *three or more secret-level*
（三）为境外窃取、刺探、收买、非法提供国家秘密或者情报，对国家安全和利益造成其他严重损害的。	(3) Stealing, gathering, procuring or illegally providing state secrets or intelligence to anyone outside of the country, the results of which cause serious harm to state security and interests.	• *state secrets/intelligence and serious harm*
第四条	**Article 4**	*Secret level/intelligence to anyone outside of country and "less serious circumstances"*
为境外窃取、刺探、收买、非法提供秘密级国家秘密或者情报，属于"情节较轻"，处五年以下有期徒刑、拘役、管制或者剥夺政治权利，可以并处没收财产。	If an act of stealing, gathering, procuring or illegally providing secret level state secrets or intelligence to anyone outside of the country is committed under circumstances that are deemed to be "less serious," a sentence of five years' imprisonment or less, criminal detention, public surveillance or deprivation of political rights may be imposed and the defendant's property and belongings may be confiscated.	

"Knows/should know" standard for providing matter not marked to anyone outside of the country

第五条

行为人知道或者应当知道没有标明密级的事项关系国家安全和利益，而为境外窃取、刺探、收买、非法提供的，依照刑法第一百一十一条的规定以为境外窃取、刺探、收买、非法提供国家秘密罪定罪处罚。

Article 5

If a person knows, or should know, that any matter not marked with a security classification has a bearing on state security and interests but still steals, gathers, procures or illegally provides such matters to anyone outside of the country, the determination and punishment for this crime shall be that of stealing, gathering, procuring or illegally providing state secrets outside of the country according to the provisions in Article 111 of the Criminal Law.

Transmission via Internet

第六条

通过互联网将国家秘密或者情报非法发送给境外的机构、组织、个人的，依照刑法第一百一十一条的规定定罪处罚；将国家秘密通过互联网予以发布，情节严重的，依照刑法第三百九十八条的规定定罪处罚。

Article 6

If state secrets or intelligence are illegally transmitted via the Internet to bodies, organizations or individuals outside of the country, the determination and punishment for this crime shall be in accordance with the provisions in Article 111 of the Criminal Law. If state secrets are sent over the Internet and the circumstances are serious, the determination and punishment for this crime shall be in accordance with the provisions in Article 398 of the Criminal Law.

Verification of whether state secret and classification

第七条

审理为境外窃取、刺探、收买、非法提供国家秘密案件，需要对有关事项是否属于国家秘密以及属于何种密级进行鉴定的，由国家保密工作部门或者省、自治区、直辖市保密工作部门鉴定。

Article 7

When trying cases of stealing, gathering, procuring or illegally providing state secrets to anyone outside of the country, verification must be obtained as to whether or not the matter is a state secret and if so, which security classification it belongs to. Such verification must be obtained either from the national State Secrets Bureau or from a state secrets bureau at the provincial, autonomous region or directly-administered municipality level.

B.

Selected Provisions of Major Laws Involving State Secrets

Editors' Note:

Below some of the key points in national laws that contain provisions on state secrets are excerpted. Article 4 of the State Security Law is crucial in understanding what the Chinese authorities consider to be crimes that "endanger state security": the list encompasses both espionage-related and political crimes, the latter of which are not specified but come under the general headings of "conspiring to overthrow the government" (subversion, or any act that threatens the government), "splitting the country" (all ethnic unrest, such as protests in Tibet or the Xinjiang Uyghur Autonomous Region), and "overthrowing the socialist system" (used less often in recent years than the other two, which are invoked regularly to punish dissidents of all stripes).

The Criminal Law sets forth the actual sentences for all crimes; the provisions here are related to the crimes of stealing, gathering, procuring or illegally providing state secrets or intelligence outside of the country, endangering state security, and possessing or disclosing state secrets. As with the Supreme People's Court Interpretation, above, the Criminal Law also uses the vague term of "serious" circumstances to determine the severity of punishment, thus again allowing substantial latitude to the courts. The Criminal Procedure Law explicates the legal procedures to be followed when the judicial organ arrests an individual, such as the right to an attorney.

中华人民共和国国家安全法

颁布部门：全国人大常委会
颁布日期：1993年2月22日
实施日期：1993年2月22日

State Security Law of the People's Republic of China

Promulgation Body: The Standing Committee of the National People's Congress
Promulgation Date: February 22, 1993
Effective Date: February 22, 1993

Definition of "any act of endangering state security"

第四条
任何组织和个人进行危害中华人民共和国国家安全的行为都必须受到法律追究。

本法所称危害国家安全的行为，是指境外机构、组织、个人实施或者指使、资助他人实施的，或者境内组织、个人与境外机构、组织、个人相勾结实施的下列危害中华人民共和国国家安全的行为：

（一）阴谋颠覆政府，分裂国家，推翻社会主义制度的；

（二）参加间谍组织或者接受间谍组织及其代理人的任务的；

（三）窃取、刺探、收买、非法提供国家秘密的；

Article 4

Any organization or individual that has committed any act of endangering state security of the People's Republic of China shall be prosecuted according to law.

The phrase "any act of endangering state security" as referred to in this law means any of the following acts of endangering state security of the People's Republic of China committed by institutions, organizations or individuals outside the territory of the People's Republic of China, or by other persons under the instigation or financial support of the afore-mentioned institutions, organizations or individuals, or by organizations or individuals within the territory in collusion with institutions, organizations or individuals outside of the country:

(1) conspiring to overthrow the government, splitting the country or overthrowing the socialist system;

(2) joining an espionage organization or accepting a mission assigned by an espionage organization or by its agent;

(3) stealing, gathering, procuring or illegally providing state secrets;

（四）策动、勾引、收买国家工作
人员叛变的；

（五）进行危害国家安全的其他破
坏活动的。

(4) instigating, luring or bribing a government official to turn traitor; and,

(5) committing any other act of sabotage that endangers state security.

第二十条

任何个人和组织都不得非法持有属于国家秘密的文件、资料和其他物品。

Article 20

No individual or organization may illegally hold any documents, information or other materials classified as state secrets.

Illegally holding state secrets

第二十三条

境外机构、组织、个人实施或者指使、资助他人实施，或者境内组织、个人与境外机构、组织、个人相勾结实施危害中华人民共和国国家安全的行为，构成犯罪的，依法追究刑事责任。

Article 23

Whenever any act of endangering state security committed by institutions, organizations or individuals outside of the country, or committed by other persons under the instigation or financial support of said institutions, organizations or individuals, or committed by institutions or individuals within the country in collusion with institutions, organizations or individuals outside of the country constitutes a crime, such institutions, organizations or individuals shall be held criminally responsible according to law.

Institutions/organizations or individuals outside of country and criminal responsibility for endangering state security

第二十八条

故意或者过失泄露有关国家安全工作的国家秘密的，由国家安全机关处十五日以下拘留；构成犯罪的，依法追究刑事责任。

Article 28

Anyone who intentionally or mistakenly discloses a state secret related to state security work shall be detained by a state security organ for not more than 15 days; if such act constitutes a crime, that person shall be held criminally responsible.

Disclosing state secrets related to state security work

Search by state security organ and criminal responsibility for illegally holding or disclosing state secrets

第二十九条
对非法持有属于国家秘密的文件、资料和其他物品的，以及非法持有、使用专用间谍器材的，国家安全机关可以依法对其人身、物品、住处和其他有关的地方进行搜查；对其非法持有的属于国家秘密的文件、资料和其他物品，以及非法持有、使用的专用间谍器材予以没收。

Article 29

A state security organ may search the body, belongings, residence and other related places of anyone who illegally holds documents, information or other materials classified as state secrets, or who illegally holds or uses equipment especially for espionage purposes, and it may confiscate such documents, information, materials and equipment.

非法持有属于国家秘密的文件、资料和其他物品，构成泄露国家秘密罪的，依法追究刑事责任。

Anyone who illegally holds documents, information or other materials classified as state secrets and commits the crime of disclosing state secrets shall be held criminally responsible according to law.

中华人民共和国刑法（1997修订）

Criminal Law of the People's Republic of China (1997)

颁布部门：全国人民大会
颁布日期：1997年3月14日
实施日期：1997年10月1日
修正日期：1999年12月25日，
2001年8月31日，2001年12月29日，
2002年12月28日，2005年2月28日，
2006年6月29日

Promulgation Body: National People's Congress
Promulgation Date: March 14, 1997
Effective Date: October 1, 1997
Amended: December 25, 1999; August 31, 2001; December 29, 2001; December 28, 2002; February 28, 2005; June 29, 2006

Sentences for stealing or providing state secrets outside the country and "circumstances"

第一百一十一条
为境外的机构、组织、人员窃取、刺探、收买、非法提供国家秘密或者情报的，处五年以上十年以下有期徒刑；情节特别严重的，处十年以上有期徒刑或者无期徒刑；情节较轻的，处五年以下有期徒刑、拘役、管制或者剥夺政治权利。

Article 111

Whoever steals, gathers, procures or illegally provides state secrets or intelligence for an organ, organization or individual outside of the country shall be sentenced to fixed-term imprisonment of not less than five years but not more than 10 years. If the circumstances are deemed to be especially serious, he shall be sentenced to fixed-term imprisonment of not less than 10 years or life imprisonment. If the circumstances are deemed to be less serious, he shall be sentenced to fixed-term imprisonment of not more than five years, criminal detention, public surveillance or deprivation of political rights.

第一百一十三条

本章上述危害国家安全罪行中，除第一百零三条第二款、第一百零五条、第一百零七条、第一百零九条外，对国家和人民危害特别严重、情节特别恶劣的，可以判处死刑。

犯本章之罪的，可以并处没收财产。

Article 113

Whoever commits any of the crimes of endangering state security as mentioned above in this chapter, except for those crimes mentioned in Paragraph 2 of Article 103 and in Articles 105, 107 and 109,* if the crime causes especially serious harm to the state and the people or if the circumstances are especially serious, he or she may be sentenced to death.

Whoever commits any of the crimes mentioned in this chapter may also be subject to confiscation of their property and belongings.

*[*Ed. Note: These are: inciting others to split the state or undermining national unity; subverting state power or overthrowing the socialist system; spreading rumors or slander to subvert state power; funding criminal activities in China from abroad; and the defection of government officials while discharging their official duties abroad.]*

Death penalty if endangering state security and especially serious harm or circumstances

Confiscation of property and belongings

第二百八十二条

以窃取、刺探、收买方法，非法获取国家秘密的，处三年以下有期徒刑、拘役、管制或者剥夺政治权利；情节严重的，处三年以上七年以下有期徒刑。

非法持有属于国家绝密、机密的文件、资料或者其他物品，拒不说明来源与用途的，处三年以下有期徒刑、拘役或者管制。

Article 282

Whoever uses the methods of stealing, gathering or procuring to illegally obtain state secrets shall be sentenced to fixed-term imprisonment of not more than three years, criminal detention, public surveillance or deprivation of political rights. If the circumstances are deemed to be serious, he or she shall be sentenced to fixed-term imprisonment of not less than three years but not more than seven years.

Whoever unlawfully holds documents, information or other materials classified as "top secret" or "highly secret" state secrets and refuses to explain their

Sentences for stealing, etc. under serious circumstances

source or purpose shall be sentenced to fixed-term imprisonment of not more than three years, criminal detention or public surveillance.

Violations by state personnel	第三百九十八条 国家机关工作人员违反保守国家秘密法的规定，故意或者过失泄露国家秘密，情节严重的，处三年以下有期徒刑或者拘役；情节特别严重的，处三年以上七年以下有期徒刑。	**Article 398** State personnel who violate provisions of the Law on the Protection of State Secrets and who, under circumstances deemed to be serious, either intentionally or through negligence disclose state secrets, shall be sentenced to three years' imprisonment or less, or criminal detention. If the circumstances of their crime are deemed to be especially serious, they shall be sentenced to not less than three years and not more than seven years' imprisonment.
Violations by non-state personnel	非国家机关工作人员犯前款罪的，依照前款的规定酌情处罚。	Non-state personnel who commit the crime mentioned in the preceding paragraph shall be punished according to the circumstances and in accordance with the provisions of the preceding paragraph.
	中华人民共和国刑事诉讼法（1996修订） 颁布部门：全国人民大会 颁布日期：1996年3月17日 实施日期：1997年1月1日	**Criminal Procedure Law of the People's Republic of China (1996)** Promulgation Body: National People's Congress Promulgation Date: March 17, 1996 Effective Date: January 1, 1997
Evidence • *authority to collect/obtain*	第四十五条 人民法院、人民检察院和公安机关有权向有关单位和个人收集、调取证据。有关单位和个人应当如实提供证据。	**Article 45** The people's courts, the people's procuratorates and the public security organs have the authority to collect or obtain evidence from all units and individuals concerned. The units and individuals concerned shall provide truthful evidence.
• *confidential*	对于涉及国家秘密的证据，应当保密。	Evidence involving state secrets shall be kept confidential.

凡是伪造证据、隐匿证据或者毁灭证据的，无论属于何方，必须受法律追究。

Anyone who falsifies, conceals or destroys evidence, regardless of which side of a case he belongs to, must be investigated under law.

- *falsification, concealment or destruction*

第九十六条

犯罪嫌疑人在被侦查机关第一次讯问后或者采取强制措施之日起，可以聘请律师为其提供法律咨询、代理申诉、控告。犯罪嫌疑人被逮捕的，聘请的律师可以为其申请取保候审。涉及国家秘密的案件，犯罪嫌疑人聘请律师，应当经侦查机关批准。

Article 96

After a criminal suspect has been interrogated by an investigative organ for the first time, or starting from the day on which coercive measures are adopted against him, he may appoint a lawyer to provide him with legal advice and to file petitions and complaints on his behalf. If a criminal suspect has been arrested, his lawyer may request that the suspect be released on bail pending trial. If a case involves state secrets, the criminal suspect must obtain the approval of the investigative organ before appointing a lawyer.

Appointment of lawyer

受委托的律师有权向侦查机关了解犯罪嫌疑人涉嫌的罪名，可以会见在押的犯罪嫌疑人，向犯罪嫌疑人了解有关案件情况。律师会见在押的犯罪嫌疑人，侦查机关根据案件情况和需要可以派员在场。涉及国家秘密的案件，律师会见在押的犯罪嫌疑人，应当经侦查机关批准。

The appointed lawyer shall have the right to find out from the investigative organ what crime the criminal suspect is suspected of, and may meet with the criminal suspect in custody to learn the details of the case. When the lawyer meets with the criminal suspect in custody, the investigative organ may, according to the circumstances of the case and as it deems necessary, send one or more of its personnel to be present at the meeting. If a case involves state secrets, before the lawyer meets with the criminal suspect, he must obtain the approval of the investigative organ.

Rights of appointed lawyer

第一百五十二条

人民法院审判第一审案件应当公开进行。但是有关国家秘密或者个人隐私的案件，不公开审理。

Article 152

Trials of the first instance heard in a people's court shall be heard in public. However, cases involving state secrets or the private affairs of individuals shall not be heard in public.

Public or not public trials

十四岁以上不满十六岁未成年人犯罪的案件，一律不公开审理。十六岁以上不满十八岁未成年人犯罪的案件，一般也不公开审理。

对于不公开审理的案件，应当当庭宣布不公开审理的理由。

No cases involving crimes committed by minors who have reached the age of 14 but not the age of 16 shall be heard in public. Generally, cases involving crimes committed by minors who have reached the age of 16 but not the age of 18 shall also not be heard in public.

The reason for not hearing a case in public shall be announced in court.

The full Chinese text of the above laws are available at:

- State Security Law of the People's Republic of China: http://www.gov.cn/ziliao/flfg/2005-08/05/content_20927.htm
- Criminal Law of the People's Republic of China: http://www.people.com.cn/item/faguiku/xingf/R1010.html
- Criminal Procedure Law of the People's Republic of China: http://www.gov.cn/banshi/2005-05/25/content_887.htm

C.

Four Classified Regulations
Pertaining to Law Enforcement
and the Judiciary

1. REGULATION ON STATE SECRETS AND THE SPECIFIC SCOPE OF EACH LEVEL OF SECRETS IN PUBLIC SECURITY WORK

Editors' Note:

The following regulation details the precise scope of state secrets and internal matters in public security (police) work. Issued jointly by the Ministry of Public Security and the National Administration for the Protection of State Secrets in February 1995, this regulation is itself classified as a "secret" level document.

This regulation mandates a far-reaching classification of basic information in police work, ranging from the "deployment" of law enforcement duties to undisclosed statistics about arrests of state security suspects and sentencing of offenders to the reeducation-through-labor system.

Reflecting the role of the public security organs in suppressing political dissent and social strife, Article 2 lists as top secret any "important" information on "international hostile organizations," "splittist organizations" and "hostile religious organizations" that are currently under investigation by a public security organ. Information on handling illegal gatherings, demonstrations, disturbances, riots, and other critical political incidents that have a "major influence" on local social order is considered "highly secret."

This regulation also contains a level of secrecy below "secret" which is termed "*neibu*" (internal). Article 3 lists the items that—although not technically classed as state secrets—still may not be released to the public without consent of the relevant body. This information includes statistics on kidnapping and trafficking in humans, details of criminal cases whose disclosure would have a "negative impact" on the public, and certain information on violations of the law or codes of conduct by police officers.

The source for the following regulation is: 国家保密局（编），《国家秘密及其密级具体范围的规定选编》（修订本）（机密），（北京：金城出版社，1997），7–12 [National Administration for the Protection of State Secrets, ed., *Selected Regulations on State Secrets and the Specific Scope of Each Level of Secrets* (Revised Edition, Classified as "Highly Secret"), (Beijing: Jincheng Publishing House, 1997), 7–12].

公安工作中国家秘密及其密级具体范围的规定

Regulation on State Secrets and the Specific Scope of Each Level of Secrets in Public Security Work

颁布日期：1995年3月28日
实施日期：1995年5月1日

Promulgation Date: March 28, 1995
Effective Date: May 1, 1995

Promulgating authority

第一条
根据《中华人民共和国保守国家秘密法》第二章第十条规定，制定本规定。

Article 1

This regulation has been formulated in accordance with Chapter 2, Article 10 of the Law on the Protection of State Secrets of the People's Republic of China.

Scope of each classification level

第二条
公安工作中国家秘密及其密级的具体范围：

Article 2

State secrets and the specific scope of each level of secrets in public security work are as follows:

Top secret

（一）绝密级事项

A. Matters classed as top secret

1. 党和国家主要领导人、来访的外国国家元首和政府首脑未公开的活动日程、警卫部署，住地、路线、现场警卫的警力部署及其通信联络方法和秘密安全设施、执勤方案、警卫手段。

1. Information that has not already been made public on the itineraries and deployment of security guards for top Party and state leaders, visiting foreign heads of state and heads of government; the deployment of security guards at the homes of these individuals, along routes that they follow, and in public locations; methods for communicating with and contacting these individuals, as well as secret security arrangements, plans for implementing such arrangements, and the methods used by security guards.

2. 涉及国家安全统一、社会政治稳定、民族团结、国家经济利益、对外关系等特别重要的秘密情报；

3. 公安机关防范、制止、处置骚乱、暴乱、重大紧急治安事件的具体方案；

4. 重点警卫、守卫、守护目标和国家重点建设工程，国防保密工程，通信、电力、水力、交通枢纽设施，重要的信息中心等要害单位或部位，重要军工产品、尖端科研项目的安全保卫工作计划和警卫、守卫值勤方案、力量部署、安全技术防范措施及其有关情况；

5. 重要情报的来源、获取手段和联络方法；

6. 对重要侦控对象的查控、堵截措施、材料和正在侦查的重要专案、敌情线索查证情况；

2. Secret intelligence involving the coordination of national security, the stability of social administration, ethnic unity, national economic interests, foreign relations, and other especially important intelligence.

3. Specific plans of the public security organ to guard against, prevent or deal with disturbances, riots and other major and urgent public order incidents.

4. Key sites being guarded, protected or defended; key national engineering projects; classified projects related to national defense; the facilities at communications, electrical, water or transportation hubs; important centers of information and other critical units or parts; the output of important military projects; the plans and security personnel used in the security and protection work of advanced scientific research projects; the objectives of on-duty security guards; the strength of their deployments; measures to safeguard technology; and other relevant information.

5. The sources of and methods used to procure important intelligence, and the methods used for maintaining contact.

6. Information on investigating and controlling, on ways to intercept, and other materials regarding important targets of surveillance, as well as information used to verify important cases currently under investigation or leads on enemy positions.

7. 公安机关调查掌握境内外敌对组织或社团、间谍特务组织、民族分裂组织、黑社组织、国际犯罪集团、国际恐怖组织、宗教敌对势力、反动会道门和境内非法织及其人员的重要情况和动态；

7. Important information and developments on domestic and international hostile organizations or movements, espionage and spy organizations, minority splittist organizations, secret societies, international criminal gangs, international terrorist organizations, hostile religious organizations, reactionary sects, and other illegal domestic organizations and their personnel that are currently under investigation by a public security organ.

8. 侦察工作专案、阵地、特情、密干、"朋友"、"关系"、秘密保卫员及业务据点的布建、审批、使用、管理情况；

8. Information on the reconnoitering work of special cases, enemy positions, special agents, secret agents, "friends," "relations," and secret security personnel, as well as the establishment, applications for approval, usage and management of their strongholds.

9. 技术侦察手段和技术侦察阵地的设置、实力、使用情况；

9. Information on methods of technical reconnaissance work and the installation, strength and uses of technical reconnaissance positions.

10. 技术侦察手段的技术方法、技术侦察专用器材的性能、管理情况及其更新换代情况；

10. Information on the function and administration of the specific technical means for doing technical reconnaissance work and the specialized equipment used for such work, as well as the newest generations of such equipment.

11. 技术侦察业务工作和技术管理情况；

11. Information on professional technical reconnaissance work and the technical administration of such work.

12. 计算机系统处理绝密级信息的安全技术措施；

12. Measures to safeguard the technology of encoding systems used to handle top-secret information.

13. 居民身份证、边境管理区通行证和入出境证件的一类防伪措施；

14. 有重大影响的外国人秘密入境向我申请政治避难的情况；

15. 担负看守所、劳改单位看押任务的武警部队执勤方案及其有关情况；

16. 武警部队总队（含）以上的实力统计和执勤目标、岗哨的综合统计。

（二）机密级事项

1. 重点对象以外的警卫对象和国内、国际举行的重要会议、重大活动未公开的活动安排、警卫部署，通信联络的密语、代号，住地的秘密安全设施及其有关情况；

2. 在处理涉外案件、事件中对外交涉、谈判的策略、方案，我同外国警方的秘技术合作或对外承担保密义务的事项；

13. Category 1 measures to protect against forging resident identity cards, transit visas used at border control areas, and entry and exit visas.

14. Information on foreign nationals of great influence who secretly enter the country and apply for political asylum.

15. Information on plans for police troops responsible for guarding detention centers and reeducation-through-labor units, and other related information.

16. Compiled statistics on the strength of police troops at the regiment level and above, and on sites being guarded by on-duty troops and sentry guards.

B. Matters classed as highly secret **Highly secret**

1. Except for key targets of security personnel, all information that has not yet been made public regarding the arrangements and security deployments for important conferences and major events held domestically and internationally; secret codes and code names used for making contact; secret security arrangements at residences; and other related information.

2. Tactics and plans for handling cases and incidents involving foreign matters or foreign affairs negotiations, and matters related to secret technical cooperation with international police forces or with foreigners who have the duty of protecting state secrets.

3. 反革命案件的统计数字、综合情况;

3. Numerical and compiled statistics on counterrevolutionary cases.

4. 重点目标以外的其它警卫、守卫、守护目标的安全保卫工作计划、守护力量部署、执勤方案和安全技术防范措施及其有关情况;

4. Except for key sites, all other information on security defense plans, the deployment of guards, and duty rosters of security personnel at sites being guarded, protected or defended, as well as measures to safeguard technology and other related information.

5. 公安机关调查掌握的境内外敌对组织或社团、间谍特务组织、民族分裂组织、黑社会组织、国际犯罪集团、国际恐怖组织、宗教敌对势力、反动会道门和境内非法组织及其人员的一般情况和动态;

5. General information and developments on domestic and international hostile organizations or movements, espionage and spy organizations, minority splittist organizations, secret societies, international criminal gangs, international terrorist organizations, hostile religious organizations, reactionary sects, and other illegal domestic organizations and their personnel that are currently under investigation by a public security organ.

6. 对外国、外商驻华机构和人员的工作情况以及来华政治避难的外国人管理情况;

6. Information on the work of foreign agencies and businesses posted in China and their personnel, and information on handling foreign nationals who come to China for political asylum.

7. 正在侦查的重大刑事案件的侦察方案、使用手段,侦察、预审及技术鉴定工作情况;

7. Plans and methods used to investigate important criminal cases already under investigation, as well as information on investigations, prejudication, and the work of technical verification.

8. 根据《刑事诉讼法》第五十条的规定,因"有碍侦查"而在逮捕后不通知家属或所在单位的重要案犯关押地点、动态,有重大影响的服刑人员的动态;

8. Information on the place of custody or circumstances of prisoners of great influence who are serving sentences and who, after being arrested, in order to "obstruct the investigation" did not

notify their families or units in accordance with the provisions of Article 50 of the Criminal Procedure Law.

9. 国家级重要计算机系统的安全状况和安全措施，以及进行安全检查的有关情况；

9. Security measures and the security situation of important state-level encoding systems, as well as related information used to carry out safety inspections.

10. 无线通信中正在或准备使用的用于侦察反革命案件和重大刑事案件、布置警卫工作、处理紧急治安事件、调动警力的联络呼号、密语；

10. Call letters and secret contact codes that are either in current use or are being prepared to be used through wireless communications to investigate counterrevolutionary cases and important criminal cases, to arrange security work, to handle public order emergencies, or to transfer security forces.

11. 来源秘密的公安科学技术和科研资料；

11. Materials on the source of secrets used in public security technology and research.

12. 平息、处理对当地社会秩序有重大影响的非法集会、游行示威和闹事、骚乱及其它紧急治安事件的具体工作部署及其有关情况；

12. Information on the specific deployment of troops to suppress and handle illegal gatherings, demonstrations and protests, as well as disturbances, riots and other public order emergencies that have a major influence on local social order, and other related information.

13. 预防和处理看守所人犯暴狱、劫狱等重大事故的预案及其有关情况；

13. Information on preventing and handling prison violence, jail-breaks and other major incidents, and other related information.

14. 居民身份证、边境管理区通行证和入出境证件的二类防伪措施；

14. Category 2 measures to protect against forging resident identity cards, transit visas used at border control areas, and entry and exit visas.

HRIC

15. 公安机关隐蔽工作单位的机构、任务、人员、编制、经费情况和人员、器材伪装及其掩护措施；

15. Information on the organization, duties, personnel, establishment and expenditures of covert public security work units, as well as their undercover personnel and counterfeit equipment, and measures to keep them undercover.

16. 武器弹药、爆炸物品和剧毒物品及放射性物品的集中存放地点、数量、守护、运送情况；

16. Information on the locations of concentrated deposits, quantities, measures to safeguard, and transportation of weapons ammunition, explosive materials, highly toxic substances and radioactive materials.

17. 武警部队支队、大队的实力统计和执行目标、岗哨的综合统计。

17. Compiled statistics on the strength of detachments and brigades of armed troops and on the sites being guarded by on-duty troops and sentry guards.

Secret

（三）秘密级事项

C. Matters classed as secret

1. 公安机关打击、查处违法犯罪活动的具体工作部署、行动方案；

1. Plans for the specific deployment and movements of public security organs in cracking down on, investigating and handling unlawful criminal activities.

2. 尚未公布的全国和各省、自治区、直辖市逮捕人犯、劳动教养、少年管教、收容审查、抓获人犯的综合情况和统计数字；

2. Compiled information and statistics that have not yet been made public on criminals that have been arrested, captured, sent for reeducation through labor or juvenile rehabilitation, or taken in for shelter and investigation in any directly-administered municipality, autonomous region or province throughout the country.

3. 国有大型企业的守护力量部署、安全技术防范措施及其它有关情况；

3. The strength and deployment of guards at, and the measures to safeguard technology of, large state-owned enterprises, and other related information.

4. 技术侦察手段的代号；

5. 公安机关掌握的重要社情动态；

6. 重要的检举、揭发材料和检举、揭发人的姓名、住址以及可能危害其安全的有关情况；

7. 公安机关调查、掌握、控制的工作对象以及重点人口的情况和数字；

8. 正在侦察、预审的刑事案件的具体方案、重要案情和侦察、预审工作情况；

9. 根据《刑事诉讼法》第五十条的规定，因"有碍侦查"而在逮捕后不通知其家属或所在单位的一般案犯关押地点和动态；

10. 各地构成犯罪的非法种植毒品原植物案件和铲除此类毒品原植物的统计数字，境内制造毒品的情况、数字；

4. Codes names used for technical reconnaissance methods.

5. Important social movements being looked into by public security organs.

6. Important information from informants and whistleblowers, the names and addresses of informants and whistleblowers, and any other information that might endanger their persons or their safety.

7. Information and statistics on those who are targets of investigation, under investigation, or under the control of public security organs, and key members of the population that are under public security scrutiny.

8. Specific plans and important case details on criminal cases that are in the information-gathering or the pretrial stages, and information on information-gathering or pretrial work.

9. Information on the place of custody or circumstances of ordinary prisoners who, after being arrested, in order to "obstruct the investigation," did not notify their families or units in accordance with the provisions of Article 50 of the Criminal Procedure Law.

10. Statistics on anything that constitutes a crime in any part of the country involving cases of growing botanical substances for illegal drugs or digging up this kind of botanical substance for drug use, and information or figures

on the domestic manufacturing of drugs.

11. 公安机关社会化、职业化阵地、据点的情况；

11. Information on positions or strongholds that have been used for social or business purposes by the public security organs.

12. 治安、狱内耳目的布建、使用情况及其数字；

12. Information and statistics on the setting up and uses of spies in public order work or inside prisons.

13. 无线通讯中，用于刑侦和社会治安工作的频率、暗语；

13. The frequencies and code words used in wireless communications to perform criminal investigations and public order work.

14. 计算器安全监察工作的总体部署，处理涉密讯息计算机系统的信息安全和物理安全措施；

14. The total deployment of those in charge of computer security work, the security of computer systems that handle information involving secrets, and the physical safety measures of such systems.

15. 侦察、边防、出入境管理部门侦控工作的内部工作程序；

15. The procedures of the internal surveillance work of reconnoitering scouts, border patrols, and departments that handle immigration.

16. 居民身份证、边防管理区通行证和入出境证件的三类防伪措施，各种公安业务专用章和机动车驾驶执照的防伪措施；

16. Category 3 measures to protect against forging resident identity cards, transit visas used at border control areas, and entry and exit visas. Measures to protect against forging all kinds of specialized public security business stamps [chops] as well as licenses to operate motor vehicles.

17. 武警部队中队的执勤目标、岗哨统计和实力统计。

17. Statistics on the sites being guarded by on-duty armed forces at the squadron level, sentry guards, and the strength of these troops.

第三条

公安工作中下列事项不属于国家秘密，但应当作为内部事项管理，未经规定机关批准不得擅自扩散：

1. 尚未公布的统计数字和文件、公文、管理措施；

2. 刑事技术的具体方法和具有国际先进水平的刑事技术器材；

3. 公安机关掌握的一般社情动态；

4. 尚未构成犯罪的零星非法种植毒品原植物情况、零星铲除情况及其数字；

5. 拐卖人口的发案数字和被拐卖人口数字，涉及少收民族妇女、外国籍妇女和严重威胁群众安全感的拐卖人口案件以及聚众阻挠解救受害妇女儿童案件的具体案情；

6. 已破案但公开会造成不良影响的刑事案件的具体案情；

Article 3

The following matters are not classed as state secrets within public security work, but they should be handled as internal (*neibu*) matters and their unauthorized dissemination is not allowed without first getting permission from the regulatory organ.

1. Statistics and files, documents, and administrative measures that have not yet been made public.

2. Specific methods of criminal investigation techniques and advanced criminal investigation techniques used internationally.

3. General social movements currently being looked into by public security organs.

4. Information or figures on anything that does not yet constitute a crime involving scattered cases of growing or digging up botanical substances for illegal drugs.

5. Figures on cases of kidnapping and trafficking in humans and figures on those kidnapped or sold; cases involving the kidnapping and trafficking of women belonging to ethnic minorities or women from outside the country; cases of kidnapping and trafficking in humans that seriously threaten the safety of the public; and specific details of cases of gathering crowds to obstruct the rescue of women or children that are in danger of being harmed.

6. Specific details of criminal cases that have already been solved but whose public disclosure would have a negative impact.

Internal (neibu) *matters*

	7. 大型活动的保卫工作方案及其具体措施；	7. Plans and specific measures for security arrangements at large-scale activities.
	8. 国有企业的安全保卫工作计划、守护力量部署、安全技术防范措施及其它有关情况；	8. Plans to secure the safety of, and the number of guards deployed to protect, state-owned enterprises, as well as measures to safeguard their technology and other related information.
	9. 内部参阅的各种资料；	9. All kinds of internal (*neibu*) reference materials.
	10. 正在拟议中的构机、人员调整意见；	10. Opinions currently being drafted regarding proposed changes to organs and their personnel.
	11. 未决定公布的公安干警违法违纪的统计数字和情况；	11. Information and statistics—about which a decision has not yet been made regarding whether to make such information public—concerning violations of the law or codes of conduct by public security officers.
	12. 由县以上公安机关规定的其它事项。	12. All other matters concerning regulations of public security organs at the county level and above.

Public security work and other departments' work

第四条
公安工作中涉及其它部门保密工作事项的，按照有关保密范围执。

Article 4
Matters in public security work that affect other departments' work of protecting state secrets must be handled according to the relevant scope of state secrets protection.

Secrets used by police troops

第五条
武警部队的其它涉密事项执行军队系统的定密规定。

Article 5
Secret regulations on other matters involving secrets used by police troops to implement systems of the armed forces.

第六条

本规定由公安部保密工作机构负责解释。

Article 6

Explaining this regulation is the work of the organ responsible for the protection of secrets of the Ministry of Public Security.

Responsibility for explaining regulation

第七条

本规定自1995年5月1日起生效。公安部、国家保密局1989年10月17日印发的《公安工作中国家秘密及其密级具体范围的规定》（〔89〕公发21号文件）同时废止。

Article 7

This regulation takes effect as of May 1, 1995. At the same time, the Regulation on State Secrets and the Specific Scope of Each Level of Secrets in Public Security Work (document no. 21 [89]) issued on October 17, 1989 is hereby revoked.

Effective date

2. REGULATION ON STATE SECRETS AND THE SPECIFIC SCOPE OF EACH LEVEL OF SECRETS IN THE WORK OF THE PEOPLE'S PROCURATORATES

Editors' Note:

The regulation below details the precise scope of state secrets and internal matters in the work of the people's procuratorates. Issued jointly by the Supreme People's Procuratorate and the National Administration for the Protection of State Secrets, this regulation is itself classified as a "secret" level document.

This regulation mandates the classification of matters such as statistics and information regarding the death penalty at all administrative levels, and the number of political cases handled yearly (referred here under their pre-1997 appellation of "counterrevolutionary crimes"). Included in the list of matters classed as "highly secret" are statistics and details regarding the use of torture to extract confessions, a practice that has caused much controversy within the judicial system and internationally.

This type of information is commonly regarded as key indicators of a country's human rights record, in particular in respect to the administration of justice.

The source for the following regulation is: 国家保密局（编），《国家秘密及其密级具体范围的规定选编》（修订本）（机密），（北京：金城出版社，1997年），70-71页 [National Administration for the Protection of State Secrets, ed., *Selected Regulations on State Secrets and the Specific Scope of Each Level of Secrets* (Revised Edition, Classified as "Highly Secret"), (Beijing: Jincheng Publishing House, 1997), 70–71].

検察工作中国家秘密及其密级具体范围的规定

Regulation on State Secrets and the Specific Scope of Each Level of Secrets in the Work of the People's Procuratorates

实施日期：1996年1月15日

Effective Date: January 15, 1996

第一条

为维护国家的安全和利益，保障检察工作依法顺利进行，根据《中华人民共和国保守国家密法》和《中华人民共和国保守国家秘密法实施办法》的规定，制定本规定。

Article 1

In order to safeguard the security and interests of the state and to ensure that the work of the people's procuratorates runs smoothly and according to law, this regulation has been formulated in accordance with the provisions in the Law on the Protection of State Secrets of the People's Republic of China and the Measures for Implementing the Law on the Protection of State Secrets of the People's Republic of China.

Purpose and promulgating authority

第二条

检察工作中的国家秘密是指关系国家的安全和利益，依照法定程序确定，在一定时间内只限一定范围的人员知悉的事项。

Article 2

State secrets in the work of the people's procuratorates refers to matters that are related to state security and national interests and, as specified by legal procedure, are entrusted to a limited number of people for a given period of time.

Definition of state secrets

第三条

检察工作中国家秘密及其密级的具体范围：

Article 3

State secrets and the specific scope of each level of secrets in the work of the people's procuratorates are as follows:

Scope of each classification level

（一）绝密级事项

A. Matters classed as top secret

Top secret

1. 检察机关正在立案侦查（包括立案前的初查）的对国家安全、社会稳定有影响的案件和涉及省部级以上干部的案件的侦查方案及案件材料（包括举报材料）；

1. Plans and materials for investigating cases put on file for investigation that are currently being investigated by procuratorial organs (including initial investigations that occurred prior to putting a case on file) and that could impact state security or social stability, as well as plans and ma-

terials for investigating cases that involve cadres at the provincial level or above (including materials provided by informants).

2. 全国死刑统计数字及综合情况；

2. Statistics and compiled information on death sentences nationwide.

3. 检察系统使用的保密机及其密钥和加密算法；

3. Scrambling devices used in the work of the procuratorates, as well as their keys and encryption algorithms.

Highly secret

（二）机密级事项

B. Matters classed as highly secret

1. 检察机关正在立案侦查（包括立案前的初查）的案件的侦查计划、处理意见及有关材料（包括举报材料）；

1. Plans for investigating and ideas on how to handle cases put on file for investigation that are currently being investigated by procuratorial organs (including initial investigations that occurred prior to putting a case on file), as well as related materials (including materials provided by informants).

2. 反革命案件的统计数字和综合情况；

2. Statistics and compiled information on counterrevolutionary cases.

3. 涉外案件对外交涉的策略、方案；

3. Strategies and proposals regarding cases involving foreigners or foreign affairs.

4. 省、自治区、直辖市死刑统计数字和综合情况；

4. Statistics and compiled information on death sentences within provinces, autonomous regions or directly-administered municipalities.

5. 采取刑讯逼供、体罚虐待手段造成严重后果的统计数字和具体案情；

5. Statistics and specific case details regarding the use of torture to extract confessions and corporal punishment abuse that led to serious consequences.

6. 检察机关武器弹药调拨、发运、存放情况。

6. Information on the allocation, transportation, and storage of weapons and ammunition by procuratorial organs.

（三）秘密级事项

C. Matters classed as secret

Secret

1. 审查起诉的刑事案件（自侦案件除外）的有关材料和处理意见；

1. Relevant materials and opinions on how to handle investigations into indictments of criminal cases (except for cases investigated by oneself).

2. 尚未公布的全国和省、自治区、直辖市刑事案件、逮捕人犯的统计数字；

2. Statistics on criminal cases, and on those arrested in connection with such cases, that have not yet been made public either nationwide or within provinces, autonomous regions or directly-administered municipalities.

3. 省辖市（地区、自治州）死刑统计数字和综合情况。

3. Statistics and compiled information on death sentences within provincially-administered municipalities (prefectures and autonomous prefectures).

第四条
检察工作中涉及其它部门的国家秘密事项，按照国家有关主管部门的保密范围确定密级。

Article 4
If there are any state secret matters within the work of the procuratorate that involve other departments, the security classification of those matters should be carried out according to the scope of state secrets protection practiced by that department.

Classification of matters that involve other departments

第五条
本规定由最高人民检察院保密委员会负责解释。

Article 5
Explaining this regulation is the responsibility of the Committee on the Protection of State Secrets of the Supreme People's Procuratorate.

Responsibility for explaining regulation

Effective date

第六条

本规定自1996年1月15日起生效。最高人民检察院、国家保密局1989年10月23日制定的《检察工作中国家秘密及其密级具体范围的规定》（〔1989〕高检发保委字第17号），最高人民检察院1990年8月23日制定的《关于〈检察工作中国家秘密及其密级具体范围的规定〉的说明》（高检发保委字〔1990〕1号）同时废止。

Article 6

This regulation shall take effect as of January 15, 1996. At the same time, the Regulation on State Secrets and the Specific Scope of Each Level of Secrets in the Work of the People's Procuratorate (Supreme Procuratorate Protection Committee document no. 17 [1989]) jointly issued on October 23, 1989 by the Supreme People's Procuratorate and the National Administration for the Protection of State Secrets, as well as the Explanation of the Regulation on State Secrets and the Specific Scope of Each Level of Secrets in the Work of the People's Procuratorates (Supreme Procuratorate Protection Committee document no. 1 [1990]) issued on August 23, 1990 by the Supreme People's Procuratorate, are hereby revoked.

3. REGULATION ON STATE SECRETS AND THE SPECIFIC SCOPE OF EACH LEVEL OF SECRETS IN THE WORK OF THE PEOPLE'S COURTS

Editors' Note:

The following regulation details the precise scope of state secrets and internal matters in the work of the people's courts. Issued jointly by the Supreme People's Court and the National Administration for the Protection of State Secrets in July 1995, this regulation is itself classified as a "secret" level document.

This regulation reflects the high level of secrecy under which courts operate in China, as well as their subordination to the internal instructions of the Supreme People's Court and the higher people's courts. Indeed, Article 7 states that, although the work of the people's courts is itself not a state secret, "any matters that, once made public, could have a negative impact or undesirable results" must not be made public, thereby providing the courts with legal justification for withholding trial proceedings from the public domain.

Cases of "very high," "high" and "relatively high" significance, as well as the instructions received by the courts on how to adjudicate them, are respectively classified as top secret, highly secret and secret. The term "significance" is not specifically defined but seems to refer to the risk of public embarrassment or loss of political control that certain cases might cause for the government, such as "major criminal cases involving Party or state leaders," "socially sensitive cases" or cases that, "if disclosed, could provoke social unrest or intensify ethnic conflicts."

This regulation also mandates the classification of all information regarding "the use of bodily organs of prisoners who have been sentenced to death," a subject that has been widely discussed and for which the government has been criticized in recent years (Article 3, Section B.4).

The source for the following regulation is: 国家保密局（编），《国家秘密及其密级具体范围的规定选编》（修订本）（机密），(北京：金城出版社，1997年)，52–55页 [National Administration for the Protection of State Secrets, ed., *Selected Regulations on State Secrets and the Specific Scope of Each Level of Secrets* (Revised Edition, Classified as "Highly Secret"), (Beijing: Jincheng Publishing House, 1997), 52–55].

人民法院工作中国家秘密及其密级具
体范围的规定

Regulation on State Secrets and the Specific Scope of Each Level of Secrets in the Work of the People's Courts

颁布日期: 1995年7月31日
实施日期: 1995年8月8日

Promulgation Date: July 31, 1995
Effective Date: August 8, 1995

Purpose and promulgating authority

第一条
根据《中华人民共和国保守国家秘密法》和《中华人民共和国保守国家秘密法实施办法》的规定，为维护国家的安全和利益，保障人民法院审判工作依法顺利进行，制定本规定。

Article 1

In order to safeguard the security and interests of the state and to ensure that the judicial work of the people's courts runs smoothly and according to law, this regulation has been formulated in accordance with the provisions in the Law on the Protection of State Secrets of the People's Republic of China and the Measures on Implementing the Law on the Protection of State Secrets of the People's Republic of China.

Definition of state secrets

第二条
人民法院工作中国家秘密是指人民法院工作中关系国家安全和利益，依照法定程序确定，并在一定时间内只限一定范围的人员知悉的事项。

Article 2

State secrets in the work of the people's courts refers to matters that are related to state security and national interests and, as specified by legal procedure, are entrusted to a limited number of people for a given period of time.

Scope of each classification level

第三条
人民法院工作中的国家秘密及其密级的具体范围：

Article 3

State secrets and the specific scope of each level of secrets in the work of the people's courts are as follows:

Top secret

（一）绝密级事项

A. Matters classed as top secret

　　1. 最高人民法院和高级人民法院就审理具有特别重大影响案件的内部重要指示、决定、部署、方案和案件处理中重大问题的请示、报告、批复。

1. Important internal directives, decisions, plans and proposals used by the Supreme People's Court and higher people's courts in trying cases of very high significance, as well as requests for instructions, reports and official replies regarding important

questions that come up in handling such cases.

本规定所指的"具有特别重大影响案件"，一般应是最高人民法院或高级人民法院作为一审的下列案件：

In this regulation, the phrase "cases of very high significance" generally refers to the following types of cases tried in trials of the first instance by the Supreme People's Court or higher people's courts:

(1) 在全国或省、自治区、直辖市范围内具有重大影响的反革命案件；

(i) Counterrevolutionary cases of high significance either nationwide or that come under the jurisdiction of provinces, autonomous regions and directly-administered municipalities.

(2) 关系国家主权和国家重大利益的涉外案件；

(ii) Cases involving foreign matters that impact national sovereignty and key interests of the state.

(3) 关系国家内政、外交工作的非常敏感案件；

(iii) Extremely sensitive cases that impact either national-level internal affairs or foreign affairs work.

(4) 如泄露可能在全国或省、自治区、直辖市范围内引起社会动乱和激化民族矛盾的案件；

(iv) Cases that, if disclosed, could provoke social unrest and intensify ethnic conflicts either nationwide or under the jurisdiction of provinces, autonomous regions and directly-administered municipalities.

(5) 涉及党和国家领导人的重大刑事案件.

(v) Major criminal cases involving Party or state leaders.

也可以是因特殊需要，由上级人民法院指定中级人民法院作为一审的上述(1)至(4)类案件。

It is also possible that, if there is a special need, the higher people's courts could direct an intermediate people's court to hold a trial of the first instance for the types of cases listed above in items (i) through (iv).

2. 最高人民法院和高级人民法院审判委员会、合议庭讨论具有特别重大影响案件的具体情况和记录。	2. Specific details and records of cases of very high significance that have been sent by the Supreme People's Court or higher people's courts for deliberation to either judicial committees or collegiate benches.
3. 全国判处、核准和执行死刑案犯的年度、月份统计数字。	3. Annual or monthly statistics on national cases involving the sentencing, ratification or implementation of the death penalty.

Highly secret

（二）机密级事项

B. Matters classed as highly secret

1. 最高人民法院和高级人民法院就审理具有重大影响案件的内部重要指示、决定、部署、方案和案件处理中重要问题的请示、报告、批复。

1. Important internal directives, decisions, plans and proposals used by the Supreme People's Court and higher people's courts in trying cases of high significance, as well as requests for instructions, reports and official replies regarding important questions that come up in handling such cases.

• ***Cases of high significance***

本规定所指的"具有重大影响案件"，一般应是最高人民法院或高级人民法院作为一审或根据需要指定由中级人民法院作为一审的下列案件：

In this regulation, the phrase "cases of high significance" generally refers to the following types of cases tried in trials of the first instance either by higher people's courts or to cases that are directed, as needed, to intermediate people's courts for trials of the first instance:

（1）在省、自治区、直辖市范围内具有较大影响的反革命案件；

(i) Counterrevolutionary cases of relatively high significance either nationwide or that come under the jurisdiction of provinces, autonomous regions and directly-administered municipalities.

(2) 关系国家声誉和国家利
益的涉外案件；

(ii) Cases involving foreign
matters that impact na-
tional reputation and the
interests of the state.

(3) 如省、自治区、直辖市
范围内社会敏感案件；

(iii) Socially sensitive cases t
hat come under the juris-
diction of provinces,
autonomous regions and
directly-administered
municipalities.

(4) 在泄露可能在一个地区
范围内引起社会动乱和
激化民族矛盾的案件；

(iv) Cases that, if disclosed,
could provoke social unrest
or intensify ethnic conflicts
and that come under the
jurisdiction of a single prefecture.

(5) 涉及正、副省部级领导
干部或在国内外政治上
有重大影响知名人士的
重大刑事案件。

(v) Important criminal cases involving leading cadres in provincial departments at the
chief or deputy chief levels,
or involving well-known
persons of great influence
who work in national do-
mestic or foreign politics.

2. 中级以上人民法院审判委员
会、合议庭讨论具有重大影
响案件的具体情况和记录。

2. Specific details and records of
cases of high significance that
have been sent for deliberation to
judicial committees or collegiate
benches by people's courts at the
intermediate level and above.

3. 省、自治区、直辖市和全军
判处、核准和执行死刑案犯
的年度、月份统计数字。

3. Annual or monthly statistics on
cases tried at the provincial, autonomous region or directly-administered municipality level, as
well as all military cases that involve the sentencing, ratification
or implementation of the death
penalty.

4. 人民法院判处死刑的罪犯尸
体或尸体器官利用的具体情
况

4. Specific information on the
corpses or on the use of bodily
organs of prisoners who have

been sentenced to death by people's courts.

Secret

（三）秘密级事项

C. Matters classed as secret

1. 最高人民法院和高级人民法院就审理具有较大影响案件的内部重要指示、决定、安排、方案和案件处理中重要问题的请示、报告、批复。

1. Important internal directives, decisions, arrangements and proposals used by the Supreme People's Court and higher people's courts in trying cases of relatively high significance, as well as requests for instructions, reports and official replies regarding important questions that come up in handling such cases.

• *Cases of relatively high significance*

本规定所指的"具有较大影响案件"，一般应是中级人民法院作为一审的下列案件：

In this regulation, the phrase "cases of relatively high significance" generally refers to the following types of cases tried in trials of the first instance by intermediate people's courts:

（1）在一个地区范围内具有较大影响的反革命案件；

(i) Counterrevolutionary cases of relatively high significance that come under the jurisdiction of a single prefecture.

（2）有较大影响的涉外案件；

(ii) Cases of relatively high significance involving foreign matters.

（3）在一个地区、县范围内社会敏感的案件；

(iii) Socially sensitive cases that come under the jurisdiction of a single prefecture or county.

（4）如泄露可能在一个地区、县范围内引起社会动荡或影响民族团结的案件；

(iv) Cases that, if disclosed, could provoke social unrest or affect ethnic unity and that come under the jurisdiction of a single prefecture or county.

（5）涉及地、县级主要领导干部或省、地、县范围

(v) Important criminal cases involving leading cadres at

内政治上有较大影响知名人士的重大刑事案件。

the prefecture or county level, or involving well-known persons of great influence who work in domestic politics at the provincial, prefecture or county level.

2. 各级人民法院审判委员会、合议庭讨论具有较大影响案件的具体情况和记录。

2. Specific details and records of cases of relatively high significance that have been sent for deliberation to judicial committees or collegiate benches by people's courts at all levels.

3. 中级人民法院判处和执行死刑案犯年度、月份统计数字。

3. Annual or monthly statistics on cases tried by intermediate people's courts involving the sentencing or implementation of the death penalty.

4. 中级以上人民法院除死刑外的刑事司法统计报表。

4. Criminal judiciary forms for reporting statistics on cases other than those involving the death penalty tried by people's courts at the intermediate level and above.

5. 对有较大影响的死刑案犯执行死刑的方案。

5. Plans to carry out the executions of prisoners of relatively high significance who have received the death penalty.

6. 外国最高法院院长和首席大法官来访中重要事项的内部请示、报告。

6. Internal reports and requests for instructions on important matters related to visits to China from abroad by supreme court chief justices and other chief justices.

Matters regarding newly-created or existing regulations

第四条

对于人民法院工作中新产生或本规定不明确的，一旦泄露可能会给国家的安全和利益造成危害的事项，产生该事项的人民法院应先拟定密级，并按所拟密级采取相应的保密措施，同时由高级人民法院归口上报最高人民法院保密委员会确定。

Article 4

Within the work of the people's courts, if there are any matters regarding either newly-created regulations or existing regulations that are not clear and which, once disclosed, could harm the security and interests of the state, then the people's courts must produce an initial draft to determine the level of secrets that apply to these matters. In addition, they should follow the relevant measures adopted to protect the secrecy of these drafts. At the same time, all higher people's courts should verbally report to the Committee on the Protection of State Secrets of the Supreme People's Court to obtain verification.

User instructions for computers, date/files on lawsuits, or audio-visual products

第五条

计算器的应用程序和数据、诉讼案卷和声像制品中涉及国家秘密的，其密级按其中最高的密级确定。

Article 5

If there are any state secrets contained in user instructions for computers, data or files on lawsuits, or audio-visual products, then when determining which level of secrets should be used to classify these, the highest level of secrets among them should be used.

Matters that involve other departments

第六条

人民法院工作中涉及其它部门的国家秘密事项，其密级应按国家有关主管部门保密范围的规定执行。

Article 6

If, in the work of the people's courts there are matters of state secrecy that involve other departments, the level of secrets applied to these matters should be determined according to the regulations of the relevant national-level department responsible for the protection of state secrets.

第七条

对人民法院在审判工作中形成的，虽不属于国家秘密，但一旦公开又会造成不良影响和后果的事项，应按审判工作秘密进行保守，不准擅自公开和扩散。

Article 7

In terms of the form that the judicial work of the people's courts takes, although that work itself is not a state secret, whenever there are matters that, once made public, could have a negative impact or undesirable results, then those secrets in judicial work must be protected and must not be made public or disseminated without authorization.

Matters that could have negative/undesirable results

第八条

本规定由最高人民法院保密委员会负责解释。

Article 8

Explaining this regulation is the responsibility of the Committee on the Protection of State Secrets of the Supreme People's Court.

Responsibility for explaining regulation

第九条

本规定自1995年8月8日起施行。最高人民法院、国家保密局1989年10月24日下发的《人民法院工作中国家秘密及其密级具体范围的规定》（法（办）发〔1989〕30）号文件及最高人民法院1992年1月15日下发的（法〔1992〕4号）对该规定的说明通知同时废止。

Article 9

This regulation shall take effect as of August 8, 1995. At the same time, the Regulation on State Secrets and the Specific Scope of Each Level of Secrets in the Work of the People's Courts (court document no. 30 [89]) issued on October 24, 1989 by the Supreme People's Court and the National Administration for the Protection of State Secrets, as well as the notice of explanation regarding this regulation (court document no. 4 [1992]) issued on January 15, 1992 by the Supreme People's Court, are hereby revoked.

Effective date

4. REGULATION ON STATE SECRETS AND THE SPECIFIC SCOPE OF EACH LEVEL OF SECRETS IN JUDICIAL ADMINISTRATION WORK

Editors' Note:

The following regulation details the scope of state secrets and internal matters in the "judicial administration" of prisons and labor camps. Issued jointly by the Ministry of Justice and the National Administration for the Protection of State Secrets in August 1995, this regulation is itself classified as a "secret" level document.

This regulation reflects the high degree of secrecy in which prison administration and conditions are kept in the PRC. It precludes the disclosure of statistics on prisoner executions, "unusual" deaths in detention facilities (including reeducation-through-labor and juvenile facilities), "reeducation plans" for political and religious prisoners, as well as data on "instances of police officers causing injuries or disabilities to prisoners." Even general statistics on the number of prisoners currently held in detention nationwide are classed as "secret" level state secrets.

Not surprisingly, plans for "dealing with human rights issues" such as the reform of individuals in prisons or reeducation-through-labor camps is classed as "highly secret," as is information on the detention and reform of "prisoners of influence" currently serving sentences (Article 2, Section B), although the phrase "prisoners of influence" is not defined.

This regulation also contains a section on *"neibu"* (internal) information which, although not technically a state secret, still may not be disclosed without permission from the relevant body. Listed among the *neibu* information (Article 4) is data on instances of police mistreatment of prisoners, cases of police officers who violate discipline, and—in a final catch-all phrase—"information not yet made public on any judicial administration work that is not a state secret."

The source for the following regulation is: 国家保密局（编），《国家秘密及其密级具体范围的规定选编 》（修订本）(机密)，(北京：金城出版社，1997年)，56–58页 [National Administration for the Protection of State Secrets, ed., *Selected Regulations on State Secrets and the Specific Scope of Each Level of Secrets* (Revised Edition, Classified as "Highly Secret"), (Beijing: Jincheng Publishing House, 1997), 56–58].

司法行政工作中国家秘密及其密级具体范围的规定

Regulation on State Secrets and the Specific Scope of Each Level of Secrets in Judicial Administration Work

颁布日期：1995年8月31日
实施日期：1995年10月15日

Promulgation Date: August 31, 1995
Effective Date: October 15, 1995

第一条
根据《中国人民共和国保守国家秘密法》及其实施办法，制定本规定。

Article 1

This regulation has been formulated in accordance with the Law on the Protection of State Secrets of the People's Republic of China and the measures for implementing that law.

Promulgating authority

第二条
司法行政工作中国家秘密及其密级的具体范围：

Article 2

State secrets and the specific scope of each level of secrets in judicial administration work are as follows:

Scope of each classification level

（一）绝密级事项

A. Matters classed as top secret

Top secret

1. 全国监狱、劳动教养工作的总体规划、计划；

1. Overall programs and plans for nationwide prison and reeducation-through-labor work.

2. 监狱、劳教所全国总体看押兵力部署方案，警诫、执勤方案；

2. Overall plans for the deployment of military troops to guard detention areas and reeducation-through-labor facilities nationwide, as well as plans for guards and on-duty personnel.

3. 大批量跨地区调动罪犯的部署和行动方案；

3. Plans for the deployment and movement of large numbers of prisoners being transferred from one region to another.

（二）机密级事项

B. Matters classed as highly secret

Highly secret

1. 全国和各省、自治区、直辖市统计的监狱、少管所和劳教所内重新犯罪人员的处决人数及非正常死亡人数；

1. Statistics nationwide and for any province, autonomous region or directly-administered municipality on the number of new prisoner executions and unusual

deaths in prisons, juvenile detention facilities and reeducation-through-labor facilities.

2. 预防和处置监狱、劳教所内越狱、暴狱重大事件的预案；

2. Advance plans on how to prevent and handle major incidents of jailbreaks and violence in prisons and reeducation-through-labor facilities.

3. 监狱、少管所内正在侦察的重、特大案件的侦察计划、侦察手段和打击对策；

3. Plans and methods for gathering information on important and especially large cases currently being investigated in prisons and juvenile detention facilities, as well as countermeasures for handling such cases.

4. 全国监狱、劳教所的总体布局；

4. The overall layout of national prisons and reeducation-through-labor facilities.

5. 国际人权斗争中针对改造罪犯、劳教人员和预防犯罪的问题我方拟采取的对策；

5. Countermeasures that our country plans to adopt to deal with international human rights issues including prisoner reform, reform of reeducation-through-labor inmates, and crime prevention.

6. 省、自治区、直辖市范围内调犯计划、行动方案；

6. Plans and proposals on transferring prisoners within provinces, autonomous regions and directly-administered municipalities.

7. 监狱、劳教所武器、弹药集中存放地点、数量、守护、运送情况；

7. Information on the location, quantity, security arrangements and transportation of weapons and ammunition stored in prisons and reeducation-through-labor facilities.

8. 有重大影响的服刑人员的关押、改造情况。

8. Information on the detention and reform of prisoners of influence currently serving sentences.

（三）秘密级事项

1. 监狱的干警编制、看押兵力、警戒、报警、通讯、供电设施、武器装备情况；

2. 全国在押罪犯年度、委度的综合统计数字；

3. 省、自治区、直辖市以下单位统计的监狱、少管所和劳教所内重新犯罪人员的处决人数及非正常死亡人数。

4. 监狱内的耳目建设情况。

5. 全国在押犯和劳教人员的专项、抽样调查与分类统计数字；

6. 司法界要员出访、来访的重要事项的内部请示、报告及方案。

C. Matters classed as secret

1. Information on matters inside prisons including police officer formations, troops guarding detention areas, guards, reports made to the police, communications, electrical power facilities and weaponry.

2. Compiled annual and quarterly statistics on prisoners currently in detention nationwide.

3. Statistics at the level of province, autonomous region, directly-administered municipality or lower regarding the number of new prisoner executions and unusual deaths in prisons, juvenile detention facilities and reeducation-through-labor facilities.

4. Information on the placement of spies in prisons.

5. Specialized and sample surveys on, and the statistical classifications of, prisoners currently in detention and reeducation-through-labor inmates nationwide.

6. Internal requests for instructions, reports and proposals on important matters related to visits to China by foreign judicial officials or visits abroad by Chinese judicial officials.

Secret

Judicial administration work and other departments' work	**第三条** 司法行政业务工作中涉及其它部门的国家秘密事项，其密级应按所涉及部门的保密范围执行。	**Article 3** If there are any state secret matters within the arena of judicial administration work that involve other departments, the security classification of those matters should be carried out according to the scope of state secrets protection practiced by that department.
Internal (neibu) matters	**第四条** 司法行政工作中下列事项不属于国家秘密，而作为工作秘密内部掌握，未经规定机关批准不得擅自扩散：	**Article 4** The following matters, which fall within judicial administration work and are not considered state secrets but are secret work being handled internally (*neibu*), must not be made public or disseminated without authorization from the regulatory organ:
	1. 对搞现行反革命活动、搞非法宗教活动、搞非法刊物和非法组织活动的劳教人员的劳教方案；	1. Reeducation plans for reeducation-through-labor inmates who engage in counterrevolutionary activities, illegal religious activities, illegal publications and the activities of illegal organizations.
	2. 罪犯和劳教人员在监狱、少管所和劳教所内的犯罪情况；	2. Information on crimes committed by prisoners or reeducation-through-labor inmates in prisons, juvenile rehabilitation facilities or reeducation-through-labor facilities.
	3. 监狱、少管所和劳教所内的发案数、罪犯和劳教人员的改造动向及脱逃情况的综合分析；	3. Comprehensive analyses of information on the numbers of, and the prisoners involved in, cases occurring inside prisons, juvenile rehabilitation facilities or reeducation-through-labor facilities, as well as on reform trends and escapes of reeducation-through-labor inmates.
	4. 全国监狱系统财务决算和计划及工业、农业年度报表；	4. Financial statements and plans of the national prison system, as well as annual industrial and agricultural reports.

5. 律师受理的未公开的对国家安全、民族团结、对外关系有一定影响的刑事案件、经济案件的案情及对外表态口径；

6. 追捕逃犯和追找劳教人员的行动方案；

7. 打击监狱、少管所和劳教所内犯罪活动的破案计划、行动方案和情况报告；

8. 干警致残、致伤罪犯、劳教人员和干警违法乱纪的数据；

9. 全国监狱系统财务、工业季度统计报表和年度投资计划；

10. 部属政法院校尚未实施的有关教学质量评估的统考或抽考的试题以及单独招生的考题；

5. Case details and guidelines on how to handle foreign inquiries regarding criminal and economic cases of definite significance concerning state security, national unity or foreign relations that have been handled by lawyers and not yet made public.

6. Action plans to pursue and arrest escaped prisoners and to pursue and return reeducation-through-labor inmates.

7. Plans for solving cases, action plans and information reports on cracking down on criminal activities inside prisons, juvenile rehabilitation facilities and reeducation-through-labor facilities.

8. Data on instances of police officers causing injuries or disabilities to prisoners or reeducation-through-labor inmates and instances of police officers violating the law or discipline.

9. Financial and industrial quarterly statistical reports on the national prison system, as well as annual investment plans.

10. Test questions on actual or sample exams that have not yet been used to evaluate the qualifications of relevant students and teachers applying to political and legal institutions affiliated with a government ministry, as well as individual examination questions used for admitting new students.

11. 在一定时间和范围内的不宜公开的有关机构设置、内部分工、干部选拔、配备、任免事项的材料及干部档案材料；

12. 尚未公布的司法行政干警违纪案件的调查、审理情况；

13. 全国在押罪犯和劳教人员思想动态、生活卫生方面的统计数字；

14. 罪犯和劳教人员中发生较大规模疫病的情况；

15. 审计机关内部机构的工作计划、总结、请示、报告及有关纪录；

16. 未经公开的司法行政工作中非国家秘密的统计资料；

17. 司法行政系统企、事业单位的人事、劳资统计报表和财务决算；

18. 内部工作文件、参考资料。

11. Materials on relevant organizations that should not be made public within a given time period or within certain confines regarding the organizations' set-up and internal division of labor; their selection, allocation, appointment and dismissal of cadres; and files and information on cadres in those organizations.

12. Information not yet released on the investigations or trials of cases of judicial administration officers who violate discipline.

13. Statistics on the ideological tendencies and living and sanitation conditions of prisoners in detention and reeducation-through-labor facilities nationwide.

14. Information on relatively large-scale epidemics that occur amongst prisoners and reeducation-through-labor inmates.

15. Work plans, summaries, requests for instructions and reports regarding the internal structure of auditing agencies, and other related records.

16. Statistical information not yet made public on any judicial administration work that is not a state secret.

17. Financial statements and statistical reports on the personnel, labor and capital of enterprises and institutions within the judicial administration system.

18. Documents and reference materials used in internal (*neibu*) work.

第五条
本规定由司法部保密委员会负责
解释。

Article 5

Explaining this regulation is the responsibility of the Committee on the Protection of State Secrets of the Ministry of Justice.

Responsibility for explaining regulation

第六条
本规定自1995年10月15日起生效。司
法部、国家保密局1990年1月6日联合
制发的《司法行政工作中国家秘密及
其密级具体范围的规定》（〔89〕司
发办字第237号文）及司法部1991年5
月6日下发的（〔91〕司办通字061号
）对该规定的说明同时废止。

Article 6

This regulation shall take effect as of October 15, 1995. At the same time, the Regulation on State Secrets and the Specific Scope of Each Level of Secrets in Judicial Administration Work (judicial document no. 237 [89]) jointly issued on January 6, 1990 by the Ministry of Justice and the National Administration for the Protection of State Secrets, as well as the notice of explanation regarding this regulation (judicial document no. 061 [91]) issued on May 6, 1991 by the Ministry of Justice, are hereby revoked.

Effective date

D.

Regulation on the Protection of State Secrets in News Publishing

Editors' Note:

The following regulation, issued by the National Administration for the Protection of State Secrets in June 1992, specifies the obligations of news and media organizations in respect to state secrets protection. These obligations apply to the publishing or issuing of newspapers and periodicals, news dispatches, books, maps, illustrated reference materials, audio-visual productions, as well as the production and broadcasting of radio programs, television programs and films.

According to this regulation, all news publishing units in China should use a dual system of first checking all articles, reports, drafts, news releases and so forth internally for any possible disclosures of state secrets; after this, if it unclear whether or not a state secret might be involved, the unit must send the materials to another, higher department for external vetting. If the materials in question are found to contain state secrets, such information must either be declassified, abridged, edited, or otherwise removed.

In addition, any news reports on national politics, foreign affairs, economics, science and technology, and military affairs that are to be sent to foreign news organizations for publication must always be checked by a higher body, regardless of whether or not there is a question of the materials containing state secrets. This regulation also contains a section (Chapter 3) on what news publishing units should do in case a state secret is disclosed in the course of their work. The above dual system is intended precisely to prevent any such disclosures, but should they occur, the persons or units responsible will be "severely punished" (Article 18).

As regulations concerning the state secrets system are not systematically provided to the public, it can be difficult to determine the current status of any particular regulation. A search for this regulation on news publishing, for instance, found it listed on two different Web sites, both belonging to Peking University: The Lawyee Web site (www.lawyee.net) where it was listed as no longer effective, and the Law Info China Web site (www.lawinfochina.com) where it was listed as currently effective.

The source for the following regulation is: 李志东（主编），《中华人民共和国保密法全书》，(本书仅供各级保密部门、组织、人员使用)》（长春：吉林人民出版社，1999），363-366页　[Li Zhidong, ed. *Compendium of Laws of the People's Republic of China on the Protection of State Secrets,* (Circulation limited to departments, organizations and personnel doing state secrets protection work), (Changchun: Jilin People's Press, 1999), 363–366].

新闻出版保密规定

Regulation on the Protection of State Secrets in News Publishing

颁布日期：1992年6月13日
实施日期：1992年10月1日
文号 国保（1992）34号

Promulgation Date: June 13, 1992
Effective Date: October 1, 1992
National Administration for the Protection of State Secrets Document No. 34 (1992)

第一章 总 则

Chapter One: General Provisions

第一条
为在新闻出版工作中保守国家秘密，根据《中华人民共和国保守国家秘密法》第二十条，制定本规定。

Article 1
In order to safeguard state secrets in news publishing work, this regulation has been formulated in accordance with Article 20 of the Law on the Protection of State Secrets of the People's Republic of China.

Purpose and promulgating authority

第二条
本规定适用于报刊、新闻电讯、书籍、地图、图文资料、声像制品的出版和发行以及广播节日、电视节目、电影的制作和播放。

Article 2
This regulation shall apply to the publishing or issuing of newspapers and periodicals, news dispatches, books, maps, illustrated reference materials and audio-visual productions, and to the production and broadcasting of radio programs, television programs and films.

Scope of application

第三条
新闻出版的保密工作，坚持贯彻既保守国家秘密又有利于新闻出版工作正常进行的方针。

Article 3
The work of protecting state secrets in news publishing is a principle to be adhered to and implemented in order to safeguard state secrets and to aid in the normal functioning of news publishing work.

Principle of protecting state secrets in news publishing

第四条
新闻出版单位及其采编人员和提供信息单位及其有关人员应当加强联系，协调配合，执行保密法规，遵守保密制度，共同做好新闻出版的保密工作。

Article 4
News publishing units and their reporters or editors, as well as units that provide information and their relevant personnel, shall strengthen relations, improve cooperation, implement the

Role of news publishing units, reporters, editors, relevant personnel

laws and regulations on protecting state secrets, comply with the system for protecting state secrets, and work together to protect state secrets in news publishing.

第二章 保密制度

Chapter Two: The System for Protecting State Secrets

System to check on protection of state secrets

第五条

新闻出版单位和提供信息的单位，应当根据国家保密法规，建立健全新闻出版保密审查制度。

Article 5

News publishing units and units that provide information shall establish and perfect a system to check on the protection of state secrets in news publishing in accordance with the laws and regulations on protecting state secrets.

Checking materials

第六条

新闻出版保密审查实行自审与送审相结合的制度。

Article 6

Checking on the protection of state secrets in news publishing shall be implemented through a combination of checking materials oneself and sending materials out to be checked.

Submission of unclear information to relevant department or higher authorities

第七条

新闻出版单位和提供信息的单位，对拟公开出版、报道的信息，应当按照有关的保密规定进行自审；对是否涉及国家秘密界限不清的信息，应当送交有关主管部门或其上级机关、单位审定。

Article 7

Information intended to be made public by news publishing units or by units that provide information shall be checked by those units in accordance with the relevant regulations on the protection of state secrets. Where it is unclear whether or not a piece of information involves state secrets, such information shall be submitted to the relevant department in charge or to higher authorities or units for examination and approval.

第八条

新闻出版单位及其采编人员需向有关部门反映或通报的涉及国家秘密的信息，应当通过内部途径进行，并对反映或通报的信息按照有关规定作出国家秘密的标志。

Article 8

If information involving state secrets must be reported or circulated to relevant departments by news publishing units and their reporters or editors, such actions shall be carried out through internal channels, and the reported or circulated information shall be marked as a state secret in accordance with the relevant regulations.

Internal circulation and marking as state secrets

第九条

被采访单位、被采访人向新闻出版单位的采编人员提供有关信息时，对其中确因工作需要而又涉及国家秘密的事项，应当事先按照有关规定的程序批准，并采编人员申明；新闻出版单位及其采编人员对被采访单位、被采访人申明属于国家秘密的事项，不得公开报道、出版。

Article 9

When information is provided to reporters or editors of news publishing units by the units or persons being interviewed, and that interview material which is necessary to the work in hand involves state secrets, then such matters shall be approved in advance according to relevant legal procedures and shall be declared to the reporters or editors. Matters which have been declared to be state secrets by the units or persons being interviewed shall not be publicly reported or published by news publishing units, or by their reporters or editors.

Advance approval for interview materials provided to reporters/editors

对涉及国家秘密但确需公开报道、出版的信息，新闻出版单位应当向有关主管部门建议解密或者采取删节、改编、隐去等保密措施，并经有关主管部门审定。

Regarding information involving state secrets that must be publicly reported or published, the news publishing units concerned shall suggest to the relevant department in charge that the materials be declassified or that other measures be adopted to protect state secrets, such as abridging, editing or concealing such materials. The materials shall then be checked and approved by the relevant department in charge.

Declassifying, abridging, editing, or concealing information that must be published

Covering meetings/other activities involving state secrets	**第十条**	**Article 10**

Covering meetings/other activities involving state secrets

第十条

新闻出版单位采访涉及国家秘密的会议或其他活动，应当经主办单位批准。主办单位应当验明采访人员的工作身份，指明哪些内容不得公开报道、出版，并对拟公开报道、出版的内容进行审定。

Article 10

News publishing units that cover meetings or other activities involving state secrets must first be given permission to do so by the host unit. The host unit shall check the work identity papers of the interviewers and indicate which items should not be publicly reported or published. Items that are intended to be publicly reported or published shall be checked and approved by the host unit.

Responsibility of state organs under central government, other relevant units

第十一条

为了防止泄露国家秘密又利于新闻出版工作的正常进行，中央国家机关各部门和其他有关单位，应当根据各自业务工作的性质，加强与新闻出版单位的联系，建立提供信息的正常渠道，健全新闻发布制度，适时通报宣传口径。

Article 11

In order to prevent state secrets from being disclosed and to ensure that routine news publishing work can be carried out, all departments belonging to state organs under the central government, as well as other relevant units, shall strengthen their relationship with news publishing units according to the nature of their work, establish regular channels for providing information, perfect their system for issuing news releases, and circulate propaganda guidelines in a timely manner.

Checking and approving manuscripts

第十二条

有关机关、单位应当指定有权代表本机关、单位的审稿机构和审稿人，负责对新闻出版单位送审的稿件是否涉及国家秘密进行审定。对是否涉及国家秘密界限不清的内容，应当报请上级机关、单位审定；涉及其他单位工作中国家秘密的，应当负责征求有关单位的意见。

Article 12

Relevant organs and units shall appoint a body or individual from another organ or unit with the authority to represent the former to check their manuscripts. That body or individual shall be responsible for checking and approving manuscripts submitted by news publishing units to determine whether or not the manuscripts involve state secrets. Where it is unclear whether or not the contents involve state secrets, the materials shall be submitted to higher authorities or units for examination and approval. If the materials are related to state secrets that involve the work of other units, an opinion shall be solicited from the relevant unit.

第十三条

有关机关、单位审定送审的稿件时，应当满足新闻出版单位提出的审定时限的要求，遇有特殊情况不能在所要求的时限内完成审定的，应当及时向送审稿件的新闻出版单位说明，并共同商量解决办法。

Article 13

When the relevant organs or units are checking manuscripts submitted for approval, they shall satisfy the time requirements of the news publishing unit, and if such work cannot be concluded within the required time limit due to special circumstances, this shall be explained to the relevant news publishing unit and they shall discuss a way to solve the problem.

Time requirements for checking manuscripts

第十四条

个人拟向新闻出版单位提供公开报道、出版的信息，凡涉及本系统、本单位业务工作的或对是否涉及国家秘密界限不清的，应当事先经本单位或其上级机关、单位审定。

Article 14

If an individual intends to provide information to news publishing units for public dissemination or publication and the information involves the work of affiliated organizations or units, or if it is unclear whether or not the information involves state secrets, such information shall be checked and approved in advance by that individual's unit or by higher authorities or units.

Prior approval for information involving work of affiliated organizations or units

第十五条

个人拟向境外新闻出版机构提供报道、出版涉及国家政治、经济、外交、科技、军事方面内容的，应当事先经过本单位或其上级机关、单位审定。向境外投寄稿件，应当按照国家有关规定办理。

Article 15

If an individual intends to provide reports or publications involving national politics, economics, foreign affairs, science and technology, or military affairs to foreign news publishing organizations, such materials shall be checked and approved in advance by that individual's unit, or by higher authorities or units. If manuscripts are mailed outside of the country, they shall be handled in accordance with relevant state regulations.

Providing reports/publications involving national politics, economics, foreign affairs, science and technology, or military affairs to foreign news publishing organizations

第三章 泄密的查处

Chapter Three: Investigating and Handling Occurrences of Disclosing State Secrets

Illegal reporting/publishing of state secrets

第十六条

国家工作人员或其他公民发现国家秘密被非法报道、出版时，应当及时报告有关机关、单位或保密工作部门。泄密事件所涉及的新闻出版单位和有关单位，应当主动联系，共同采取补救措施。

Article 16

If state personnel or other citizens discover that state secrets have been illegally reported or published, they shall immediately make a report to the relevant organ or unit, or to a state secrets bureau. If the disclosure of state secrets is related to news publishing units or other relevant units, those units shall initiate contact and jointly adopt measures to remedy the situation.

Disclosure during course of news publishing activities

第十七条

新闻出版活动中发生的泄密事件，由有关责任单位负责及时调查；责任暂时不清的，由有关保密工作部门决定自行调查或者指定有关单位调查。

Article 17

If state secrets are disclosed during the course of news publishing activities, a person from the relevant unit responsible shall immediately investigate. If it is uncertain who is responsible for the investigation, the relevant state secrets bureau shall make a decision to investigate the matter itself or appoint another unit to investigate.

Punishment for disclosure

第十八条

对泄露国家秘密的责任单位、责任人，应当按照有关法律和规定严肃处理。

Article 18

Any units or individuals that are responsible for disclosing state secrets shall be severely punished according to the relevant laws and regulations.

Handling closing down, takeover, or resulting economic losses

第十九条

新闻出版工作中因泄密问题需要对出版物停发、停办或者收缴以及由此造成的经济损失，应当按照有关主管部门的规定处理。

Article 19

If the disclosure of a state secret that occurs during the course of news publishing work requires that publication to cease publishing, close down, or be taken over, and if economic losses are incurred as a result of this, the relevant department in charge shall handle the situation according to its regulations.

新闻出版单位及其采编人员和提供信息的单位及其有关人员因泄露国家秘密所获得的非法收入，应当依法没收并上缴国家财政。

Illicit income obtained through the disclosure of state secret matters by news publishing units, their reporters or editors, or by units or persons that provide information, will be confiscated in accordance with the law and will be turned over to the state.

Confiscation of illegal income

第四章 附则

Chapter Four: Additional Provisions

第二十条
新闻出版工作中，各有关单位因有关信息是否属于国家秘密问题发生争执的，由保密工作部门会同有关主管部门依据保密法规确定。

Article 20
If, in the course of news publishing work, individual units disagree as to whether or not certain information is a state secret, the question shall be decided by a state secrets bureau together with the relevant department in charge, in accordance with the laws and regulations on the protection of state secrets.

When different units disagree

第二十一条
本规定所称的"信息"可以语言、文字、符号、图表、图像等形式表现。

Article 21
The term "information" as used in this regulation may refer to language, writing, symbols, charts, pictures, and other forms of expression.

"Information"

第二十二条
本规定由国家保密局负责解释。

Article 22
Explaining this regulation is the work of the National Administration for the Protection of State Secrets.

Responsibility for explaining regulation

第二十三条
本规定自１９９２年１０月１日起施行。

Article 23
This regulation shall take effect as of October 1, 1992.

Effective date

E.

Selection of State Secrets Provisions Regulating Specific Activities

Editors' Note:

The table below is a compilation of some of the provisions contained in the body of regulations issued jointly by the National Administration for the Protection of State Secrets (NAPSS) and specific government and party organs, ranging from the Ministry of Labor and Social Security to the All-China Women's Federation.

These regulations indicate the far-reaching influence that the NAPSS has in preventing information on nearly all aspects of life from reaching the public domain. Social science research work, labor and social security, environmental protection, land management, civil affairs work, women's work, family planning, and ethnic and religious affairs all have a long list of matters that are classified as state secrets. For example:

- Information on labor petitions or strikes in state enterprises

- Nearly all information held by the ACFTU (All-China Federation of Trade Workers)

- Information on incidents of environmental contamination or pollution

- Information on infectious diseases and large-scale epidemics

- Plans for handling ethnic unrest, and the reactions of overseas ethnic minorities on ethnic problems within China, including certain writings or speeches of ethnic minorities in China

- Information on overseas religious organizations and their personnel

- Statistics on the number of abortions and incidents of infanticide and child abandonment

Each regulation divides information into the standard classification of top secret, highly secret and secret, with some also including the level of *neibu* (internal) classification for matters that are not technically state secrets but that must not be disclosed without approval of the relevant body.

Unless otherwise noted, the source for the following regulations is: 李志东（主编），《中华人民共和国保密法全书》，（本书仅供各级保密部门、组织、人员使用）（长春：吉林人民出版社，1999），[Li Zhidong, ed. *Compendium of Laws of the People's Republic of China on the Protection of State Secrets,* (Circulation limited to departments, organizations and personnel doing state secrets protection work), (Changchun: Jilin People's Press, 1999).

Regulation on State Secrets and the Specific Scope of Each Level of Secrets in Social Science Research Work

- Chinese Academy of Social Sciences, National Administration for the Protection of State Secrets

- April 21, 1995

社会科学研究工作中国家秘密及其密级具体范围的规定

- 中国科学院、国家保密局

- 1995年4月21日

Top secret:

- Materials related to the details or forms of research performed by research departments and individuals that are appointed by the Party or state to take part in major reforms of the country's economic and political systems, as well as information on major internal and foreign policy principles. (研究部门及个人被党和国家制定参加关于国家重大经济体制改革和政治体制改革问题及重大内政外交方针政策的研究情况和形成的有关材料。) *(Article 3.1.1)*

Highly secret:

- Planning and policy research reports and suggestions that involve China's foreign policy, state-to-state relations, or other serious matters concerning state security and interests. (涉及我国外交政策、国家关系以及严重关系国家安全和利益的预测性、政策性研究报告和建议。) *(Article 3.2.1)*

- Research reports, details of responses to reports, statistical data and audio-visual materials that concern socially sensitive domestic issues and are meant only for Party and state leaders or relevant departments. (只适于向党和国家领导及有关部门反映的国内社会敏感问题的调研究报告、情况反映、数据统计和音像资料。) *(Article 3.2.3)*

Secret:

- Documents and reports on the details or forms of research regarding policies and measures for the establishment and perfection of the socialist market economy that are still under consideration and have not yet been implemented. (参加关于建立和完善社会主义市场经济体制过程中尚未出台的政策、措施的研究清况和形成的文件、报告。) *(Article 3.3.1)*

NAME OF REGULATION

ISSUING BODIES AND DATE OF ISSUE

RELEVANT PROVISIONS

Regulation on State Secrets and the Specific Scope of Each Level of Secrets in Labor and Social Security Work

- Ministry of Labor and Social Security, National Administration for the Protection of State Secrets

- January 27, 2000

劳动和社会保障工作中国家秘密及其密级具体范围的规定

- 劳动和社会保障部、国家保密局

- 2000年1月27日

Highly secret:

- Undisclosed information and data on the handling of child labor cases nationwide. （尚未公布的全国童工案件查处情况及统计数据。）*(Article 3.1.1)*

Undisclosed opinions on amendments to important, socially sensitive government policies. （尚未公布的重大社会敏感政策的调整意见。）*(Article 3.1.2)*

Compiled information on major incidents involving workers in enterprises nationwide, such as collective petitioning or strikes. （全国企业职工集体上访和罢工等重大突发事件的综合情况。）*(Article 3.1.4)*

Policies and plans to revise wages in enterprises at the national level, in all State Council departments, and at the level of province, autonomous region, and directly-administered municipality. （全国、国务院各部门及各省、自治区、直辖市的企业工资调整政策、调整方案。）*(Article 3.1.5)*

Information concerning major cases of embezzlement and the illegal use of social insurance funds, and information on the informants in such cases. （社会保险基金被挤占挪用和违规动用的重大案件及案件举报人的有关情况。）*(Article 3.1.6)*

Plans and strategies for participating in meetings of international labor organizations. （参加国际劳动组织会议的计划，对策。）*(Article 3.1.7)*

Secret:

- Undisclosed unemployment rates, revenue and expenditure forecasts for social insurance funds, and planning data regarding all mid- and long-term development programs and annual development plans for labor and social security projects. （劳动和社会保障事业中、长期发展规划和年度发展计划中尚未公布的失业率、社会保险基金收支预测和计划数据。）*(Article 3.2.1)*

- Investigative materials and statistical data which reflect the macroscopic situation of wage distribution in enterprises nationwide. （反映全国企业工资分配宏观状况的调查资料和统计数据。）*(Article 3.2.2)*

Regulation on State Secrets and the Specific Scope of Each Level of Secrets in Labor and Social Security Work, *cont.*

Internal (*neibu*):

- Undisclosed key policy measures and revised plans regarding all mid- and long-term development programs and annual development plans for labor and social security projects. (劳动和社会保障事业中、长期发展规划和年度发展计划中尚未公布实施的重大政策措施及调整方案。) *(Article 4.1)*

- Statistical materials on labor protection at the national level, in all State Council departments, and at the level of province, autonomous region, and directly-administered municipality. (全国及各省、自治区、直辖市和国务院各部门的劳动保障统计资料) *(Article 4.2)*

- The total number of laid-off workers in state-owned enterprises. (国有企业下岗职工总数。) *(Article 4.3)*

- Distribution plans concerning basic living guarantees and re-employment funds for laid-off workers in state-owned enterprises. (国有企业下岗职工基本生活保障和再就业资金分配方案。) *(Article 4.4)*

- Plans and measures for the reform of the labor protection system at the national level, in all State Council departments, and at the level of province, autonomous region, and directly-administered municipality. (全国及各省、自治区、直辖市和国务院各部门的劳动保障制度改革方案及办法。) *(Article 4.6)*

The source for this regulation is: Law Search （盼律网）Web site, http://www.panlv.net/p1281237059253125000.html.

NAME OF REGULATION
ISSUING BODIES AND DATE OF ISSUE

RELEVANT PROVISIONS

Regulation on State Secrets and the Specific Scope of Each Level of Secrets in Trade Union Work

• All-China Federation of Trade Unions (ACFTU), National Administration for the Protection of State Secrets

• May 27, 1996

工会工作中国家秘密及其密级具体范围的规定

• 全国总工会、国家保密局

• 1996年5月27日

Highly secret:

• Compiled information and statistics held by the ACFTU concerning collective petitioning, strikes, marches, demonstrations and other major incidents involving workers. （全国总工会掌握的职工集体上访、罢工、游行、示威等重大突发事件的综合情况和统计数字。）*(Article 3.1.1)*

• Information and investigative materials held by trade unions at the national level and in each province, autonomous region and directly-administered municipality concerning the activities of illegal labor organizations. （全国及各省、自治区、直辖市工会掌握的职工中的非法组织的活动情况以及对其查处材料。）*(Article 3.1.2)*

• The positions of, and strategies against, trade union organizations in Taiwan. （对台湾工会组织的表态口径和对策。）*(Article 3.1.3)*

Secret:

• Compiled information and statistical data held by trade unions in each province, autonomous region and directly-administered municipality regarding collective petitioning, strikes, marches, demonstrations and other major incidents involving workers. （各省、自治区、直辖市工会掌握的职工集体上访、罢工、游行、示威等重大突发事件的综合情况和统计数字。）*(Article 3.2.1)*

• Undisclosed compiled information and statistical data held by the ACFTU concerning major dangerous accidents and occupational illnesses. （未公开的全国总工会掌握的重大恶性事故、职业病综合统计数字。）*(Article 3.2.2)*

• Compiled information and statistics held by the ACFTU concerning worker unemployment and the financial hardships of workers. （全国总工会掌握的职工失业和生活困难的综合情况和统计数字。）*(Article 3.2.3)*

• Results of scientific research, technological materials, tricks of the trade and their sources that were acquired by trade unions and related organizations through secret channels. （工会及其有关组织通过秘密渠道取得的科研成果、科技资料、技术诀窍及其来源。）*(Article 3.2.4)*

• Work plans and strategies concerning participation in international labor organizations, and in bilateral and multilateral contacts with trade union organizations in individual nations. （参加国际工会组织和与各国工会组织进行双边、多边交往的工作方案和对策。）*(Article 3.2.5)*

**Regulation on State Secrets
and the Specific Scope
of Each Level of Secrets
in Trade Union Work, *cont.***

Secret, *cont.*:

- The positions of, and strategies against, trade unions in Hong Kong and Macao. (对港、澳工会组织的表态口径和对策) *(Article 3.2.6)*

Internal (*neibu*):

- Undisclosed directives issued by central Party and state leaders concerning trade union work. (未公开的党中央及中央领导同志有关工会工作的指示。) *(Article 5.1)*

- Proposals sent to the Party's Central Committee, the State Council, and other relevant departments regarding questions of national economic development and the immediate concerns of workers. (给党中央、国务院及其有关部门关于国民经济发展和职工切身利益问题的建议。) *(Article 5.2)*

- Information and statistical data not yet made public on the situation of workers and trade union work. (尚未公布的职工队伍状况和工会工作的综合情况和统计数字。) *(Article 5.3)*

- Information and materials that are part of an ongoing investigation or research that could be detrimental to the stability of workers. (在调查研究中掌握的有关不利于职工队伍稳定的情况和材料。) *(Article 5.4)*

- Details of current investigations concerning worker casualties. (正在调查的职工伤亡案情。) *(Article 5.5)*

- Information concerning internal discussions of assessments, promotions, appointments, awards or punishments of cadres, and information concerning appraisals and votes taken during job performance reviews in specialized fields. (干部考核、晋升、聘任、奖励、处分事项的内部讨论情况和专业职务评聘工作中的评议表决情况。) *(Article 5.6)*

- Plans and arrangements for activities involving foreign affairs. (外事活动的计划安排。) *(Article 5.7)*

- Self-published internal publications and other materials published by trade union organizations. (工会组织自行编印的内部刊物、资料。) *(Article 5.8)*

| NAME OF REGULATION ISSUING BODIES AND DATE OF ISSUE | RELEVANT PROVISIONS |

Regulation on the Specific Scope of State Secrets in Environmental Protection Work

- State Environmental Protection Administration, National Administration for the Protection of State Secrets

- December 28, 2004

环境保护工作国家秘密范围的规定

- 国家环境保护部总、国家保密局

- 2004年12月28日

Highly secret:

- Information on environmental pollution that would, if disclosed, seriously affect social stability. (泄露会严重影响社会稳定的环境污染信息。) *(Article 2.1.1)*

- Information that would, if disclosed, constitute a serious threat to military installations. (泄露会对军事设施构成严重威胁的信息。) *(Article 2.1.2)*

Secret:

- Information on environmental pollution that would, if disclosed, affect social stability. (泄露会影响社会稳定的环境污染信息。) *(Article 2.2.1)*

- Information that would, if disclosed, create an unfavorable impression in our country's foreign affairs work. (泄露会给我外交工作造成不利影响的信息。) *(Article 2.2.2)*

The source for this regulation is: 《中国环境年鉴》 编辑委员会。《中国环境年鉴》。(北京：中国环境科学出版社，2005) [China Environment Yearbook Editorial Committee. *China Environment Yearbook.* (Beijing: China Environmental Sciences Press, 2005)].

Regulation on State Secrets and the Specific Scope of Each Level of Secrets in Managing Land and Resources Work

- Ministry of Land and Resources, National Administration for the Protection of State Secrets

- May 14, 2003

国土资源管理工作国家秘密范围的规定

- 国土资源部、国家保密局

- 2003年5月14日

Top secret:

- Statistics on state land and resources that would, if made public or disclosed, seriously harm the nation's image and social stability. (公开或泄露后会严重损害国家形象和社会安定的国土资源数据。) *(Article 2.1.1)*

- Information on surveying work to serve military aims and for national construction, as well as surveys of mineral resources, that would, if made public or disclosed, bring about serious disputes with foreign countries or border conflicts. (公开或泄露后会引发严重外交纠纷、边界争端的矿产资源调查和为国防建设和军事目的服务的探测工作情况。) *(Article 2.1.2)*

Highly secret:

- Information on land that would, if made public or disclosed, constitute a serious threat to the safety of Party or state leaders. (公开或泄露后会对党和国家领导人安全构成严重威胁的土地资料。) *(Article 2.2.1)*

- Information on geological surveying work that would, if made public or disclosed, bring about border disputes or that would be disadvantageous to the resolution of border questions. (公开或泄露后会引发边界争议或不利于边界问题解决的地质调查工作情况。) *(Article 2.2.2)*

Secret:

- Information on mapping regional state land and resources that would, if made public or disclosed, weaken military defense capabilities. (公开或泄露后会削弱军事防御能力的区域性国土资源测绘资料。) *(Article 2.3)*

The source for this regulation is: The Ministry of Land and Resources Web site, http://www.mlr.gov.cn/pub/mlr/documents/t20041125_75029.htm.

NAME OF REGULATION

ISSUING BODIES AND DATE OF ISSUE   **RELEVANT PROVISIONS**

Regulation on State Secrets and the Specific Scope of Each Level of Secrets in Family Planning Work	**Highly secret:**

Highly secret:

- Preliminary discussions by the State Council and other relevant departments on national sex education and family planning policies and programs. （国务院及其有关部门正在酝酿的全国性生育政策方案。）*(Article 3.1.1)*

Regulation on State Secrets and the Specific Scope of Each Level of Secrets in Family Planning Work

- State Family Planning Commission (now State Population and Family Planning Commission), National Administration for the Protection of State Secrets

- May 16, 1995

计划生育工作中国家秘密及其密级具体范围的规定

- 国家计划生育委员会（国家人口与计划生育委员会）、国家保密局

- 1995年5月16日

- Statistics from family planning departments at the national level and at the level of province, autonomous region, directly-administered municipality or planned city on the number of deaths resulting from problems with surgical birth control procedures or family planning. （全国及省、自治区、直辖市、计划单列市计划生育部们统计的节育手术死亡数和因计划生育问题造成死亡的数据。）*(Article 3.1.2)*

- Statistics from family planning departments at the national level and at the level of province, autonomous region, directly-administered municipality or planned city regarding the number of induced abortions. （全国及省、自治区、直辖市、计划单列市计划生育部们统计的引产数。）*(Article 3.1.3)*

Secret:

- Statistics from family planning departments at the prefectural level on the number of deaths resulting from problems with surgical birth control procedures or family planning. （地级计划生育部门统计的节育手术死亡数和因计划生育问题造成死亡的数据。）*(Article 3.2.1)*

- Statistics from family planning departments at the prefectural level on the number of induced abortions. （地级计划生育部门统计的引产数。）*(Article 3.2.2)*

- Statistics on infanticide and child abandonment at the county level and higher during specific periods of investigation by relevant departments. （有关单位专项调查期间统计的县级以上的溺弃婴数。）*(Article 3.2.3)*

- Statistics from family planning departments at the national, provincial, prefectural and county level on fees collected for unplanned births [births not allowed under family planning policy]. （全国及省、地、县级计划生育部门统计的计划外生育费汇总数。）*(Article 3.2.4)*

**Regulation on State Secrets
and the Specific Scope
of Each Level of Secrets
in Family Planning Work,** *cont.*

Internal (*neibu***):**

- Statistics from family planning departments at the county level on the number of deaths resulting from problems with surgical birth control procedures or family planning. (县级计划生育部门统计的节育手术死亡数和因计划生育问题造成死亡的数据。) *(Article 5.1)*

- Statistics from family planning departments at the county level on the number of induced abortions. (县级计划生育部门统计的引产数。) (Article 5.2)

- Statistics on infanticide and child abandonment at the township level during specific periods of investigation by relevant units. (有关单位专项调查期间统计的乡级的溺弃婴数。) *(Article 5.3)*

- Statistics from family planning departments at the county level and higher on the gender and sex ratio of second and third-born children. (县级以上计划生育部门统计的第二、三胎出生婴儿性别数和性别比。) *(Article 5.4)*

- Cases of deaths or disabilities resulting from problems with surgical birth control procedures or family planning. (因节育手术和计划生育问题造成残废或死亡的案列。) *(Article 5.5)*

- Collective disturbances or incidents that occurred as a result of using overly crude or brutal methods in family planning work. (简单粗暴的工作方法及因此而引发的群体闹事事件。) *(Article 5.6)*

- Incidents of cruel treatment of family planning officers that occurred while they were fulfilling their family planning duties according to law, or incidents of cruel treatment to their families or serious damage to their property or belongings. (残害依法执行计划生育公务人员及其家属和严重捐坏其财产的事件。) *(Article 5.7)*

NAME OF REGULATION

ISSUING BODIES AND DATE OF ISSUE

RELEVANT PROVISIONS

Regulation on State Secrets and the Specific Scope of Each Level of Secrets in Cultural Work

- Ministry of Culture, National Administration for the Protection of State Secrets

- July 21, 1995

文化工作中国家秘密及其密级具体范围的规定

- 文化部、国家保密局

- 1995年7月21日

Top secret:

- Tactics, strategies and measures adopted in handling major incidents in foreign relations and cultural activities with foreign nations that involve our country's national reputation. （对外文化活动方面涉及国家声誉和对外关系的重大事件所采取的策略、对策和措施。）*(Article 3.1)*

Highly secret:

- Relevant details of, and measures adopted to handle, cultural work or cultural activities with foreign nations that might have an international influence. （在文化工作或对外文化活动方面涉及国际影响的有关情况和所采取的措施。）*(Article 3.2.1)*

- Propaganda guidelines, strategies and measures used in cultural propaganda work with sensitive foreign nations or regions. （在对外文化宣工作中对敏感国家或地区的宣传口径、策略和措施。）*(Article 3.2.2)*

- Details on the approval process for major cultural exchange projects with other countries that involve sensitive issues. （涉及敏感问题的重大中外文化合作项目的审批情况。）*(Article 3.2.4)*

- Collections of old books and maps that contain information on borders between China and neighboring countries that have not yet been determined, or information on borders with neighboring countries that are still under dispute. （馆藏古旧图书、地图中涉及我国与邻国未定边界或已定边界中有争议的有关内容。）*(Article 3.2.8)*

Secret:

- The annual work reports or proposals of cultural organizations stationed abroad on the situation in those countries, and the strategies approved and adopted by this ministry to deal with such situations. （驻外文化机构对有关驻在国形势的年度工作总结、建议及我部批复和采取的对策。）*(Article 3.3.2)*

Regulation on State Secrets and the Specific Scope of Each Level of Secrets in Civil Affairs Work

- Ministry of Civil Affairs, National Administration for the Protection of State Secrets

- February 29, 2000

民政工作中国家秘密及其密级具体范围的规定

- 民政部、国家保密局

- 2000年2月29日

Highly secret:

- Basic information on illegal organizations or unlawful civil organizations held by civil affairs departments in the course of performing their work of administering civil affairs. (民间组织管理工作中民政部门掌握的非法组织或违法民间组织的基本情况。) *(Article 3.2.1)*

Secret:

- Recommendations and plans for boundary delimitations issued by relevant departments of the central government or a province (or autonomous region or directly-administered municipality) on border disputes that have not yet been resolved. (中央、省（自治区、直辖市）有关部门对边界争议事件未解决之前的处理意见及划界方案。) *(Article 3.3.1)*

- Statistics and other related information on individuals who flee from famine, beg for food or die as a result of natural disasters at the national, provincial, autonomous region or directly- administered municipal level. (全国及省、自治区、直辖市因自然灾害导致的逃荒、要饭、死亡人员总数及相关资料。) *(Article 3.3.4)* [Ed. note: This article was removed by Document 116, Notice Regarding the Declassification of Statistics on Casualties Caused by Natural Disasters and Related Information, issued by the Ministry of Civil Affairs and the NAPSS on August 8, 2005.]

- Archived records containing place names located on border areas that are marked with the exact latitude and longitude. (边境地区标有准确经纬度的地名档案) *(Article 3.3.5)*

- Policies on handling problems with refugees from abroad in China. （处理在华国际难民问题的决策。） *(Article 3.3.6)*

The source for this regulation is: Law Search （盼律网）Web site, http://www.panlv.net/p17087.html.

NAME OF REGULATION

ISSUING BODIES AND DATE OF ISSUE   **RELEVANT PROVISIONS**

Regulation on State Secrets and the Specific Scope of Each Level of Secrets in Public Health Work

- Ministry of Health, National Administration for the Protection of State Secrets

- January 23, 1996

卫生工作中国家秘密及其密级具体范围的规定

- 卫生部、国家保密局

- 1996年1月23日

Top secret:

- Records on the health situation, plans for medical treatment, and medical history of Party and important state leaders, and of foreign state dignitaries and heads of government that are visiting China. （党和国家主要领导人及来访的外国国家元首、政府首脑的健康情况、医疗方案、病历记录。）*(Article 3.1)*

Highly secret:

- Undisclosed medium-, long-term or annual plans for medical or scientific research. （未公开的医学科学研究中长期规划、年度计划。）*(Article 3.2.1)*

- Information on the number of cases of Class A infectious diseases, as well as information on large-scale epidemic outbreaks (at the prefectural, municipal and autonomous region level or higher) of viral hepatitis and other hemorrhagic diseases, that has not yet been authorized for public disclosure by the Ministry of Health or other organizations authorized by the Ministry of Health. （未经卫生部和卫生部授权机构公布的甲类传染病疫情及较大范围（地市州以上）爆发流行的病毒性肝炎、流行性出血热等病例数。）*(Article 3.2.9)*

- Statistics, methods and numbers of cases from all levels of health departments on induced abortions during the second trimester of pregnancy (pregnancies at 14 weeks or more). （各级卫生部门统计的中期妊娠 （妊娠14周以上）引产的数字、方法、病例。）*(Article 3.2.10)*

Secret:

- Nationwide figures not yet authorized for disclosure by the Ministry of Health or other organizations authorized by the Ministry of Health on the incidence of people who contract any kind of occupational illness; and compiled statistical figures on infected persons in each province, autonomous region, directly-administered municipality and planned city. （未经卫生部和卫生部授权机构公布的全国各类职业病发病人术；各省、自治区、直辖市及计划单列市的发病人数的综合统计数字。）*(Article 3.3.2)*

- The biological effects of all previous nuclear test site areas. （我国历次核试验期间场区的生物效应。）*(Article 3.3.4)*

Regulation on State Secrets and the Specific Scope of Each Level of Secrets in Women's Work

- All-China Women's Federation, National Administration for the Protection of State Secrets

- April 24, 1991

妇女工作中国家秘密及其密级具体范围的规定

- 中华全国妇女联合会、国家保密局

- 1991年4月24日

Highly secret:

- Plans and strategies for handling major issues in women's work that involve important and sensitive countries or regions. （妇女工作涉及重要和敏感国家、地区的重要问题的方案、对策。）*(Article 3.1)*

Secret:

- Compiled data regarding major cases that involve the killing of women and children. （有关残害妇女、儿童犯罪活动重大案件综合性数据。）*(Article 3.2.3)*

- Compiled data at the provincial level and higher regarding the trafficking of women and children. （有关拐卖妇女、儿童的省以上综合性数据。）*(Article 3.2.4)*

| NAME OF REGULATION ISSUING BODIES AND DATE OF ISSUE | RELEVANT PROVISIONS |

Regulation on State Secrets and the Specific Scope of Each Level of Secrets in Ethnic Work

- State Ethnic Affairs Commission, National Administration for the Protection of State Secrets

- March 17, 1995

民族工作中国家秘密及其密级具体范围的规定

- 国家民族事务委员会、国家保密局

- 1995年3月17日

Top secret:

- Analyses of important developments and information on anything that could seriously harm ethnic relations, or that for other ethnic reasons could endanger national unity or affect social stability. (对可能严重损害民族关系和由于民族方面的因素而危害国家统一、影响社会稳定的重要动态和情况分析。) *(Article 3.1.1)*

- Strategies and measures for dealing with the occurrence of major ethnic-related public order emergencies. (对民族方面发生的重大紧急治安事件的处置对策和措施。) *(Article 3.1.2)*

- Strategies and measures used in handling ethnic separatist activities. (对民族分裂活动采取的对策和措施。) *(Article 3.1.3)*

Highly secret:

- Important guiding principles, policies and measures currently being discussed or formulated regarding ethnic work. (正在酝酿制定中的有关民族工作的重要方针、政策和措施。) *(Article 3.2.1)*

- Plans and measures for handling ethnic disputes (处理民族纠纷的方案、措施。) *(Article 3.2.2)*

- Reactions from individuals in Taiwan, Hong Kong and Macau, or from ethnic minorities living abroad, on important questions involving issues, policies and work related to ethnic minorities in China. (台湾、香港、澳门及旅居海外的少数民族人士所反映的有关民族问题、民族政策、民族工作中的重要问题。) *(Article 3.2.3)*

Secret:

- Reactions to important issues regarding the implementation of ethnic policies. (贯彻有关民族政策中反映的重要问题。) *(Article 3.3.1)*

- Information and measures under consideration that must be held internally on the work of ethnic identification and the establishment of ethnic autonomous areas. (民族识别和建立民族自治地方工作中需要内部掌握的情况及拟采取的办法。) *(Article 3.3.2)*

Regulation on State Secrets and the Specific Scope of Each Level of Secrets in Ethnic Work, *cont.*

Secret, *cont.*:

- Internally-held guidelines on ethnic propaganda work in foreign relations and ethnic foreign affairs work. (民族对外宣传工作和民族涉外工作内部掌握的口径。) *(Article 3.3.3)*

- Analyses of important trends in speeches or writings by ethnic minorities. (对民族语言文字的重要动态分析。) *(Article 3.3.4)*

Internal (*neibu*):

- The contents of meetings of professional government bodies that should not be announced to the public. (机关业务会议中不宜公开的内容。) *(Article 4.1)*

- Work plans, summaries, written instructions, reports and relevant materials on the internal work of government organs. (机关内部的工作计划、总结、请示、报告及有关材料。) *(Article 4.2)*

- Statistical materials and formulations of guiding principles and policies used in the work of governmental organs that should not be announced to the public within a specified time frame. (在一定时间和范围内不宜公开的机关工作中统计资料和制定的方针、政策。) *(Article 4.3)*

- Documents, data, publications and bulletins used as internal reference materials. (机关内部参阅的文件、资料、刊物和简报。) *(Article 4.4)*

Regulation on State Secrets and the Specific Scope of Each Level of Secrets in Religious Work

- Ministry of Religious Affairs, National Administration for the Protection of State Secrets

- October 12, 1995

宗教工作中国家秘密及其密级具体范围的规定

- 宗教事务局、国家保密局

- 1995年10月12日

Top secret:

- Strategies and measures for handling major public order emergencies involving religious matters. （对宗教方面的重大紧急治安事件的处置对策和措施。） *(Article 3.1.1)*

- Strategies under consideration for handling criminal activities involving the use of religion to carry out political infiltration or to engage in serious violations of the law. （对利用宗教进行政治渗透和从事严重违法犯罪活动拟采取的对策。） *(Article 3.1.2)*

- Guiding principles and strategies under consideration for handling major religious issues that involve foreign relations. （对宗教方面涉外事宜中重大问题拟采取的方针、对策。） *(Article 3.1.3)*

Highly secret:

- Analyses of religious developments and situations, as well as important guiding principles and strategies under consideration for dealing with them. （对宗教形势、动态的分析和拟采取的重大方针、政策。） *(Article 3.2.1)*

- Specific guiding principles and tactics for making contact with religious organizations overseas and in Hong Kong, Macau and Taiwan. （与国外及港澳台宗教组织交往的具体方针和策略。） *(Article 3.2.2)*

Secret:

- Reactions to important issues concerning the implementation of religious policies. （贯彻有关宗教政策中反映的重要问题。） *(Article 3.3.1)*

- Internally-held guidelines for handling foreign affairs propaganda work （在对外宣传工作中内部掌握的口径。） *(Article 3.3.2)*

Regulation on State Secrets and the Specific Scope of Each Level of Secrets in Religious Work, *cont.*

Internal (*neibu*):

- Information on, and suggestions drawn up regarding the arrangements for, important representatives of religious groups. (宗教界重要代表人士的情况及其拟议中的安排意见。)*(Article 4.1)*

- Analyses and reactions to information on religious individuals that have an important influence in Hong Kong, Macau, Taiwan, China and abroad. （国内外、港澳台有重要影响的宗教人士的情况分析和反映。）*(Article 4.2)*

- Reactions to information on, and records of talks given during, receptions for representatives of religious groups. (接待宗教界代表人士的情况反映、谈话记录。)*(Article 4.3)*

- The reactions, opinions and recommendations of representatives of religious groups regarding guiding principles, policies and important decisions contained in proposals on religious matters. (宗教界代表人士对我宗教方面拟议中的方针、政策和重要决策的反映、意见和建议。)*(Article 4.4)*

- Analyses of information on the trends of overseas religious organizations and their personnel. (境外宗教组织、人员情况的动态分析。) *(Article 4.5)*

- Information and statistical data that should not be disclosed to the public regarding religious organizations, religious institutes and religious activities. (有关宗教组织、宗教院校、宗教活动不宜公开的情况及统计数字。) *(Article 4.6)*

- Information relating to Party members and cadres in religious groups and in grassroots Party organizations. (宗教团体中党员干部、党的基层组织的有关情况。) *(Article 4.7)*

- Drafts of laws and regulations on religion. (拟定中的宗教法规。) *(Article 4.8)*

- The contents of meetings held by government organs that should not be disclosed to the public. (机关会议中不宜公开的内容。) *(Article 4.9)*

Table of Contents

Appendices

Editors' Introduction   188

I. Official Documents   189

Document 1
Jiang Zemin: The Work of Protecting State Secrets Faces
"Unprecedented Difficulties"   189

Document 2
The Overall Structure of State Secrets Administration   192

Document 3
The "Basic" and "Specific" Scope of State Secrets   194

Document 4
Classification Procedures for State Secret Matters   196

Document 5
The Determination and Handling of "Work Secrets"   198

Document 6
Assessing State Secrets Protection Work   200

Document 7
The Protection of State Secrets in News Publishing   203

II. Cases Involving State Secrets   213

A.
Individuals Charged with State Secrets Offenses   214

B.
Individuals Likely Denied Procedural Protections on State Secrets Grounds   229

III. Incidents of Official Cover-Ups   236

Appendices Notes   243

Editors' Introduction

In Part I of these appendices, we present a variety of charts, speeches and other documents that provide a rare "inside" glimpse into China's system of state secrets administration, including an explanation of a type of internal, or *neibu,* matter called "work secrets," a speech by Jiang Zemin on the difficulties of protecting state secrets, and—in what should be an indispensable resource for all reporters and journalists working in China—a *neibu* document giving an in-depth description of how state secrets are to be protected in news publishing.

As in Section 2: State Secrets Laws and Regulation of the PRC, many of the documents in these appendices have also been translated and made available to English-speaking audiences for the first time. In fact, while many of the laws and regulations presented in Section 2 are readily available in Chinese—some even online—these more obscure documents can only be found in classified or *neibu* publications.

In Parts II and III, we present two tables. The first, entitled Cases Involving State Secrets, includes a list of individual cases involving charges of state secrets and a second list of cases where procedural protections were denied, likely because of the involvement of state secrets. The second table is a selected list of cover-up incidents which provide clear examples of how the culture of secrecy has denied information to the public—information that was crucial to protect public health and allow for open and transparent discussion of government policies.

I

Official
Documents

DOCUMENT 1

Jiang Zemin: The Work of Protecting State Secrets Faces "Unprecedented Difficulties"

Editors' Note:

The following document presents excerpts from a speech given by Jiang Zemin (then General Party Secretary) at the National Conference on the Work of Protecting State Secrets held in Beijing, December 11–13, 1996.

The conference was an important turning point in the strengthening and expansion of the state secrets system, and coincided with the distribution of the Central Party Committee's "Decision on Strengthening the Work of Protecting State Secrets Under New Trends" (Document No. 16) which, to this date, continues to frame the work of state secrecy.

The national conference was attended by over 400 participants and established the work ahead through a five-year and a ten-year plan. The tone of the conference was unambiguously terse, with Jiang Zemin stating that the current "level of complexity and difficulty" of protecting state secrets is "unprecedented."

Stressing that the protection of state secrets affected "the larger picture of Party and state security" as well as "economic construction," Jiang urged leading cadres to "understand the importance of state secrets work from this political angle," and to put state secrets protection "at the core of our work methods."

The conference called for a rapid expansion of the laws and regulations governing state secrets so as to "fully put to use the authority and restricting force of national laws."

Hu Jintao, Zeng Qinghong, Li Peng and Luo Gan also addressed the conference, whose proceedings remain classified.

Sources:

"中央文献：全国保密工作会议（1996年12月11–13日）"，北京党建网站，["Important Documents from the Central Authorities: National Conference on State Secrets Protection Work (December 11–13, 1996), Website of Beijing's Party-Building Committee], http://www.bjdj.gov.cn/article/detail.asp?UNID=7688; 刘志才（主编），《保密法概论》（北京：金城出版社，1996），III [Liu Zhicai, ed. *Overview of the Law on the Protection of State Secrets* (Beijing: Jincheng Publishing House, 1996, p. III]; 国家保密局（主编），《保密知识读本》（北京：金城出版社，1999年，127 页 [National Administration for the Protection of State Secrets, ed. *Manual of State Secrets Protection Knowledge* (Beijing: Jincheng Publishing House, 1999), 127].

"Central Committee General Secretary Jiang Zemin's Address to the National Conference on the Work of Protecting State Secrets" December 12, 1996 (Excerpts)

在新的历史时期，保密工作做得好不好，直接影响着改革开放和社会主义现代化建设的进展。保密工作关系党和国家的安全、关系经济建设和社会主义发展的大局。全党同志特别是各级领导干部，必须从这样的政治高度充分认识保密工作的重要性。

In this new period in history, whether or not we do a good job of protecting state secrets directly influences the rate of progress of reforms and socialist modernization. The work of protecting state secrets is related to the larger picture of Party and state security, as well as to economic construction and socialist development. All party comrades, in particular leading cadres, must comprehensively understand the importance of state secrets work from this political angle.

在对外开放和发展社会主义市场经济的条件下，同志们还要充分认识到保密工作的复杂性和艰巨性。可以说：这种复杂性和艰巨性是前所未有的。

Under the current situation of opening to the outside world and developing a socialist market economy, our comrades must also comprehensively understand the complex and difficult nature of the work of protecting state secrets. It could be said that this level of complexity and difficulty is unprecedented.

保密工作历来是党和国家的一项重要工作。革命战争年代，保密就是生存，保胜利；和平时期，保密就是保安全、保发展"，"越是深化

Protecting state secrets has always been an important element of the work of the Party and the state. During the revolutionary years, protecting state secrets

改革，扩大开放，越要做好保密工作。

was done for survival and to ensure victory; in times of peace, protecting state secrets is done to protect security and development. The deeper the reforms go and the more we open to the outside world, the more important it is to do a good job of protecting state secrets.

必须保持高度的政治敏锐性和警惕性，牢固树立"保守党的机密，慎之又慎"的思想，"必须十分注意保守党的机密，九分半不行，九分九也不行，非十分不可"，把保密工作作为保障改革开放、促进经济发展、维护党和国家安全的一项重要工作抓紧抓好。

It is necessary to maintain a high level of political enthusiasm and alertness, and to securely establish the thinking that "In protecting secrets of the Party, we need to be even more careful." It is imperative to pay the utmost attention to protecting the secrets of the Party: 95% [protection] is not good enough, 99% is not good enough either. Only 100% is acceptable. We must have a firm grasp of the importance of protecting state secrets in order to safeguard the reform process, advance economic development, and protect the security of the Party and the state.

要加强保密法制建设，健全保密法规，充分运用国家法律的权威性和约束力，强化保密执法监督，加大执法力度。保密部门要协同纪检监察、组织人事部门一起制定严密的制度规章。对失密泄密案件，必须从严查处，坚决依法打击，绝不能徇情袒护、姑息养奸。

We must strengthen the legal system to protect state secrets, establish complete laws and regulations for protecting state secrets, fully utilize the authority and restricting power of national laws, strengthen supervision of the implementation of state secret laws, and increase the power to implement laws. The departments that do the work of protecting state secrets must coordinate with the discipline inspection and personnel departments to formulate a strict system of rules. Cases of loss or disclosure of state secrets must be sternly resolved and strictly dealt with according to law, without any wavering.

我们应该转变过去以管好涉密文件为主的工作方式，努力探索加强保密工作的新路子。

We must change the past and make the proper protection of secret matters the core of our work methods, and strive to find a new road for strengthening the work of protecting state secrets.

DOCUMENT 2

The Overall Structure
of State Secrets Administration

Editors' Note:

The following chart is a reproduction of an internal government graphic, with English translation added, that attempts to show the organizational structure of the state secrets system in China. The leading body is the General Office of the Committee on the Protection of State Secrets, directly under the authority of the Central Committee of the Communist Party of China (CPC). Reflecting the Party's direct management of the state secrets system, the National Administration for the Protection of State Secrets (NAPSS, also referred to here as the national State Secrets Bureau) is the administrative incarnation of the General Office (an arrangement described as "one body, two names").

The Ministry of National Defense and other "leading state organs" each have a specific Committee on the Protection of State Secrets that contributes to national policy-making in state secret matters. Policy implementation is then divided into three main branches: Science and Technology, Foreign Affairs, and agencies—called "groups"—from the different ministries and central government departments (e.g., Publicity, Personnel, Planning, Finance), as well as three "workshops" whose roles are unknown (but are most likely in charge of the technical aspects of state secrets protection: cryptography, security and communications).

The national State Secrets Bureau has branches at the provincial and municipal levels. While the total number of personnel at the different levels of state secrets bureaus is unknown, other sources state that it runs in the order of the thousands.

Source:

王守信，《保密工作管理概论（修订版）》(内部发行) (北京：金城出版社 ，1999): 24 [Wang Shouxin. *Overview of the Management of State Secrets Protection Work* (Revised Edition, Internal Circulation) (Beijing: Jincheng Publishing House, 1999), 24].

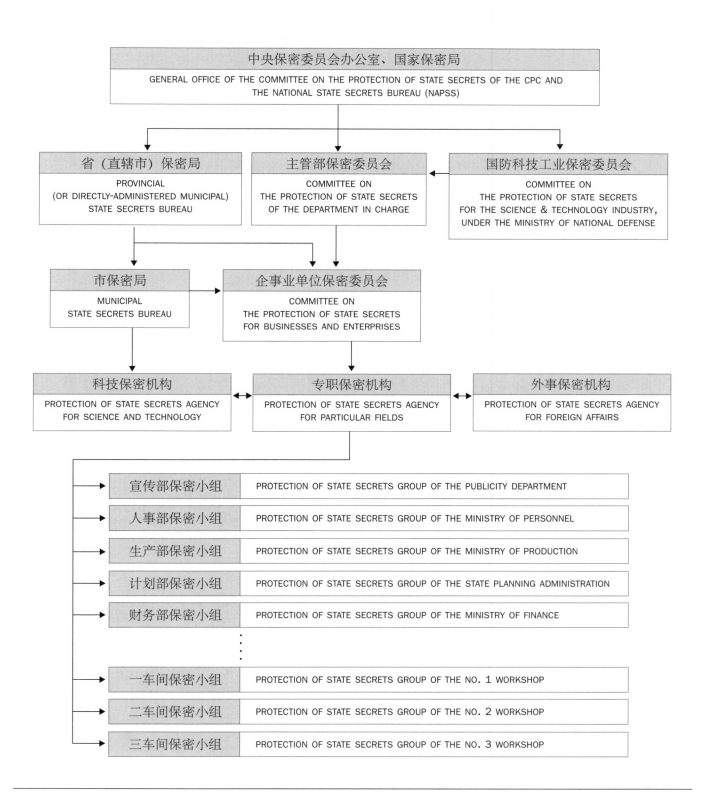

DOCUMENT 3

The "Basic" and "Specific" Scope of State Secrets

Editors' Note:

The following chart is a reproduction of an internal government graphic, with English translation added, that attempts to describe the overall system of state secrets as seen from an administrative perspective.

Matters belonging to the overall category of "state secrets" (at the right of the chart) come from two main overlapping areas: the "basic scope" and the "specific scope" of state secrets. "Basic scope" seems to refer to the nature of the information (i.e. "Major policy decisions on national affairs," "National economic and social developments") and proceeds from the Law on the Protection of State Secrets and implementing measures of that law; while "Specific Scope" refers directly to specific organs of the Party-state: State and Public Security, National Defense, Foreign Affairs and "other organs of the central government."

Each organ has issued its own regulations defining the specific scope of classified information, in conjunction with the national State Secrets Bureau. Some of these regulations are themselves classified (e.g. the public security regulation featured in this report) and can therefore remain unknown to the public.

Source:

王守信，《保密工作管理概论（修订版）》（内部发行）（北京：金城出版社，1999）: 56 [Wang Shouxin. *Overview of the Management of State Secrets Protection Work* (Revised Edition, Internal Circulation) (Beijing: Jincheng Publishing House, 1999), 56].

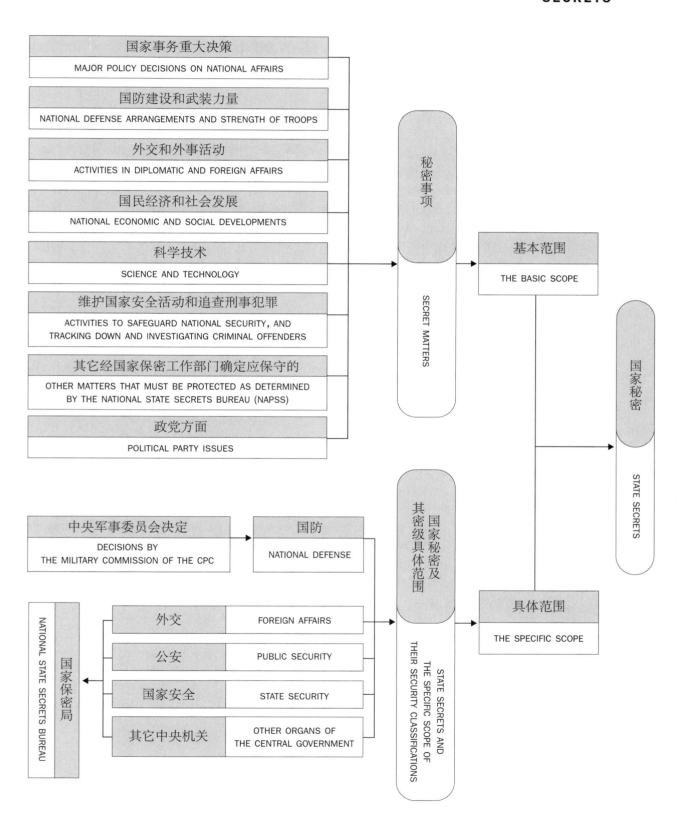

DOCUMENT 4

Classification Procedures for State Secret Matters

Editors' Note:

The following chart is a reproduction of an internal government graphic, with English translation added, that attempts to show the procedural steps that must be taken when classifying a document "according to law." Essentially, the process is one of self-classification by the issuing department, on the basis of regulations (public or not) that specify the scope of classified information in the domain over which the department has jurisdiction. The document is then marked (level of secrecy) and issued to "the relevant personnel."

If the matter is top secret, the determination is made by the national State Secrets Bureau (NAPSS); if the matter is highly secret or secret, it is decided by a state secrets bureau at the provincial, autonomous region or directly-administered municipal level; or if it is secret, it could also be determined by "other organs." In case of dispute, the NAPSS or another responsible bureau or department at the provincial (or equivalent administrative) level have the final say.

The likely reason behind this system is that the three levels of classification (top secret, highly secret, secret) are prescribed on the one hand by specific regulations, and on the other hand by the administrative level of the document. The procedure makes it apparent that, in practice, many bureaus and institutions at different levels have the authority to decide the classification of a specific matter, thus contributing to the systematically overextended classification of government-held information.

Source:

王守信,《保密工作管理概论（修版）》(内部发行) (北京：金城出版社 ，1999): 59 [Wang Shouxin. *Overview of the Management of State Secrets Protection Work* (Revised Edition, Internal Circulation) (Beijing: Jincheng Publishing House, 1999), 59].

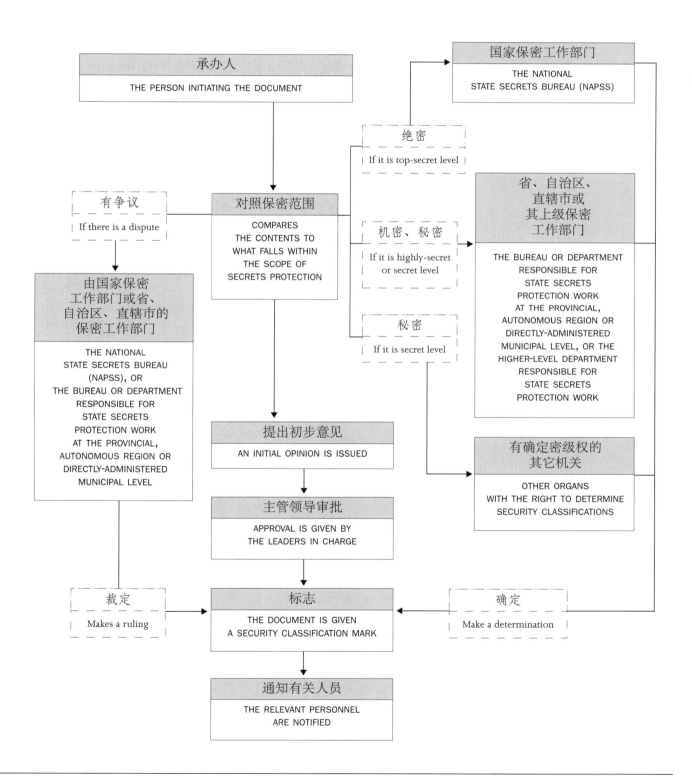

DOCUMENT 5

The Determination and Handling of "Work Secrets"

Editors' Note:

The status of "internal" *(neibu)* material in Chinese law and practice remains unclear. Although security organs and the courts have in practice associated *neibu* materials with state secrets on the basis that both types of information "shall not be made public," the main statutes on the protection of state secrets makes explicitly clear that internal material "does not belong to state secrets." Many of the regulations that define the scope of state secrets in various policy fields (of which a selection is reproduced in this report) include provisions for *neibu* matters, which "are not categorized as state secrets, but are matters to be managed internally, and [which] may not be disseminated without approval from the [relevant] organ."

An operational distinction between state secrets and internal matters rests on the fact that *neibu* materials can be disclosed at will by the issuing organ itself, whereas state secrets declassification requires a specific procedure and the approval of other (generally higher) departments.

Many researchers and journalists in China write reports or articles that are "internal" and never published, but are often shared with professionals of the same field. Yet, individuals have been convicted of state secrets offenses for passing on or holding *neibu* documents.

The excerpt below discusses another type of "internal matter" called "work secrets." Work secrets are documents that "come up in the course of one's work and should not be publicly disseminated." This self-classification procedure considerably extends the scope of information that is withdrawn from the public, and vests the bureaucracy with unchallengeable authority "not only to protect state secrets but also to protect any work matters that should not be made public without authorization."

Source:

王守信，《保密工作管理概论（修订版）》（内部发行）（北京：金城出版社，1999): 70–71 [Wang Shouxin, *Overview of the Management of State Secrets Protection Work* (Revised Edition, Internal Circulation) (Beijing: Jincheng Publishing House, 1999), 70–71].

DETERMINING AND MAKING REVISIONS TO WORK SECRETS

1.
The Concept and Scope of Work Secrets

Work secrets refer to internal *(neibu)* matters, excluding state secrets, that come up in the course of one's work and should not be publicly disseminated. Once these secrets are disclosed, they could bring indirect harm to the work of that organ or unit. The method for determining work secrets is formulated by each organ or unit according to its needs.

Work secrets are internal matters and do not belong to the category of state secrets. Although "internal matters" are listed as matters that should fall under the protection of state secrets, this is because in the past, "internal matters" were largely state secrets, whereas now such matters are listed as "internal matters" to show that these things are no longer state secrets. The main purpose of this is to differentiate between what is a state secret and what is not.

Every state secrets protection agency within individual organs and units, as well as the staff of all organs and units, have the responsibility to not only protect state secrets but also to protect any work matters that should not be made public without authorization.

Each organ or unit should determine, based on what is practical in its individual circumstances, the scope of work secrets, or internal matters, in that organ or unit. Since the professional scope of each organ and unit is different and their individual circumstances are different, there is no one, uniform standard or scope; these are up to each organ or unit to determine.

2.
Steps for Making the Determination

A. Under the guidance of the protection of state secrets organization within each organ or unit, the individual department should determine the scope of its work secrets based on the particular circumstances of its line of work. This includes departments such as the Organizational Department, Human Resources, Discipline Inspection, Auditing, Security, and so forth. For example, an Organizational Department can mark the following as internal matters: internal reference documents; details not yet made public on the appointment and dismissal of cadres in that unit; information on setting up echelons of cadres; all kinds of information, materials, Party publications and work briefs for circulation within the Party, and other matters not suitable for external circulation. A Human Resources Department can mark the following as internal matters: plans for sending personnel abroad; information on salary adjustments that have not yet been made public; details on assessments of job titles; files on cadres in general, and other information that is not suitable for external circulation.

B. Based on the scope of internal matters as determined by the individual department, the person initiating a particular document, form or other internal matter should issue an opinion.

C. The leader of the department checks and approves it.

D. Work secrets are not divided according to level, so the words "for internal use only" should be written on the relevant documents, materials or other items.

3.
Making Revisions to Work Secrets

Revisions to internal matters may be made providing the following circumstances are met:

(i) Internal documents, materials, notices and other matters that have been publicly announced are automatically declassified on the day they are made public.

(ii) According to the practical circumstances and work needs of an individual organ or unit, the decision [to make the revision] is made by the leader of that organ or unit.

(iii) Regarding internal matters that cannot be made public for a long time, those kept in archives shall have the same time limit as for other records kept in storage, and they shall be destroyed once their time limit has expired. Records not yet placed in archives that have lost their usefulness or value can be registered by oneself, with larger quantities sent to an appointed location to be destroyed.

DOCUMENT 6

Assessing State Secrets Protection Work

Editors' Note:

The following table is a reproduction of an internal government document, translated into English, that details the criteria used by local state secrets protection departments when assessing the security of government (and government-operated) units.

An important part of the work of the local state secrets protection departments is to ensure that these units are in conformity with the requirements set by the national State Secrets Bureau (NAPSS) for the protection of classified information. In particular, they are required to establish a Protection of State Secrets Committee and appoint a "department leader." According to the principle by which "the person in charge is the person who bears responsibility," the designated person is directly liable for any "loss" of state secrets and can face Party, administrative or criminal charges.

Another important aspect of the work of these departments is to investigate cases of "major disclosures" of classified material and whether or not any of these incidents were "concealed and not reported."

Source:

王守信,《保密工作管理概论（修订版）》(内部发行)(北京：金城出版社 ，1999): 246–247 [Wang Shouxin, *Overview of the Management of State Secrets Protection Work* (Revised Edition, Internal Circulation) (Beijing: Jincheng Publishing House, 1999), 246–247].

GRADING STANDARDS FOR INSPECTING AND ASSESSING THE PROTECTION OF STATE SECRETS

NO.	ITEMS	WHAT IS BEING ASSESSED
1.	Staff provisions; organizational structure	(1) Has a Protection of State Secrets Committee been set up? (2) Has a department leader been appointed to take responsibility for protection of state secrets work? (3) Has a suitable agency for that unit been set up to do protection of state secrets work and does it adequately fulfill this task? (4) Is fair compensation given to protection of state secrets personnel?
2.	Practical information; the regulations system	(1) Is there a complete and effective system of regulations for the protection of state secrets? (2) Is it clear who is responsible for protection of state secrets work? (3) Are the regulations for protection of state secrets work strictly followed? (4) Is a system for making regular inspections in place?
3.	Education on the protection of state secrets	(1) Are relevant regulations on protection of state secrets work transmitted in a timely manner? (2) Are regular classes organized on protection of state secrets laws and regulations? (3) Are personnel involved in the protection of state secrets familiar with the laws and regulations? (4) Are regular classes organized for protection of state secrets personnel to keep up on professional knowledge?
4.	Conditions for state secrets protection work	(1) Is there an office location specifically dedicated for this work? (2) Are there facilities necessary to do the work? (3) Is there necessary funding to do the daily work?
5.	The management of personnel who handle state secrets	(1) Before employees take up a position, are they assessed, examined and given protection of state secrets education? (2) Once employees take up a position, are they given protection of state secrets education and supervision on a regular basis? (3) After employees leave their position, have agreements on protecting state secrets been signed and supervision carried out? (4) Have outside staff been given education on the protection of state secrets and supervision?

GRADING STANDARDS FOR INSPECTING AND ASSESSING THE PROTECTION OF STATE SECRETS

NO.	ITEMS	WHAT IS BEING ASSESSED
6.	Key locations that do protection of state secrets work	(1) Are the locations of state secrets protection departments and the content of their work made clear? (2) Has the style for protection of state secrets work in key locations been formulated? (3) Has a system of responsibility for protection of state secrets work in key locations been formulated?
7.	Inspections of summaries of experience and supervision	(1) Are there opportunities for regular research into the protection of state secrets? (2) Are there regular inspections of protection of state secrets work? (3) Are reports on work experiences sincere and is encouragement given for outstanding work?
8.	Handling disclosures of state secrets	(1) Were there any incidents of major disclosures? (2) Were there any incidents of ordinary disclosures? (3) Were any incidents of disclosures concealed and not reported?

DOCUMENT 7

The Protection of State Secrets
in News Publishing

Editors' Note:

The following document, excerpted from Chapter 15 of the internal manual *Overview of the Management of State Secrets Protection Work,* is an in-depth description of the state secrets system and routines in the news, media and publishing sectors. The manual emphasizes that protection of state secrets in news publishing is "not rigorous enough," due to the fact that the media industry values above all "the openness, timeliness and value of the news" above state secrecy imperatives.

This chapter makes clear that the scope of information "that should not be made public" goes far beyond matters that are statutorily classified as state secrets, but rather encompasses any information that could lead one to obtain "valuable intelligence" if aggregated with other public sources. The chief rationale for imposing strict limits on news publishing, according to the manual, is that China has become "a center of focus for foreign intelligence organizations" and that these organizations "use our newspapers, publications, and radio and television broadcasts as channels for collecting and studying intelligence, with some even going so far as to shamelessly purchase newspapers and periodicals that are publicly distributed."

The chapter details the goals, responsibilities and procedures that must be adhered to in order to protect information that has not yet been made public, or that is deemed to be protected by state secrets regulations. It describes the procedures for ascertaining whether information can be published or not, how to obtain approval from the state secrets organs, and the system of authorization and supervision for interviewing and filming. Filming requires arrangements by both the News Propaganda Department of the higher-level organ and a state secrets bureau.

Although in non-sensitive cases these burdensome procedures are routinely ignored by Chinese media professionals, in effect they give unchallengeable discretion to the bureaucracy on the disclosure of government-held information and cause news publishing units to constantly live under the threat of violating state secrets laws.

Source:

王守信，《保密工作管理概论（修订版）》（内部发行）（北京：金城出版社，1999): 206 [Wang Shouxin, *Overview of the Management of State Secrets Protection Work* (Revised Edition, Internal Circulation) (Beijing: Jincheng Publishing House, 1999), 206].

CHAPTER 15:
THE PROTECTION OF STATE SECRETS IN NEWS PUBLISHING (EXCERPTS)

SECTION 1
Introduction

The responsibility of publishing the news is the duty of the Party and the state, which do the work of mass media circulation and the dissemination of scientific and cultural knowledge. It is an important part of the work of protecting secrets. In today's world of rapid development, doing a good job of protecting state secrets in news publications has great significance in terms of effectively safeguarding state secrets, upholding the security and interests of the state, and promoting the smooth modernization of socialism. (. . .)

4. The scrutiny of society. Our modern society is an information society, and news publications are the most basic vehicle for conveying all sorts of information, with each piece of information scrutinized by people all over the world. The main reasons for this scrutiny are: Firstly, the special characteristic of modern society is such that people's interest in information has become an important part of their lives and an essential aspect of their socialization. Secondly, news publications contain a large amount of valuable intelligence that frequently involves various aspects of politics, economics, military affairs, foreign affairs, scientific and technical knowledge, and ideology. If all this information is put together and analyzed, one can definitely sift out a great deal of valuable intelligence. Each country has specialized organs and personnel to collect and research

the latest news from other countries. This also means that an important aspect of intelligence activities—the theft of secrets and the struggle against such theft—is being reflected more and more in news publications, making them the easiest and most accessible method for collecting information. Therefore, the work of protecting secrets in news publications is becoming more complex and our duties are becoming much greater. (. . .)

(iii) *The importance of looking at news publishing work from the perspective of how other countries pay attention to intelligence work*

From an international viewpoint, the intelligence organ of each country does everything it can to collect large quantities of different kinds of information. On the other hand, it strictly controls the circulation of information and does everything possible to not allow its own secrets to be disclosed. Many countries also put the secrets that are contained in reports and publications into articles of law and thereby use legal structures as an added guarantee of protection. For example, the former Soviet Union adopted measures to prevent secrets from being disclosed in their news publications, while the United States mainly adopts methods of pursuing and punishing offenders. In brief, in this modern day there is unfortunately no country that does not deliberately plan to collect intelligence from other countries' publications, broadcasts and so forth. According to the information available, 90 percent of the intelligence obtained by the former Soviet Union was obtained through public channels, not through classified documents, industrial exhibitions, or scientific and technological publications.

(iv) *The importance of looking at the protection of state secrets in news publishing work from the perspective of foreign intelligence organizations' determination to collect our secrets*

In the wake of our country's policy of reforming and opening to the world, the speed of our economic growth has increased, the overall strength of our nation has improved, and our international standing has been raised. Due to the important role that we now play on the world stage, we have become a center of focus for foreign intelligence organizations. They use our newspapers, publications, and radio and television broadcasts as channels for collecting and studying intelligence, with some even going so far as to shamelessly purchase newspapers and periodicals that are publicly distributed. The quantity and quality of all kinds of intelligence collected by foreign intelligence organizations from publicly circulated reports—as well as the speed with which they collect such information—is quite alarming. Therefore, it can be said that news publishing work has become an important line of defense in the current struggle to prevent the theft of state secrets.

SECTION 2
Principles for Protecting Secrets in News Publishing

1. The reasons that state secrets are disclosed in news publications

(i) *The awareness of how to protect secrets is weak and ideology is slack*

During this important phase of a socialist market economy, when people have many different kinds of ideologies, the lack of awareness of how to protect state secrets is quite pronounced. We can see this reflected in those who work in the news publishing industry, and a trend has arisen whereby people only consider their own special area of expertise. They emphasize the openness, the timeliness and the value of the news in news publishing, but they neglect the need to protect state secrets so that, over time, things that should not be made public are made public. For these reasons, leaks occur.

(ii) *The system for monitoring the protection of state secrets is lax*

The main cause for state secrets to be disclosed is the fact that the system for monitoring the protection of state secrets in news publishing is not rigorous enough. This is precisely the responsibility of news publishing departments, as well as that of all professional departments and writers. For example, although some news publishing departments have a system for examining written materials, they only check on the reliability and accuracy of the information, not on whether or not state secrets are being protected. Or, they only check the main page of their newspaper, not the later pages. Professional departments only care about making great achievements and expanding their influence, not about protecting state secrets. Writers "scramble for" the news, chase after sensational stories, and try to avoid having their unit monitored for the protection of secrets. For these reasons, leaks occur.

(iii) *There is a lack of general knowledge about protecting state secrets*

Protecting state secrets is not only a matter of thinking about protecting

them, it's also a matter of having general knowledge and skill. For example, some people don't know that news publishing needs to have a system for monitoring the protection of state secrets, some don't know the principles of protecting state secrets in news publishing and can't distinguish what is for internal circulation only and what is not, and some people don't understand the scope of protecting state secrets in professional departments. For these reasons, leaks occur.

(iv) *A small number of people seek profit, forget what's right, and lack organizational discipline*

In society, there are some people who have the ideology that "material gain" is the highest goal and, in order to impress people or to gain reputation, will even adopt the despicable method of sending materials to newspapers and periodicals that are either not allowed to be made public or have not been sent out to be checked. Even worse, they privately send documents that involve state secrets to foreign newspapers and periodicals. For these reasons, leaks occur.

2. The principles for protecting state secrets in news publishing

(i) *The principle of everyone following the same guidelines*

This principle means that important news stories issued by state-authorized news organs should all be issued in a unified way. Local governments that issue news stories should also follow this principle. The main organs authorized by the state to issue news stories include the Xinhua News Agency and the Ministry of Foreign Affairs. The news prop-

aganda units in every location and of every department must follow the same guidelines as state-authorized news units in issuing news stories, and they are not allowed to initiate such actions on their own. The goal of doing things this way is not only to prevent the disclosure of state secrets, but also to prevent other political mistakes from occurring. This so-called "important news" mainly refers to major events having to do with the policies and activities of the Party or state in regard to domestic politics or foreign affairs, as well as major events involving military affairs, science and technology, economics, and other such matters.

News publishing departments must firmly adhere to the relevant regulations set forth by the central authorities, and if important questions arise, the circulation guidelines must be the same as those used by the Party and central authorities. In no case are news publishing departments allowed to issue or publish, without authorization, any important Party guiding principles or policies, or any documents that would contradict regulations put out by the central authorities in newspapers, periodicals or broadcasts, or disseminate such information in any other way. Any questions that require a decision to be made by the central authorities or higher-level department heads should be immediately submitted in writing. When reports must be made on socially sensitive issues or important incidents that suddenly arise, attention must be paid to how they affect social stability, economic stability and development, and the smooth implementation of reform policies. Disseminating such reports must be done in accordance with the guiding principles and policies of the central authorities, and in a unified way with the central authorities. Any important statistics or situations that are to be published in the news must first be verified as true, then checked and approved by the head of the relevant department, before they can be publicly issued.

(ii) *The principle of differentiating between internal and external*

This refers to the fact that when news publishing units make public reports, and in the course of doing publishing work, they must strictly differentiate between internal and external matters; for example, matters that are internal knowledge of the Party, military or country must not be disseminated outside of the Party, military or country without authorization. This is because any given piece of news contains both public and secret information, and whether that information is public or secret is a relative matter. Some information would be considered public within the country, but would not be considered public if it were sent outside of the country. Likewise, some situations or news would be considered public for certain countries or regions, but not for others. This requires that news publishers have a very good understanding of how to distinguish between the two. If this principle is violated, then the work of protecting state secrets loses its validity.

(iii) *The principle of both checking materials oneself and sending them out to be checked*

The principle of both checking materials oneself and sending them out to be checked is an important principle in the Regulation on the Protection of State Secrets in News Publishing. This

regulation clearly stipulates that, after news publishing personnel have done the interviewing, editing and photography and have written the initial draft of an article, they should first check the article to see whether or not it contains secrets. On this basis, any relevant questions should be sent to the news publishing unit for verification. If there are questions that the news publishing unit is not sure about, it should immediately send the questions to the relevant professional department for verification. Once it has been checked and has been verified as containing no state secrets, it may be publicly issued.

(iv) *The principle of working in tandem with professional departments*

This refers to the fact that news publishing units should work together and cooperate with professional departments in the execution of their work. They should coordinate in unison, collectively obey the regulations on protecting state secrets, and take on the responsibility of protecting state secrets. Since state secrets are special matters that exist in many different professions, it is very difficult to effectively safeguard such matters once they have been checked, approved and are out of the hands of a professional department. If news publishing departments take the initiative to cooperate closely with professional departments, and if they mutually supervise each other, they will have sufficient resources to effectively do the work of news reporting, and they will be able to effectively prevent disclosures from occurring in news publications. At the same time, according to the nature of their work, all professional departments should establish regular channels through which they can provide infor-

mation. This should be a regular service provided to news publishers to help them carry out their work.

In summary, establishing principles for protecting state secrets that news publishers need to adhere to enables them to better deal with the relationship between news publishing and the protection of state secrets, between what is made public and the protection of state secrets, between accuracy of facts and the protection of state secrets, and between freedom of the press and the protection of state secrets. It also enables them to firmly put a stop to any disclosures that might occur in news publications. Furthermore, strictly adhering to the regulation on protecting state secrets is a necessary qualification and requirement for anyone who works in news publishing.

SECTION 3
Circulation Guidelines for the Protection of State Secrets in News Publishing

Strictly guarding state secrets in news publications is the sacred responsibility of each person working on the frontlines of news publishing. Understanding the basic scope of state secrets and having a good grasp of the circulation guidelines for the protection of state secrets in news publishing is a basic premise for doing this kind of work.

1. The basic scope of state secrets

Based on the definition of what a "state secret" is, the basic scope of state secrets is determined as follows: All matters having to do with national politics, military affairs, foreign affairs, economics, science and technology, and judicial administration, as well as other matters that arise from activities in other spheres, should first be analyzed to determine which parts are secret and which parts are not secret. Then, in principle, a total number of all the matters that are secret can be determined. Those parts that are state secrets within a professional system are included in the basic scope of what a state secret is. According to Article 10 of the Law on the Protection of State Secrets, the scope of secrets to be protected should be first determined by the department that does the work of protecting state secrets, in cooperation with the relevant state organs of the central government and in accordance with their professional jurisdiction. Once this determination has been publicly announced, it will have widespread legal effect and, if it extends beyond the jurisdiction of a particular region or industry, it will become a uniform standard used across the country.

However, of the state secrets as formulated by the organ legally authorized to protect secrets, some are inherently and definitely state secrets and their level of secrecy is already quite high; thus, we must limit their scope in terms of making them public and in terms of who knows about them. Therefore, this section regarding the circulation guidelines is just a rough outline of the regulations. We request all those who work in news publishing to increase both their awareness of the protection of state secrets and their skill in protecting state secrets. We ask that they have a good understanding of all state secret and internal (*neibu*) matters that come up in their work, and we ask them to conscientiously take up the responsibility of protecting state secrets.

2. Circulation guidelines for the protection of state secrets in news publishing

(i) Internal (*neibu*) documents and materials that come from any organ at the level of directly-administered municipality, autonomous prefecture, province, or central government—including articles or materials published in neibu publications and important speeches given by leading cadres—cannot be publicly reported without first gaining permission from the unit responsible for issuing that document.

(ii) National economic plans, budget estimates, preparatory and final accounts, banking information and financial data that has not yet been publicly issued or published cannot be cited in reports. Information regarding the distribution of source materials that have been classified as secrets by the state, as well as other related data, cannot be publicly reported.

(iii) The following cannot be publicly circulated or reported: Programs, investments, and the layout of military installations or anything else related to the national defense industry, as well as the production capacity of such places; the different kinds and functions of products made by the military industry and their production capacity; anything involving scientific and technological advances of the state and scientific advances in the national defense industry; information on key engineering projects that are currently being developed or researched, as well as problems encountered in the research stages of such projects.

(iv) The following cannot be publicly reported: Plans for national defense or

for military matters; the designations, strength, postings, deployments and arrangements of troops, as well as the logistics of ensuring supplies; information on the development of weapons, national defense engineering projects, bases, strongholds, and so forth.

(v) The different stages of progress made in work on state scientific research, inventions that have been approved by the state, and items currently being tested that could become inventions or patented products cannot be publicly reported without having first obtained permission from the relevant state department. Traditional crafts, unique technical secrets and key technical "tricks of the trade" (such as how special components are used in processing, the key parameters of a craft, or combinations of the most beautiful materials) cannot be publicly circulated. Anything that could cause disputes over intellectual property rights cannot be publicly reported.

(vi) Specific policies and measures regarding foreign economic trade, as well as the production, craft, market price, information on storage, plans for import or export, foreign trade policies and other internal information or data related to key products for export cannot be publicly circulated or reported.

(vii) The content of contracts that our country has made with other countries that have an obligation with us to protect state secrets (e.g., contracts containing technological information or advanced equipment imported from abroad, or technical information or equipment imported via secret channels) cannot be publicly reported.

(viii) Sensitive matters that could influence the development of bilateral or multilateral relations between our country and neighboring countries cannot be publicly reported unless prior permission has been obtained from the government department in charge of such matters. In order to meet the requirements of the news spokespersons of the Xinhua News Agency and the Ministry of Foreign Affairs, any propaganda on national relations or foreign policy must not be issued in advance of these bodies, nor can its key content be added to or deleted.

(ix) The achievements or notable successes of famous experts and scholars whose jobs involve state secrets are generally not publicly reported. If there is a special need, permission must be first obtained by the government department in charge of such matters.

(x) Any other secret information that falls within the scope of the protection of state secrets cannot be publicly reported.

SECTION 4
The System and Procedure for Checking Materials to Protect State Secrets in News Publishing

1. The system of both checking materials oneself and sending them out to be checked

The work of protecting state secrets in news publishing is not only the legal obligation of news publishing units and their editorial staffs, it is also the legal obligation of the relevant organs, units and personnel who provide the information and articles to them. The two sides that bear this responsibility should practice mutual supervision and

should work together closely in order to help carry out the work of news publishing, to fully allow news publishing work to be done efficiently, and to effectively prevent any disclosures from occurring. To this end, in June 1992 the National Administration for the Protection of State Secrets and the central authorities jointly issued the Regulation on the Protection of State Secrets in News Publishing and circulated it to propaganda work units, news publishing offices and to the Ministry of Radio, Film and Television. Article 6 of this regulation clearly lays out the system of both checking materials oneself and sending them out to be checked as part of the protection of state secrets in news publishing work.

(i) *The concept of checking materials oneself*

Checking materials oneself means that those involved in news publishing work, writers, and units that provide information should, in accordance with the relevant regulations, check whether or not any information that will be publicly reported or published contains matters involving state secrets. It is the legal obligation of all news publishing staff (writers) to take on the burden of "bearing personal responsibility for one's words." Those units or personnel who are interviewed are the "sources" of information, and they not only have a responsibility to make sure the information they provide is accurate, they also have a legal responsibility to say whether or not something can be publicly reported. Therefore, the law also confers on those units and personnel who are interviewed the legal obligation to be the first ones to check information.

(ii) *The concept of sending materials out to be checked*

Sending materials out to be checked means that if either news publishing units or the units that provide information are not certain whether or not a particular piece of information falls within the scope of what is considered a state secret, it should be sent to either the relevant department in charge of that matter, or to a higher-level organ or unit, for checking and approval. In this way, a clear opinion will be given as to whether or not the material should be publicly disseminated and reported.

(iii) *The difference and the relationship between checking materials oneself and sending them out to be checked*

The differences are explained as follows: 1. The agent doing the checking is not the same. The agent doing the checking in the case of checking oneself is the news publishing unit or the unit that provides the information; in the case of sending materials out to be checked, the agent doing the checking is the higher-level professional organ or department that is above the unit providing information (or the unit that did the selection of materials). (Note: Although the editorial office of the news publishing unit is responsible for checking its own written materials, it is not the agent that does the checking when materials are sent out to be checked for the protection of state secrets.) 2. The content being checked is not the same. In checking materials oneself, all of the information should be comprehensively checked. When materials are sent out to be checked, specific questions such as whether or not something is permitted, or questions on definitions that are not clear, are what are being checked. Otherwise, one should request that a comprehensive check be carried out. 3. The conclusions given are not the same. Checking oneself means that, if one is uncertain as to whether or not certain information falls within the realm of state secrets, one then makes a request to have it checked further. Or, if the information involving state secrets has gone through the process of having all its secrets removed, but one is still certain that it isn't correct, then a request to have it checked further is made. In both cases, a conclusion is made within a certain time period so that the information (or article) can be issued. On the other hand, when information (or articles) are sent out for checking, the conclusion is a report issued to agree or disagree with the initial determination on whether or not the materials involve secrets.

Indeed, state secrets are a special matter and exist in every type of professional work. Once they have been checked and approved and are out of the hands of a professional department, these matters are difficult to effectively safeguard. And once they have been sent for checking and are out of the hands of a news publishing department, oversights can also be made in safeguarding secret matters. Therefore, checking oneself and sending information out for checking are interdependent, complement each other, and are two indispensable links in the chain that allows for an article to be issued without any disclosures occurring.

2. The procedure for checking in the protection of state secrets (...)

(ii) *The system of how to be clear-cut about protecting state secrets when checking information oneself*

1. When dealing with written materials that involve state secrets, one should follow the principles of "check first, publish later" and "check first, issue later." No written materials submitted for publication to newspapers or periodicals, whether they are for internal or public distribution, can involve matters of state secrecy. Any articles written or chosen by the unit's internal staff must first go through the process of having all state secrets removed before they can be published.

2. Whenever units or personnel are interviewed for a story and provide information to the interviewer of a news publishing unit, such information must not contain any matters involving state secrets. If there is a truly a need, for work reasons, then permission must be first obtained in writing from the leader in charge of that unit or from a higher-level organ. In addition, one must clearly explain to the interviewer which parts involving state secrets cannot be publicly reported, and at the same time request that one be allowed to check the article after the interview. News publishing units have a duty to only allow articles that have been checked to be disseminated.

3. Every relevant organ and unit should establish a system for checking to protect state secrets, and they should appoint both a person and an agency within the unit to do the job of checking written materials. Offices that protect scientific or technological secrets should make it a priority to check news reports on the nat-

ural sciences and the content of their publications. Propaganda departments should make it a priority to check news reports on the social sciences and the content of their publications. Offices that protect state secrets within enterprises and businesses should take on the role of giving guidance, coordinating, supervising and investigating. Those who are responsible for checking on the protection of state secrets are also usually the leaders in charge of that unit, and the job of checking written materials is performed by the office responsible for protecting state secrets in that unit.

4. The editorial department of each news publishing unit must establish a system for checking on the protection of state secrets and appoint a person to be in charge of this task. Normally, a system of having an editor or editor-in-chief in charge of this is established. No written materials that have not yet been checked for state secrets by the unit that provided them can ever be published. Otherwise, if a problem occurs, the legal responsibility will fall on the editor or editor-in-chief.

5. Those who work in news publishing have a duty to not circulate internal information externally, to not disclose secrets obtained during interviews, and to handle in an appropriate manner all internal materials and destroy them after use.

6. Important information involving state secrets and other information whose limits are not clear

should be sent to a higher-level department for checking and approval. (. . .)

(iv) *The system for protecting state secrets in sending out materials to check: Some points to pay attention to and comply with*

1. When relevant organs and units are sent written materials to check and approve, they should comply with the time limit for checking and approval as requested by the news publishing unit. If the work cannot be completed within the requested time period, they should immediately notify the unit and discuss a way to solve the situation.

2. When dealing with state secrets in other industries or units, one should seek out the opinion of the relevant unit.

(v) *How to manage the protection of state secrets when checking written materials that involve state secrets*

1. Written materials that involve state secrets should be handled in an appropriate manner and should be strictly guarded against loss or theft.

2. If written materials that involve state secrets are transported, circulated for reading, lent out for reading, photocopied, destroyed, etc., they should be strictly handled according to the methods used for managing state secret documents.

3. Publications containing state secrets must be sent via a state se-

crets courier to a specified photocopying unit for printing (or photocopying).

4. News publishing units that deal with high-level state secrets must provide their office with a paper shredding machine.

5. It is forbidden for written materials that involve state secrets or for any books, newspapers, magazines, essays and so forth marked "neibu (internal) materials" or "for internal use only" to be sold for recycling as wastepaper.

SECTION 5
The Filming and Management of Audio-Visual Materials

The development of any large and important state-level project will invariably be a complicated and systematic project and will involve different industries and departments. In the course of working on such a project, these industries and departments not only use photographs as a form of recording and storing information in their archives; these days, they also frequently use modern technology to make high-quality audio-visual recordings of each step of the process. Therefore, in the filming and management of state secret matters, a unified form of management must be emphasized and standards must be very strict. We should not be so afraid of disclosing secrets that we leave behind no historical records, but neither should we lose control over such matters. Any unit and any individual can do filming, but if in so doing they let state secrets go unchecked, it could cause enormous harm to state security and interests.

1. The examination and approval procedure for filming audio-visual materials

(i) *When audio-visual materials involving state secrets are produced by an individual unit at its own location*

Normally, an individual unit's news or propaganda department is responsible for submitting plans for filming and should appoint a specific person to do the filming. Once approval has been given by that unit's protection of state secrets department, the unit may proceed with the shoot under the condition that someone from that department accompanies them.

(ii) *When the research, production and testing of audio-visual materials involving state secrets are produced between a local industry and an individual unit*

Firstly, there should be a definite work need that has to be fulfilled. Secondly, the unit that will be the location for the filming (the host unit) should do the coordinating. Thirdly, the unit doing the filming is responsible for providing detailed plans and personnel for the shoot, should give a definite time (or week) for the shoot to the best of their ability, should formally notify the host unit in writing, and should contact the host unit in advance. If the filming involves any state secrets at the highly-secret (*jimi*) level or below, permission must be obtained from the leader in charge of the host unit. The information must also be recorded in the files of the protection of state secrets department, which will dispatch someone to accompany the filming. If the filming involves top-secret (*juemi*) level secrets, permission must be obtained from the protection of state secrets department of a higher-level organ.

(iii) *When the research, production, testing and so forth of audio-visual materials are organized and produced by the professional department of a higher-level organ*

This should normally be arranged in coordination with the News Propaganda Department of the higher-level organ, which will work out a plan for the shoot, will support the written testimony of permission granted by the protection of state secrets department, and will appoint a person to carry out the filming.

(iv) *When a unit that is outside of the system (or industry) needs to, for work reasons, request or film audio-visual materials at any unit within the system (or industry)*

1. The procedure to request permission for any shoot that involves state secrets is as follows:

   (a) The unit doing the filming must clarify the particulars of what they are doing and provide a plan for the shoot, a list of the personnel doing the production and a time frame. They must also make a written report giving the name of the unit where the filming is taking place to the higher-level department. At the same time, they must provide, to the personnel department, materials showing government approval for the personnel doing the filming.

   (b) Once an agreement between the News Propaganda Department of the higher-level organ and the protection of state secrets department has been reached, the protection of state secrets department will provide written testimony that consent has been given to do the filming.

   (c) Only after the host unit has seen the written testimony from the higher-level organ, the identification cards (e.g. reporter's ID, work ID, or letter of introduction) of the personnel doing the filming, and has carefully checked that the number of people is correct, can it can receive the film crew. In addition, it must dispatch a specialist to accompany the film crew based on the specific filming needs.

2. If the filming does not involve any matters of state secrecy, once permission has been given by the leader in charge of the host unit and the paperwork has been completed with the protection of state secrets department, a person will be dispatched to accompany the film crew.

(v) *When audio-visual materials involve interviews or filming by foreign journalists*

1. Journalists from abroad or from outside the mainland who request telephone interviews with any unit or individual that involves state secrets will, without exception, be politely refused.

2. Journalists from abroad or from outside the mainland who request interviews with enterprises that involve state secrets will, in general, be politely refused. If there is truly a need, the host unit must fill out a "Form to Apply for Permission to Grant Interviews to Journalists from Abroad or from Outside the Mainland." On the form, the following information must be included: the name and country of the applicant's news organization, the main topic of the interview, the opinion of the unit submitting the application, and so forth. The form must be submitted for approval to a higher-level professional department and to the protection of state secrets department.

3. Once the host unit has seen the written testimony of the higher-level organ and has accepted the interview in strict accordance with the permission given, during the interview no matters involving state secrets may be discussed and no sensitive questions may be asked.

4. If a foreign journalist has not applied for permission and he or she carries out an illegal interview, even if he or she has made a special trip or is using another identity, and whether the topic of the interview is sensitive or not, he or she should be stopped on the spot, wherever he or she is discovered.

2. Managing the protection of secrets during production and distribution

(i) *Issues regarding the protection of secrets that should be kept in mind during the production process*

1. The host unit must appoint a special person to be responsible for accompanying the film crew throughout the entire process, especially if it is a person from another unit who has come to do the filming. This person should not only do the work of organizing and coordinating the shoot; more importantly, they should prevent any violations of the film plan. If other secret matters not contained in the film plan come up, effective measures such as evasion and concealment should be adopted in order to prevent state secrets from being disclosed and to avoid cause for regret later on.

2. The host unit should assign a department to do the film developing or production. If this condition is not met, the unit doing the filming has the responsibility to go to a state organ that has guaranteed security and have an internal department there do the developing and production. It is strictly forbidden for any department in society whose goal is to make a profit to do the developing or production.

3. Any photos (or negatives), films, audio tapes or video tapes that contain secret-level (*mimi*) secrets or above should be assigned a security classification by the unit that took the photos or made the film. Such items should have a registration number and should either be handed over to the information archives department of the unit that made them or to a department and staff appointed to take care of them; they should not be arbitrarily distributed.

4. The enlargement or reproduction of any photograph, the editing of any film, and the compilation of any video tape or audio tape that contains secret-level (*mimi*) secrets or above should all be regarded as falling within the scope of the system that controls state secrets. If there is any leftover or discarded film, magnetic tape or photographs remaining after the editing or compilation process is over, two people must be responsible for destroying them by burning or melting.

(ii) *Issues regarding the protection of state secrets that should be kept in mind during the process of distribution and broadcasting*

1. The security classification of audio-visual materials should be determined according to their content, and they should be strictly handled based on the same requirements used for handling secret documents.

2. Audio-visual materials at the highly-secret (*jimi*) level or above should, in principle, only be used by a business if it needs them for its work or by leaders in higher-level organs for making reports. If they are used for any other purpose, permission must be obtained from a higher-level department. Permission can be given for the use of secret-level (*mimi*) audio-visual materials by the leaders in charge of the individual unit that wants to use them.

3. No transmission made on internal (*neibu*) closed-circuit television or broadcast internally may contain state secrets (and hotels that accept foreign guests may not install internal closed-circuit televisions on their premises).

4. Any audio-visual materials that are going to be publicly circulated must have gone through the process of both checking the materials oneself and having them sent out for checking. Only after such materials have been checked and approved by a higher-level department, and have been determined not to involve state secrets, can they be publicly circulated and reported.

Cases Involving
State Secrets

Editors' Note:

Despite the difficulty in obtaining a comprehensive picture of how state secrets offenses are applied against individuals in China, HRIC has compiled information on the cases of 42 individuals charged with state secrets crimes, and 20 individuals who have been denied procedural protections likely due to the involvement of state secrets in their cases.

Statistics on the total numbers, regional variations and range of state secrets criminal cases in China are not disclosed. In its annual law yearbooks, the Chinese government does not disaggregate crimes of endangering state security by individual offense, including the crime of illegally providing state secrets abroad. Based on information available in domestic and international news, as well as in available court documents, the individuals below appear to have been imprisoned in connection with activities related to the legitimate exercise of their freedom of expression, including: exposing official corruption; exposing official repression of religious practitioners, ethnic minorities and other groups; making information about the 1989 democracy movement public; exposing information concerning government policies; or even undertaking historical research. In addition, it is a crime to disclose information classified as state secrets even if it is already published or circulating in the public domain at the time of disclosure. This information can include: published newspaper clippings, books and historical records; telephone interviews about local demonstrations; and handwritten notes. As a result, many individuals charged with leaking state secrets include those who e-mailed or faxed documents that were already public in some form. The range of individuals charged includes journalists, lawyers, religious activists, ethnic minority rights activists and other human rights defenders.

Sentences imposed for state secrets crimes, and for other state security crimes, range from one year to life imprisonment, and in some cases, the death penalty. For example, Wu Shishen, a former editor for the Xinhua News Agency, was sentenced to life imprisonment for disclosing an advance copy of Jiang Zemin's speech to the 14th CPC Party Congress to a Hong Kong reporter. In many cases of individuals charged with crimes of endangering state security, most frequently relating to subversion, defendants are denied a public trial, and sometimes denied access to their lawyers because their cases were said to "involve state secrets."

Unless otherwise cited, most of the information on the following cases comes from HRIC's human rights database, which was created over the years using primary sources, as well as information from other human rights organizations including Amnesty International, Human Rights Watch and the US Congressional-Executive Commission on China (CECC).

A. INDIVIDUALS CHARGED WITH STATE SECRETS OFFENSES

NAME	BACKGROUND	CHARGES AND ACTIVITIES ALLEGED	PROCEDURAL HISTORY	PROCEDURAL PROTECTION DEROGATIONS
Abdulghani Memetemin [阿布都拉尼 · 买买提米]	· From Xinjiang Uyghur Autonomous Region (XUAR) · Teacher and journalist · 40 years old at time of arrest	*Charges* · **Endangering state security ("separatism")** · **Violating state secrets laws** · **Illegally providing "state secrets" abroad**[1] *Activities Alleged* · Sending news reports on human rights abuses against Uyghurs to East Turkistan Information Center (ETIC), Germany · Translating speeches by government officials into Chinese · Trying to recruit new reporters for ETIC	· Detention: July 26, 2002 Kashgar, XUAR · Trial: Kashgar City Intermediate People's Court · Verdict: Guilty of violating state secrets law; not guilty of "separatism" · Sentence: **9 years' imprisonment** on June 24, 2003 · Projected release: July 25, 2011	· No access to lawyer or legal representation[2] · Tried in secret
Bao Tong [鲍彤]	· Former senior CPC official · Close assistant of former CPC General Secretary Zhao Ziyang	*Charges* · **Leaking important state secrets** · **Counterrevolutionary propaganda and incitement** *Activities Alleged* · Having a private conversation with Gao Shan (see below) on May 17, 1989; information possibly involved impending declaration of martial law and resignation of Zhao Ziyang from CPC Secretary General post—both made public May 20, 1989 · No indication in verdict of nature of state secrets allegedly leaked to Gao Shan	· Detention: May 29, 1989 · Held: Qincheng Prison, Beijing · House arrest: May 1990 · Formal arrest and charge: January 1992, returned to Qincheng Prison · Trial: July 21, 1992, Beijing Intermediate People's Court.[3] · Sentence: **7 years' imprisonment** · Appeal: Denied, August 6, 1992, Beijing Higher People's Court · Release: May 28, 1996	· Closed trial · Met with lawyers only twice before trial · Family refused entry to court but allowed to hear sentencing
Bai Weiji [白伟基]	· CPC General Office staff (1981) · Foreign Ministry - Information Department staff, monitoring and summarizing foreign news · Organized colleagues (including wife Zhao Lei) to march during student and worker protests at Tiananmen (1989) · As a result of 1989 activities, lost job and CPC membership	*Charge* · **Illegally providing state secrets abroad** *Activities Alleged* · Providing internal documents to Lena Sun (former classmate and correspondent for the *Washington Post* · Secret documents provided were confiscated by police May 17, 1992	· Detention: May 5, 1992, Beijing · Trial: Together with his wife Zhao Lei (see below) in a closed trial · Sentence: **10 years' imprisonment**, May 20, 1993, Beijing Intermediate People's Court · Appeal: Denied, Beijing Higher People's Court, July 1993 · Release: Early release, February 2, 1999	

NAME	BACKGROUND	CHARGES AND ACTIVITIES ALLEGED	PROCEDURAL HISTORY	PROCEDURAL PROTECTION DEROGATIONS
Cao Yu [曹宇]	• Owner and teacher of training center affiliated with Oriental University City, Hebei Province	**Charge** • **Leaking state secrets** ***Activities Alleged*** • Acquiring confidential examination paper for College English Test (Grade 4) from Shi Xiaolong (see below), with Liu Chen (see below) • Copying exam paper at Shi's office (Sept. 19, 2003) • Posting part of content on center's website with Liu; disclosing contents in seminar at training center	• Indictment: April 23, 2004 • Sentence: **3 years' imprisonment**, June 2, 2004, Beijing No. 1 Intermediate Court	• Closed trial
Chen Hui [陈辉]	• Assistant to director of China Academy of Social Sciences (CASS) General Office	**Charge** • **Leaking state secrets** ***Activities Alleged*** • Selling classified documents to Japanese diplomats containing information on China's policy toward Japan • No indication of nature of information allegedly leaked	• Detention: May 2005 • Sentence: **13 years' imprisonment**, June 2006, Beijing[4]	
Chen Meng[5] [陈蒙]	• Born Dec. 7, 1961, Henan Province • Musician • Participant in 1989 democracy movement	**Charge** • **Illegally providing state secrets** ***Activities Alleged*** • Obtaining official blacklist of "June 4" activists from brother-in-law and border guard Tang Tao (see below); contents were widely printed in many Hong Kong newspapers (*Oriental Daily* and *Sing Tao*)[6]	• Detention: March 14, 1995 • Formal arrest: May 25, 1995 • Sentence: **12 years' imprisonment, 4 years' subsequent deprivation of political rights,** April 15, 1997 • Appeal: Denied, June 19, 1997, Shenzhen Intermediate People's Court[7]	• Detained nearly two years without trial • From 1995 to 1999, family only allowed to visit twice • Unknown whether or not represented by legal counsel
Gao Shan [高山]	• Economist and researcher in CPC Central Committee's Research Center for Reform of the Political Structure headed by Bao Tong	**Charge** • **Leaking state secrets** ***Activities Alleged*** • Spreading state secrets disclosed by Bao Tong (see above) • Having conversation with Bao Tong, May 17, 1989, regarding impending declaration of martial law and resignation of Zhao Ziyang from CPC Secretary General post—both made public May 20, 1989	• Detention: May 1989 • Trial: August 5, 1992 • Sentence: **4 years' imprisonment** • Release: Paroled, January 1993	

A. INDIVIDUALS CHARGED WITH STATE SECRETS OFFENSES, *cont.*

NAME	BACKGROUND	CHARGES AND ACTIVITIES ALLEGED	PROCEDURAL HISTORY	PROCEDURAL PROTECTION DEROGATIONS
He Zhaohui [何朝辉]	· Chenzhou Railway worker · Involved in 1989 democracy movement · Previous arrest as leading member of the Hunan Province Changsha Workers Autonomous Federation (2 years in prison) · Following release, continued involvement in worker protests	***Charge*** · **Illegally providing intelligence/state secrets abroad** ***Activities Alleged*** · Providing information about labor unrest in Hunan Province to media and human rights organizations in the USA · Evidence used in trial included a $130 check sent by a US university professor	· Detention: Changsha, April 1998 · Escaped: During transfer, fled to Burma in April 1998. Established refugee center for democracy activists[8] · Detention again: August 1998 (upon entering Hunan) · Formal arrest: October 4, 1998 · Trial: June 30, 1999 · Sentence: **10 years' imprisonment**, August 24, 1999 · Appeal: Denied, October 1999, Hunan Higher People's Court · Status: Held at Chenzhou Prison, Hunan Province	· Detained for over 7 months months between indictment and trial
Hua Di [华棣]	· Missile expert · Obtained political asylum in U.S. after June 4, 1989 democracy protests · Affiliated with Stanford University	***Charge*** · **Leaking state secrets** ***Activities Alleged*** · Leaking article "China's Ballistic Missile Plan," co-authored with John Wilson Lewis in *International Security*[9]	· Detention: January 6, 1998 (upon return to China for family funeral) · Arrest: Kept secret from public until October 1998 · Sentence: **15 years' imprisonment** on November 25, 1999, Beijing No.1 Intermediate People's Court · Appeal: Verdict overturned, March 2000, Beijing Higher People's Court, on the grounds of insufficient evidence and unclear facts; the court ordered the case be retried.[10] · Retrial sentence: **10 years' imprisonment**, November 23, 2000, Beijing No.1 Intermediate People's Court · Appeal again: Filed, November 28, 2000[11]; denied, March 2001, Beijing Higher People's Court[12] · Status: Tilanqiao Prison, Shanghai	· Closed trial · Numerous requests by family to grant medical parole due to advanced age and poor health denied

NAME	BACKGROUND	CHARGES AND ACTIVITIES ALLEGED	PROCEDURAL HISTORY	PROCEDURAL PROTECTION DEROGATIONS
Ji Liewu[13] [纪烈武]	• Born 1963 • Manager of Hong Kong subsidiary of a government metals company • Obtained political asylum in U.S. after June 4, 1989 democracy protests	*Charges* • **Illegally obtaining state secrets** • **Organizing and using a heretical sect to undermine implementation of the law** • **Causing death through sect activities** *Activities Alleged* • Holding a leadership position in the Falun Gong • Helping organize a demonstration of thousands of Falun Gong practitioners, Zhongnanhai, April 25, 1999[14] • Exact nature of state secrets obtained, unknown	• Detention: July 20, 1999 • Formal arrest: October 19, 1999 • Indictment: November 19, 1999, Beijing People's Procuratorate • Trial: with Li Chang, Wang Zhiwen, and Yao Jie (see below) • Sentence: **12 years' imprisonment**, December 26, 1999	
Jiang Weiping[15] [姜维平]	• Reporter and editor for *Dalian Daily* and Xinhua News Agency • Worked for Hong Kong newspaper *Wen Wei Po*, stationed in its northeast China office (1994)	*Charges* • **Leaking state secrets** • **Illegally providing state secrets overseas** • **Inciting subversion** • **Illegally possessing confidential documents** *Activities Alleged* • Writing three articles for unnamed Hong Kong publication using pen name, criticizing the Dalian mayor and Liaoning Province governor (1998) • Writing series of articles using pen name, exposing corruption of Liaoning government officials (1999)	• Detention: December 4, 2000, Dalian • Formal arrest: January 3, 2001 • Indictment: May 2001, Dalian Procuratorate • Sentence: **8 years' imprisonment; 5 years' subsequent deprivation of political rights**, September 5, 2001, Dalian Intermediate People's Court • Appeal: sentence reduced to **6 years' imprisonment**, March 2003 • Release: (one year early) January 3, 2006	• Closed trial
Kong Jing [孔静]	• Sichuan Institute of Foreign Languages graduate, 2001 • Teacher at the School of Foreign Languages at the Southwest Agricultural University in Chongqing	*Charge* • **Leaking state secrets** *Activities Alleged* • Taking an examiner's advance copy of the College English Test (Grade 4), stamped "highly secret" • Copying contents of examination paper and passed information to exam participants for money	• Arrest: May 2004 • Sentence: **4 years' imprisonment**, December 13, 2004, a Chongqing court	

A. INDIVIDUALS CHARGED WITH STATE SECRETS OFFENSES, *cont.*

NAME	BACKGROUND	CHARGES AND ACTIVITIES ALLEGED	PROCEDURAL HISTORY	PROCEDURAL PROTECTION DEROGATIONS
Li Chang[16] [李昌]	· Former deputy director of the Computer Administration Office of the Ministry of Public Security	***Charges*** · **Illegally obtaining state secrets** · **Using a heretical sect to undermine implementation of law** · **Causing death through sect activities** ***Activities Alleged*** · Holding a leadership position in the Falun Gong · Helping organize a demonstration of thousands of Falun Gong practitioners at Zhongnanhai, April 25, 1999[17] · Exact nature of state secrets obtained, unknown	· Detention: July 20, 1999 · Formal arrest: October 19, 1999, with Ji Liewu, Wang Zhiwen and Yao Jie · Indictment: November 19, 1999, Beijing People's Procuratorate · Trial: With Li Chang, Wang Zhiwen, and Yao Jie · Sentence: **18 years' imprisonment**, December 26, 1999	· Lenient sentence received as a result of providing facts, confessing and expressing regret
Li Hai[18] [李海]	· Joined Students Autonomous Federation during student protests at Tiananmen while pursuing Master's degree in Philosophy at Peking University · As a result of participating in protests, detained and held for 7 months, then released and expelled from university	***Charge*** · **Gathering state secrets** ***Activities Alleged*** · Compiling list of persons from Beijing imprisoned for participating in 1989 democracy movement · Giving list to international human rights organizations · Helping to transmit overseas humanitarian aid to those imprisoned	· Arrest warrant: Issued May 25, 1995 · Detention: May 31, 1995, on charges of "hooliganism" · Formal arrest: September 19, 1995 · Trial: May 31, 1996, Chaoyang District People's Court, Beijing · Verdict: "Leaking state secrets" charge held groundless; guilty of "gathering state secrets" · Sentence: **9 years' imprisonment; 2 years' subsequent deprivation of political rights**, on December 18, 1996 · Appeal: Denied, March 13, 1997, Beijing Municipal No. 2 Intermediate Court · Release: May 30, 2004	· Court claimed open trail, but no family member allowed to attend · No access to family during detention
Liu Chen [刘晨]	· Owner and teacher of training center affiliated with Oriental University City in Hebei Province	***Charge*** · **Leaking state secrets** ***Activities Alleged*** · Acquiring confidential examination paper for College English Test (Grade 4) from Shi Xiaolong (see below) in collaboration with Cao Yu (see above) · Posting part of content on training center's website and disclosing contents in a seminar	· Indictment: April 23, 2004 · Sentence: **2 years' imprisonment**, June 2, 2004. Beijing No. 1 Intermediate Court	· Closed trial

A. INDIVIDUALS CHARGED WITH STATE SECRETS OFFENSES, *cont.*

NAME	BACKGROUND	CHARGES AND ACTIVITIES ALLEGED	PROCEDURAL HISTORY	PROCEDURAL PROTECTION DEROGATIONS
Liu Fenggang [刘凤钢]	· Factory worker in Beijing, fired 1990 · Following student and worker protests in 1989, joined underground Christian religious organization	*Charge* · **Gathering and illegally providing state secrets to foreign organizations** *Activities Alleged* · Receiving money from Xu Yonghai (see below) to travel to Liaoning to see underground Christian held in an RTL camp (2001) · Writing article on findings; sent to *Christian Life Quarterly* for publication · Writing article on persecuted Christians, sent abroad by e-mail (2003) · Writing essay on experience being interrogated by police, typed up and sent abroad by e-mail by Zhang Shengqi (2003)	· Residential surveillance: October 13, 2003, Hangzhou Public Security Bureau · Detention: November 14, 2003 · Arrest: December 4, 2003 · Trial: May 14, 2004, with Xu Yonghai and Zhang Shengqi (see below), Hangzhou City Intermediate People's Court · Inconclusive evidence: court placed the three defendants under residential surveillance · Second trial: August 6, 2004, Hangzhou Intermediate People's Court · Sentence: **3 years' imprisonment** · Release: February 4, 2007[19]	· No arrest warrant · Closed trial · Evidence deemed inconclusive in first trial was accepted in second trial
Liu Zesheng [刘泽生]	· Falun Gong contact person in Tangshan, Hebei Province	*Charge* · **Leaking state secrets** *Activities Alleged* · Reporting that police were persecuting Falun Gong practitioners · Sentence: **4 years' imprisonment**, 2000		
Lu Jianhua [陆建华]	· Prominent sociologist at CASS · Editor of annual book on China's social situation · In regular contact with journalist Ching Cheong (see below)	*Charge* · **Leaking state secrets** *Activities Alleged* · Passing information on leadership talks to Ching Cheong, convicted of spying for Taiwan · Writing articles for *Singapore Straits Times* over the past few years, including three or four articles that state investigators said contained "high-level state secrets"	· Detention: April 2005 · Trial: August 16, 2006, Beijing No. 2 Intermediate People's Court · Sentence: **20 years' imprisonment**, December 18, 2006 · Appeal: Reportedly filed	· Denied the right to choose his own lawyer; court-appointed attorney provided representation · Closed trial (wife was refused entry)

A. INDIVIDUALS CHARGED WITH STATE SECRETS OFFENSES, *cont.*

NAME	BACKGROUND	CHARGES AND ACTIVITIES ALLEGED	PROCEDURAL HISTORY	PROCEDURAL PROTECTION DEROGATIONS
Ma Tao [马涛]	· Editor for national health publication, *China Health Education News* · 29 years old at time of arrest · Married to Wu Shishen, with whom she was arrested and tried	*Charge* · **Illegally providing state secrets abroad** *Activities Alleged* · Handing over a document obtained by Wu Shishen (see below) to a Hong Kong reporter	· Detention: October 26, 1992, with husband Wu Shishen · Arrest: November 6, 1992 · Sentence: **6 years' imprisonment; 1 year subsequent deprivation of political rights**, August 30, 1993, Beijing Intermediate People's Court · Appeal: Denied, October 5, 1993, Beijing Higher People's Court · Release: No confirmation that projected release in November 1998 was carried out	· Closed trial
Qu Wei [曲炜]	· Born 1954 · Senior official in charge of propaganda work directed at Taiwan, editor of *Taiwan Union Bulletin* · Published many articles on cross-strait relations, had extensive contacts with scholars working on Taiwan-related issues	*Charge* · **Leaking state secrets** *Activities Alleged* · Leaking secrets, including some published materials he passed to Gao Zhan	· Detention: February 10, 2001 · Trial: July 24, 2001, Beijing No. 1 Intermediate People's Court · Sentence: **13 years' imprisonment; 3 years' subsequent deprivation of political rights**[20]	
Rebiya Kadeer [热比亚卡德尔]	· Born 1946 · Uyghur businesswoman · Representative of XUAR National People's Congress (NPC), and served as a delegate to the 1995 United Nations World Conference on Women in Beijing	*Charge* · **Illegally providing state secrets abroad** *Activities Alleged* · Sending her husband, who fled to the US in 1996, clippings from XUAR newspapers · Bringing copies of local newspapers and other information concerning human rights abuses in the XUAR to a meeting with visiting U.S. congressional staff in China but was detained en route (August 1999)	· Formal arrest: September 2, 1999 · Sentence: **8 years' imprisonment**, March 10, 2000, Urumqi Intermediate People's Court · Sentence reduction: 1 year reduction, March 3, 2004, for "good behavior" · Release: Medical parole, March 17, 2005, following international pressure	· Family reprisals: Following her exile in the U.S., her sons and daughters have been subject to pressure and harassment; her sons and daughters have also been held under house arrest and in detention, and two sons have been convicted of tax evasion and another convicted of state security crimes.

NAME	BACKGROUND	CHARGES AND ACTIVITIES ALLEGED	PROCEDURAL HISTORY	PROCEDURAL PROTECTION DEROGATIONS
Shi Tao [师涛]	• Born 1968, Taiyuan City, Shanxi Province • Journalist for *Dangdai Shangbao* (*Contemporary Business News*) prior to arrest • Online essayist on overseas Internet forums	***Charge*** • **Illegally supplying state secrets abroad** ***Activities Alleged*** • Posting on an overseas Web site, *Democracy Newsletter*, a summary of an official document alerting journalists to possible social instability around the 15th anniversary of the violent suppression of the 1989 democracy movement • Article traced back to Shi with the assistance of Yahoo! Holdings (HK), Ltd.	• Detention: November 24, 2004 • Formal arrest: December 14, 2004 • Indictment: Sent to Changsha Municipal Intermediate People's Court, January 31, 2005. • Trial: April 27, 2005 • Sentence: **10 years' imprisonment; 2 years' subsequent deprivation of political rights** • Appeal: Denied, June 2, 2005, Hunan Province Higher People's Court	• Closed trial
Shi Xiaolong [史晓龙]	• Senior administrative staff at Chinese People's Public Security University • Responsible for safeguarding the examination paper for College English Test (Grade 4)	***Charge*** • **Leaking state secrets** ***Activities Alleged*** • Intentionally passing examination paper for College English Test (Grade 4) to Cao Yu (see above), a teacher at the training center affiliated with the Oriental University City, who then posted the contents of the examination paper on the center's website	• Indictment: April 23, 2004, People's Procuratorate • Sentence: **3 years' imprisonment,** June 2, 2004, Beijing No. 1 Intermediate Court	• Closed trial
Song Yongyi [宋永毅]	• Born 1950 • Obtained two Master's degrees in US • Librarian at Dickinson College, Pennyslvania (1995) • Conducted research trips to China in the 1990s to research the Cultural Revolution	***Charge*** • **Procuring and illegally providing intelligence abroad** ***Activities Alleged*** • Buying materials on the Cultural Revolution and conducting research for the library where he worked on a visit to China	• Detention: August 6, 1999, Beijing (wife was detained with him, released November 16, 1999) • Formal arrest: December 24, 1999 • Criminal charges dropped; released January 28, 2000	
Tan Kai[21] [谭凯]	• Computer repair technician • Organized environmental watchdog group, Green Watch (*lüse guancha*), with Lai Jinbiao, Gao Haibing, Wu Yuanming, Qi Huimin and Yang Jianming	***Charge*** • **Illegally obtaining state secrets** ***Activities Alleged*** • Creating back-up copy of computer files during a computer repair of employee of the Zhejiang provincial Party Committee	• Summons: October 19, 2005, with five other Green Watch members, Hangzhou Public Security Bureau; all but Tan released the day after questioning • Arrest: December 7, 2005 • Indictment: April 29, 2006 • Trial: May 15, 2006	• Closed trial • Family-appointed lawyers initially refused by Hangzhou Public Security Bureau because the case involved state secrets; permission granted after Tan persisted with another application

A. INDIVIDUALS CHARGED WITH STATE SECRETS OFFENSES, *cont.*

NAME	BACKGROUND	CHARGES AND ACTIVITIES ALLEGED	PROCEDURAL HISTORY	PROCEDURAL PROTECTION DEROGATIONS
Tan Kai, *cont.*		***Activities believed to have resulted in charges*** · Activism in Green Watch—declared an illegal organization by the Zhejiang provincial government on November 15, 2005—and monitoring pollution in Huashui Town, where protests in late March and April 2005 culminated in violent conflict with local police	· Sentence: **18 months imprisonment**, August 11, 2006, Hangzhou Municipal Intermediate People's Court · Appeal: Filed · Released: April 19, 2007	
Tang Tao [唐涛]	· Born in 1970, Hunan Province · Communist Party member; served in the military in Guangdong Province	***Charge*** · **Leaking state secrets** ***Activities Alleged*** · Providing blacklist of "June 4" activists who were either barred from entering China or subject to arrest or other measures on arrival to brother-in-law, Chen Meng (see above)	· Detention: April 19, 1995 · Arrest: May 25, 1995 · Sentence: **6 years' imprisonment**, April 15, 1997, Nanshan District Court of Shenzhen City · Release: Planned for April 2001, but current status is unknown	
Teng Chunyan [滕春燕]	· Moved from Harbin to the U.S. and obtained U.S. citizenship · Acupuncturist, taught Chinese medicine in New York	***Charge*** · **Gathering and illegally providing intelligence abroad** ***Activities Alleged*** · Collecting, in February and March 2000, information about Falun Gong members who had been sent to psychiatric institutions or drug rehabilitation clinics	· Trial: November 23, 2000 by the Beijing No. 1 Intermediate Court · Sentence: **3 years' imprisonment**, December 12, 2000 · Imprisonment: After undergoing three months of "study classes," Teng was sent to the Beijing Women's Prison to serve her sentence · Appeal: Denied, May 11, 2001, Beijing Higher People's Court · Release: Early release, March 19, 2003, due to "good behavior"	· Closed trial
Tian Ye [田野]	· Vice-director of the general office of the Foreign Affairs Bureau of the People's Bank of China · Friend of journalist Xi Yang	***Charge*** · **Stealing and gathering state secrets** ***Activities Alleged*** · Stealing state financial and economic secrets, including Bank of China international gold policy strategies and plans for modifications on deposit and loan interest rates · Passing a document stamped "secret" to journalist and friend Xi Yang (see below)	· Sentence: **15 years' imprisonment; 3 years' subsequent deprivation of political rights**, March 28, 1994, Beijing No.1 Intermediate People's Court · Appeal: Denied, April 15, 1994	· Closed trial

NAME	BACKGROUND	CHARGES AND ACTIVITIES ALLEGED	PROCEDURAL HISTORY	PROCEDURAL PROTECTION DEROGATIONS
Tohti Tunyaz [图尼亚孜]	• Also known as Tohti Muzart (pen name) • Graduated from Beijing Minorities Institute (1984), sent to work for the Standing Committee of the NPC • Pursued Ph.D. in Japan on the history of China's ethnic minorities (1995)	*Charges* • **Stealing state secrets for individuals abroad** • **Inciting separatism** *Activities Alleged* • Stealing records that were more than 50 years old obtained from and photo-copied by a library worker	• Arrest: February 6, 1998 (upon return to China to collect research materials for his Ph.D. thesis) • Charge: November 10, 1998 • Sentence: **11 years' imprisonment; 2 years' subsequent deprivation of political rights,** March 10, 1999, Urumqi Intermediate People's Court [22] • Appeal: Denied, February 15, 2000, XUAR Higher People's Court • Status: Serving sentence in XUAR No. 3 Prison in Urumqi • Projected release: March 31, 2009[23]	• Detained for more than two years prior to trial • Reportedly interrogated daily • Closed trial • No access to family
Wang Zhiwen[24] [王治(志)文]	• Engineer, living in Beijing	*Charges* • **Organizing and using a heretical sect to undermine implementation of the law** • **Using a heretical sect to cause death** • **Illegally obtaining state secrets** *Activities Alleged* • Holding a leadership position in the Falun Gong. • Helping organize a demon-stration of thousands of Falun Gong practitioners at Zhong-nanhai, April 25, 1999[25] • Exact nature of state secrets obtained, unknown	• Detention: July 20, 1999 • Formal arrest: October 19, 1999 • Indictment: November 19, 1999 • Trial: with Li Chang, Ji Liewu, and Yao Jie • Sentence: **16 years' imprisonment**, December 26, 1999	
Wu Shishen (Wu Shisen)[26] [吴士深]	• Born 1960 • Editor for Xinhua News Agency • Married to Ma Tao	*Charge* • **Illegally providing state secrets abroad** *Activities Alleged* • Leaking advance copy of Party leader Jiang Zemin's speech to the 14th Party Congress to a Hong Kong reporter	• Detention: October 26, 1992, with wife Ma Tao (see above) • Formal arrest: November 6, 1992 • Sentence: **Life imprison-ment,** August 30, 1993, Beijing Intermediate People's Court. • Appeal: Denied, October 5, 1993, Beijing Higher People's Court • Release: August 2, 2005, following international pressure	• Closed trial

A. INDIVIDUALS CHARGED WITH STATE SECRETS OFFENSES, *cont.*

NAME	BACKGROUND	CHARGES AND ACTIVITIES ALLEGED	PROCEDURAL HISTORY	PROCEDURAL PROTECTION DEROGATIONS
Xi Yang [席扬]	· Reporter for Hong Kong newspaper *Ming Pao* · Mainland-born Hong Kong resident	**Charge** · **Stealing and gathering state secrets** ***Activities Alleged*** · Gathering and stealing state financial and economic secrets not yet officially released related to article he wrote discussing Bank of China international gold policy and strategies	· Detention: September 27, 1993 · Formal arrest: October 7, 1993 · Sentence: **12 years' imprisonment and 2 years' subsequent deprivation of political rights**, March 28, 1994, Beijing No.1 Intermediate People's Court · Appeal: Denied, April 15, 1994 · Release: On parole, January 26, 1997	· Closed trial
Xiu Yichun [修宜春]	· Senior Chinese manager, Royal Dutch Shell	**Charge** · **Reportedly obtaining state secrets** ***Activities Alleged*** · Obtaining state secrets related to plans of Royal Dutch Shell to build an oil refinery in Huizhou, east of Hong Kong, with a counterpart at the China National Offshore Oil Corporation (CNOOC) · Information involved the financing and environmental implications of the project	· Detention: Early February, 1996	· Held incommunicado for almost one year
Xu Yonghai [徐永海]	· Born 1960 · Psychiatric doctor in Beijing hospital · Imprisoned for two years for taking part in Wang Dan's democracy campaign · Released, 1997; subsequently detained and released, and harassed	**Charge** · **Illegally providing state secrets to foreign organizations** ***Activities Alleged*** · Providing Liu Fenggang (see above) with 1,000 yuan to go to Liaoning Province to see underground Christian in an RTL camp · Passing article that Liu wrote on his findings to an overseas magazine for publication	· Detention: November 9, 2003 · Arrest: December 4, 2003 · Trial: May 14, 2004, with Liu Fenggang and Zhang Shengqi (see below), Hangzhou City Intermediate People's Court · Inconclusive evidence: Court placed the three under residential surveillance · New trial: August 6, 2004, Hangzhou Intermediate People's Court · Sentence: **2 years' imprisonment** · Release: January 29, 2006	· Closed trial · Court took no account of the evidence that had been considered invalid in the initial trial, and still found Xu guilty[27] · Residence surveillance improperly imposed

A. INDIVIDUALS CHARGED WITH STATE SECRETS OFFENSES, *cont.*

NAME	BACKGROUND	CHARGES AND ACTIVITIES ALLEGED	PROCEDURAL HISTORY	PROCEDURAL PROTECTION DEROGATIONS
Xu Zerong (David Tsui) [徐泽荣]	• Born in Guangzhou • Graduate of Fudan University (1982) • Moved to Hong Kong in 1985 • Guangdong Academy of Social Sciences staff member; Research Associate Professor at Zhongshan University Southeast Asia Institute • Helped found *The Chinese Social Sciences Quarterly*	*Charges* • **Illegally providing state secrets abroad** • **Illegal business activities** *Activities Alleged* • Providing intelligence to individuals overseas (1992), including 4 books on the Korean War, whose contents contained information on the policy-making process of top leaders; books sent by the court for verification and determined to be top-secret level documents that had not yet been declassified • Illegally printing and selling large quantities of books in Shenzhen from 1993 to 2000	• Detention: June 24, 2000 • Formal arrest: July 29, 2000 • Indictment: July 16, 2001 by the Shenzhen People's Procuratorate. • Trial: August 7, 2001, Shenzhen Intermediate People's Court • Sentence: **10 years' imprisonment** for illegally providing intelligence abroad; **5 years' imprisonment** for illegal business activities • Appeal: upheld the portion of the verdict of "illegal business activities" but overturned the court determination of the crime of illegally providing intelligence abroad and applied the same sentence for the crime of **illegally providing state secrets abroad,** December 2002, Guangdong Higher People's Court[28] • Status: Serving sentence in Dongguan Prison, Guangdong • Projected release: September 2012 (sentence reduced by nine months)	• Closed trial
Yao Jie[29] [姚洁]	• Born 1960 • Leader of the CPC committee of a large real estate company	*Charges* • **Organizing and using a heretical sect to undermine implementation of the law** • **Using a heretical sect to cause death** • **Illegally obtaining state secrets** *Activities Alleged* • Holding a leadership position in the Falun Gong • Helping organize a demonstration of thousands of Falun Gong practitioners, Zhongnanhai, April 25, 1999[30] • Exact nature of state secrets obtained, unknown	• Detention: July 20, 1999 • Formal arrest: October 19, 1999 • Indictment: November 19, 1999, Beijing People's Procuratorate • Sentence: **7 years' imprisonment,** December 26, 1999 • Trial: With Li Chang, Ji Liewu, and Wang Zhiwen • Release: Medical parole, August 22, 2000 • New detention: February 2, 2001, to complete her sentence	

A. INDIVIDUALS CHARGED WITH STATE SECRETS OFFENSES, *cont.*

NAME	BACKGROUND	CHARGES AND ACTIVITIES ALLEGED	PROCEDURAL HISTORY	PROCEDURAL PROTECTION DEROGATIONS
Yu Meisun [俞梅荪]	· Secretary for Gu Ming, former deputy director of the State Council Office and vice-chairman of the Legal Committee of the Seventh NPC · Associate law professor, Peking University	***Charge*** · **Leaking important state secrets** ***Activities Alleged*** · Showing CPC Central Committee and State Council documents to Wang Jienan, head of the Beijing Bureau of the Shanghai newspaper *Wenhuibao* · Though Yu made clear that Wang could not make copies, he did so secretly, reporting the information in the newspapers	· Detention: January 3, 1994, Beijing State Security Bureau · Sentence: **3 years' imprisonment**, early August 1994, Beijing Intermediate People's Court · Release: January 1997	
Zhang Shanguang [张善光]	· Born 1974 · Primary and middle school teacher and business person · Joined the democracy movement in 1989 and organized activities for the Hunan Workers Autonomous Federation · Petitioned for the release of China Democracy Party's Wang Donghai, Wang Youcai and others · Previously sentenced to 7 years' imprisonment on charges of counter-revolutionary propaganda, released in 1996	***Charge*** · **Illegally providing intelligence abroad** ***Activities Alleged*** · Giving telephone interviews to reporters, including a reporter from Radio Free Asia, during which information about demonstrations near his home and about a kidnapping case under investigation was disclosed · Attempting to register Association to Protect the Rights and Interests of Laid-Off Workers, Xupu County	· Detention: July 21, 1998 · Formal arrest: August 28, 1998 · Sentence: **10 years' imprisonment**, December 27, 1998 · Appeal: Denied, May 2000, Hunan Province Higher People's Court · Status: In prison, Hunan Provincial No. 1 Prison	· Closed trial · Denied access to family
Zhang Shengqi [张胜棋]	· Born 1974 · Computer technician	***Charge*** · **Illegally providing state secrets to foreign organizations** ***Activities Alleged*** · Transcribing and sending by email an essay written by Liu Fenggang in 2003 detailing his experience of being interrogated by the police	· Detention: November 17, 2003 · Trial: May 14, 2004, with Xu Yonghai and Liu Fenggang (see above), Hangzhou City Intermediate People's Court · Inconclusive evidence: Court placed the three defendants under residential surveillance · Second trial: August 6, 2004, Hangzhou Intermediate People's Court · Sentence: **1 year imprisonment** · Release: February 7, 2005	· Closed trial · Evidence not authorized properly · Residence surveillance improperly imposed

A. INDIVIDUALS CHARGED WITH STATE SECRETS OFFENSES, *cont.*

NAME	BACKGROUND	CHARGES AND ACTIVITIES ALLEGED	PROCEDURAL HISTORY	PROCEDURAL PROTECTION DEROGATIONS
Zhao Yan [赵岩]	• Born in 1962 • Graduated from Heilongjiang University • Journalist with *China Reform*, an official publication, reporting on rural issues and official corruption • Joined the *New York Times* Beijing bureau as a researcher (April 2004)	**Charges** • **Illegally providing state secrets abroad** • **Fraud** (charge added June 1, 2005[31]) **Activities Alleged** • Requesting 20,000 *yuan* from a peasant in exchange for advising him on how to avoid prison[32] • Leaking confidential information concerning Jiang Zemin's resignation as Chairman of the Central Military Commission before it was officially announced	• Detention: September 16, 2004 • Formal arrest: around October 20, 2004 • Trial: June 16, 2006, Beijing No. 2 Intermediate People's Court • Verdict delayed: Court announced verdict to be delayed on June 23, 2006 • Verdict: State secrets charges dismissed; guilty of fraud, Beijing No. 2 Intermediate People's Court • Sentence: **3 years' imprisonment** • Appeal: September 4, 2006, Zhao filed an appeal; appeal denied, December 1, 2006, Beijing Higher People's Court • Projected release: September 2007	• Detained nearly 2 years without trial • Family notified only 34 days after his detention • No access to family and lawyer • Closed trial • Not allowed to testify, present evidence or call witnesses in the appeal hearing, which lasted only 5 minutes
Zhao Lei [赵蕾]	• Translator for foreign correspondents in Beijing • Married to Bai Weiji (see above)	**Charge** • **Illegally providing state secrets abroad** **Activities Alleged** • Translating state secrets documents for her husband Bai Weiji that were passed to Lena Sun, a correspondent for the *Washington Post*; documents confiscated May 17, 1992	• Detention: April 21, 1993, Beijing. • Trial: With her husband Bai Weiji • Sentence: **6 years' imprisonment,** May 20, 1993, Beijing Intermediate People's Court • Appeal: Denied, July 1993, Beijing Higher People's Court • Release: October 1998	• Denied public trial • Closed trial
Zheng Enchong [郑恩宠]	• Lawyer • Assisted in over 500 cases of forced eviction stemming from urban redevelopment in Shanghai • At time of detention in June 2003, was advising six Shanghai families in a lawsuit against Shanghai's Jing'an District Property Development Bureau	**Charge** • **Illegally providing state secrets abroad** **Activities Alleged** • Disseminating information about events and news articles to international organizations and press • Sending two faxes to Human Rights in China (HRIC), May 23 and May 28, 2003 containing information about the Shanghai Public Security Bureau's handling of a demonstration held by workers at the Shanghai Yimin Food Products No. 1 Factory, and the Xinhua	• Detention: June 6, 2003 • Formal arrest: June 18, 2003 • Indictment: August 15, 2003, Shanghai People's Procuratorate • Trial: August 28, 2003, Shanghai No. 2 Intermediate People's Court • Sentence: **3 years' imprisonment; one year's subsequent deprivation of political rights**, October 28, 2003 • Appeal: Denied, December 18, 2003 • Release: June 5, 2006 • New detention: July 12, 2006 for several hours along with	• Limited access to lawyers before trial; only two short visits allowed on August 22 and August 26, 2003, several days before his trial • Closed trial • Continued harassment following his release

A. INDIVIDUALS CHARGED WITH STATE SECRETS OFFENSES, *cont.*

NAME	BACKGROUND	CHARGES AND ACTIVITIES ALLEGED	PROCEDURAL HISTORY	PROCEDURAL PROTECTION DEROGATIONS
Zheng Enchong, *cont.*		News Agency's "selected internal briefing," also publicly available	his wife on suspicion of "impeding officials of state organs in the execution of their duties . . . during a period of deprivation of political rights"	

B. INDIVIDUALS LIKELY DENIED PROCEDURAL PROTECTIONS ON STATE SECRETS GROUNDS

NAME	BACKGROUND	CHARGES AND ACTIVITIES ALLEGED	PROCEDURAL HISTORY	PROCEDURAL PROTECTION DEROGATIONS
Huseyin Celil [赛利尔]	• Born 1969, Kashgar, XUAR • Granted UNHCR refugee status (2001), resettled in Canada,[33] became citizen (2005) • Imam, Hamilton Mosque, Ontario	**Charge** • **Unknown** **Activities alleged** • Unknown; Ministry of Foreign Affairs states he was involved in terrorist activities[34] **Activities believed to have resulted in charges** • Religious and political activism in XUAR	• Arrest: 1994 on allegations of forming a political party • Escape: fled to Turkey after serving a month in prison; gained political asylum in Canada (2001)[35] • Detention: March 27, 2006, Tashkent, Uzbekistan • Extradition: June, 2006, to PRC • Trial: Reportedly tried February 2, 2007 in Urumqi, XUAR[36] • Sentenced: April 19, 2007 to life imprisonment for separatism and terrorist activities, Urumqi Intermediate People's Court	• Denied access to family during detention • Reportedly tortured to force signature on confession • Celil's complaints concerning court appointed lawyer ignored and request to choose another lawyer denied • Denied access to Canadian Consular officials before and after extradition
Chen Guangcheng [陈光诚]	• Self-taught blind activist lawyer	**Charges** • **Damaging public property** • **Gathering people to block traffic** **Activities alleged** • Participating in a hunger strike and calling for the defense of human rights (March 2006) **Activities believed to have resulted in charges** • Recording the stories of abuse of villagers, Linyi City, Shandong Province (March 2005) • Publishing a report on abuses by family planning officials on a Web site (June 10, 2005) • Filing a class-action lawsuit against the city of Linyi over its official policy of forced abortions and sterilizations (June 21, 2005)	• Residential surveillance: August 12, 2005[37] • Detention: March 2006 • Charge: June 10, 2006 • Sentence: **4 years and 3 months' imprisonment**, August 24, 2006, Yinan County Court • Appeal: Verdict overturned; new trial ordered, October 31, 2006, Linyi Intermediate People's Court • Retrial: November 27, 2006, Yinan County Court • Verdict: Sentence upheld, December 1, 2006, Yinan County Court • Appeal: Denied, January 12, 2007, Linyi Intermediate People's Court	• Detained for three months without notification to family or access to lawyers • Family-appointed lawyers rejected, harassed and even detained by authorities • Two lawyers appointed for Chen against his wishes one hour before his first trial • No oral argument permitted at appeal
Ching Cheong [程翔]	• Formerly journalist with Hong Kong's *Wen Wei Po*; resigned after the Tiananmen crackdown (1989) • Chief China correspondent for the Singapore newspaper *The Straights Times*	**Charge** • **Espionage** **Activities alleged** • Buying information containing state secrets and passing it to Taiwan's intelligence services over a period of five years from mid-2000 to March 2005 **Activities believed to have resulted in charges** • Attempting to obtain a manuscript of an interview with the	• Detention: April 22, 2005 • Formal arrest: August 5, 2005 • Supplementary investigation: Insufficient evidence, case sent back to Beijing State Security Bureau, February 2006 • Sentence: **5 years' imprisonment**; **1 year's deprivation of political rights**, August 31, 2006,	• Detained without charge for four months • Detained for over 12 months before trial • Denied access to family and lawyers • Closed trial

B. INDIVIDUALS LIKELY DENIED PROCEDURAL PROTECTIONS ON STATE SECRETS GROUNDS, *cont.*

NAME	BACKGROUND	CHARGES AND ACTIVITIES ALLEGED	PROCEDURAL HISTORY	PROCEDURAL PROTECTION DEROGATIONS
Ching Cheong, *cont.*		late Chinese leader Zhao Ziyang (April 2005)	Beijing No. 2 Intermediate People's Court[38] · Appeal: Denied, November 24, 2006, Beijing Higher People's Court · Status: Transferred to a Guangzhou prison to serve out his sentence[39] · Projected release: August 3, 2010	
Gao Zhan [高瞻]	· Political scientist, American University, Washington, DC · Chinese citizen; U.S. green card	**Charge** · **Spying for Taiwan** **Activities alleged** · Involved in activities of endangering state security · Accepting missions from overseas intelligence agencies; taking funds for spying activities in mainland China.	· Detention: February 11, 2001 · Formal charge: March 27, 2001 · Sentence: **10 years' imprisonment**, July 24, 2001, Beijing No.1 Intermediate People's Court · Release: Medical parole, July 25, 2001 · Deportation: to U.S., July 26, 2001	· Denied access to family and lawyers for five months after detention · Closed trial · Husband and US Consular officials denied access to trial
Gao Zhisheng [高智晟]	· Human rights lawyer who defended underground Christians, dissidents and other human rights activists · License to practice law revoked in 2005	**Charge** · **Inciting subversion** **Activities alleged** · Organizing hunger strike, calling attention to the attack on activist-lawyer Guo Feixiong (February 2006)	· Residential surveillance: March 2006 · Detention: August 16, 2006 · Formal arrest: September 21, 2006 · Formal Charge: October 12, 2006 · Trial: December 12, 2006, Beijing No. 1 Intermediate People's Court · Sentence: **3 years' imprisonment with a 5-year reprieve; 1-year deprivation of political rights**, December 22, 2006; subsequently released[40]	· Denied access to family-appointed lawyers during detention · Closed trial
Hada [哈達]	· Political activist, Inner Mongolia Autonomous Region (IMAR) · A founder of the Southern Mongolian Democratic Alliance (SMDA)	**Charges** · **Espionage** · **Separatism** **Activities alleged** · Forming and organizing the SMDA (declared illegal in December 1995), an organization engaged in separatist activities, and writing the organization's by-laws	· Detention: December 11, 1995 · Formal arrest: March 9, 1996 · Indictment: August 19, 1996 · Trial: November 11, 1996, Hohhot Municipal Intermediate People's Court · Sentence: **15 years'**	· Closed trial

B. INDIVIDUALS LIKELY DENIED PROCEDURAL PROTECTIONS ON STATE SECRETS GROUNDS, *cont.*

NAME	BACKGROUND	CHARGES AND ACTIVITIES ALLEGED	PROCEDURAL HISTORY	PROCEDURAL PROTECTION DEROGATIONS
Hada, *cont.*		• Organizing conferences and "political training sessions" with the SMDA • Publishing separatist articles and an underground journal with the SMDA (*The Voice of Southern Mongolia*) and wrote a book (*The Way Out of Southern Mongolia*), detailing information regarding abuse of Mongolians by the authorities	**imprisonment; 4 years' subsequent deprivation of political rights** for inciting separatism and espionage • Appeal: Denied, January 24, 1997, Inner Mongolia Supreme People's Court • Status: Chifeng Prison, Inner Mongolia[41]	
Huang Qi [黄琦]	• Internet essayist, owner of Tianwang website	*Charge* • **Inciting subversion of state power** *Activities alleged* • Posting subversive material on his website (www.6-4tianwang.com) between March and June 2000, on matters such as "democracy," "June 4," and "Falun Gong" • Using "rumor-mongering and defamation" to incite subversion of state power and overthrow China's socialist system	• Arrest: June 2, 2000 • Formal charge: August 21, 2000 • Trial: January 2001, Chengdu Intermediate People's Court • Sentence: **5 years' imprisonment**, May 9, 2003 • Appeal: Denied, August 2003, Sichuan Higher People's Court • Release: June 5, 2005	• Denied access to family during detention; family was allowed to visit once in May 2003 • Closed trial
Li Zhi [李志]	• Internet essayist, expressing critical political views of the government	*Charge* • **Inciting subversion of state power** *Activities alleged* • Posting reactionary essays on the Internet • Communicating with overseas dissidents in Internet chat rooms; evidence used included that provided by Yahoo! Holdings (HK) Ltd., connecting Li Zhi to the yahoo.com.cn e-mail address used to send postings to Internet chat rooms	• Initial detention: August 8, 2003 • Formal detention: August 11, 2003 • Formal arrest: September 3, 2003 • Trial: December 10, 2003, Dazhou City Intermediate People's Court • Sentence: **8 years' imprisonment; 4 years' subsequent deprivation of political rights** • Appeal: Denied, February 26, 2004, Sichuan Province Higher People's Court	• Closed trial • Met defense lawyers only 10 minutes before his trial • Lawyers only allowed to submit written argument for appeal

B. INDIVIDUALS LIKELY DENIED PROCEDURAL PROTECTIONS ON STATE SECRETS GROUNDS, *cont.*

NAME	BACKGROUND	CHARGES AND ACTIVITIES ALLEGED	PROCEDURAL HISTORY	PROCEDURAL PROTECTION DEROGATIONS
Qin Guangguang [覃光广]	· U.S. green-card holder · Former editor, *China Economic Information News* (1986–1989) · Visiting scholar at several universities in the U.S. (1989–1992) · Research work on ethnic minorities in China (1994)	**Charge** · **Leaking state secrets** **Activities alleged** · Providing information to Taiwan intelligence personnel on China's economy and changes in top leadership	· Detention: December 2000, Beijing State Security Bureau · Formal arrest: April 2001 · Sentence: **10 years' imprisonment**, July 23, 2001, Beijing No. 1 Intermediate People's Court, for spying for Taiwan · Release: Medical parole, July 26, 2001 · Return to the US: August 8, 2001	· Denied access to lawyers and family members in the pre-trial period · Closed trial
Sang Jiancheng [桑坚城]	· Born in 1942 · Imprisoned in the late 1970s for taking part in the China Democracy Wall movement · Retired real estate broker in Shanghai	**Charge** · **Inciting subversion of state power** **Activities alleged** · Distributing copies of an open letter to the 16th Party Congress signed by 162 dissidents, calling on the government to reassess the verdict on the 1989 Tiananmen Square incident and release prisoners of conscience (November 2002)	· Detention: November 10, 2002 · Formal arrest: December 18, 2002 · Indictment: June 5, 2003, Shanghai People's Procuratorate · Sentence: **3 years' imprisonment**, January 9, 2004	
Tao Haidong [陶海东]	· Outspoken internet essayist, actively posted his views in on-line discussion groups under his real name	**Charge** · **Inciting subversion of state power** **Activities alleged** · Receiving 500 *yuan* from a foreign organization to post "subversive" articles, predicting the collapse of China's economy and describing China as the modern world's largest base of feudalism, on Chinese and overseas Web sites (official state newspaper, *Urumqi Metropolitan News*) · Slandering Chinese leaders **Activities believed to have resulted in charges** · Writing and publishing articles on the *Democracy Forum* website and other websites that focused on political and legal reform in China · Writing in an essay, "Strategies for China's Social Reforms," that "the Communist Party of	· Detention: July 9, 2003 · Trial: January 8, 2003, Urumqi People's Intermediate Court · Sentence: **7 years' imprisonment; 3 years' subsequent deprivation of political rights**, February 16, 2003 · Appeal: Denied, XUAR Higher People's Court	· Whereabouts unknown until trial was reported in a state newspaper · Closed trial

NAME	BACKGROUND	CHARGES AND ACTIVITIES ALLEGED	PROCEDURAL HISTORY	PROCEDURAL PROTECTION DEROGATIONS
Tao Haidong, *cont.*		China (CPC) and democracy activists throughout society should unite to push forward China's freedom and democratic development or else stand condemned through the ages"		
Tenzin Delek Rinpoche (Trulku Tenzin Delek) [阿安扎西]	· Influential and highly respected Tibetan Buddhist leader · Recognized by the Dalai Lama as a tulku, a reincarnated religious teacher	***Charges*** · **Causing explosions** · **Inciting separatism** ***Activities alleged*** · Involvement in "splittist activities," taking part in "causing explosions," central Chengdu, April 3, 2002 ***Activities believed to have resulted in charges*** · Attempting to set up monasteries and schools for children from poor local families in Nyagchu area in Lithang, eastern Tibet · Was ordered by the authorities to close a school; 20,000 local people reportedly signed a petition in his support (2000) · Traveling and teaching in Kardze prefecture (2000–April 2002)[42]	· Arrest: April 7, 2002, during police raid, Jamyang Choekhorling Monastery, Kardze · Trial: November 29, 2002, Kardze Intermediate People's Court · Sentence: **death sentence with two-year reprieve**, December 2, 2002 · Appeal: Denied, January 23, 2003, Sichuan Higher People's Court[43] · Sentence commuted: **life imprisonment**, January 2005[44]	· Family-appointed lawyers denied, two court-appointed lawyers provided instead · Unclear if he was actually represented by lawyers · Restricted access to trial
Wu Jianmin [吴建民]	· Born 1951, Hebei Province · Reporter for *Shenzhen Youth News* from 1986 to 1988 · Left China for U.S. in 1988, became citizen in 1996 · Under pen name, published, in Taiwan, *The Tiananmen Papers*	***Charges*** · **Spying** · **Endangering state security** ***Activities Alleged*** · Joining a Taiwanese espionage organization and going into China on several occasions to gather intelligence	· Detention: April 8, 2001 · US Embassy notified: April 10, 2001; visited by consular official, April 14, 2001 · Formal arrest: May 26, 2001 · Release: September 28, 2001, expelled from country	
Xu Wanping [许万平]	· Human rights activist · Previously imprisoned for involvement in the 1989 Tiananmen democracy protests	***Charge*** · **Inciting subversion of state power** ***Activities alleged*** · Participating in a signature campaign related to an anti-Japanese protest in 2005 · Recruiting members on behalf of the outlawed China Democracy Party	· Detention: April 30, 2005 · Formal charge: May 24, 2005 · Sentence: **12 years' imprisonment; 4 years' subsequent deprivation of political rights**, December 2005, Chongqing No.1 Intermediate People's Court · Appeal: Denied, February 28, 2006, Chongqing Municipal Higher People's Court	· Detained by public security police without a warrant · Denied access to family-appointed lawyer · Family refused visitation rights · Closed trial

NAME	BACKGROUND	CHARGES AND ACTIVITIES ALLEGED	PROCEDURAL HISTORY	PROCEDURAL PROTECTION DEROGATIONS
Xu Wenli [徐文立]	• Previously imprisoned for 12 years for participation in the Democracy Wall Movement • A founding member of the China Democracy Party (CDP)	*Charge* • **Endangering state security** *Activities alleged* • Founding and recruiting members for the CDP in Beijing and Tianjin • Attempting to establish a human rights monitoring group and publishing two unauthorized issues of a newsletter on March 23–24, 1998	• Arrest: November 30, 1998 • Trial: December 12, 1998, Beijing No.1 Intermediate People's Court[45] • Sentence: **13 years' imprisonment; 3 years' subsequent deprivation of political rights**, December 21, 1998 • Release: Medical parole, December 24, 2002	• Only his wife was permitted to attend the hearing
Xiao Yunliang [肖雲良]	• Former worker, Liaoyang Ferroalloy Factory • Led workers in a series of protests alleging corruption in factory and demanding back pay (2002–2003)	*Charges* • **Illegal assembly and demonstration** • **Subversion of state power** *Activities alleged* • Leading approximately 2,000 workers from the Liaoyang Ferroalloy Factory, and 15,000 workers from other factories, in a series of major public demonstrations with Yao Fuxin (see below) (March 2002) • Protesting alleged corruption in the factory and demanding back pay	• Detention: March 20, 2002 • Formal arrest: March 29, 2002 • Trial: January 15, 2003, Liaoyang Intermediate People's Court • Sentence: **4 years' imprisonment; 2 years' subsequent deprivation of political rights**, May 9, 2003 • Appeal: Denied, June 27, 2003 • Release: February 23, 2006, 24 days before his four-year jail sentence ended	• Closed appeal hearing
Yan Zhengxue [严正学][46]	• Artist from Taizhou, Zhejiang	*Charge* • **Inciting subversion of state power** *Activities alleged* • Participating in a "hostile organization" *Activities believed to have resulted in charges* • Assisting farmers in filing lawsuits and petitions against corrupt officials	• Detention: October 18, 2006 • Indictment: Late January, 2007 • Trial: April 5, 2007, Taizhou Intermediate People's Court • Sentence: 3 years' imprisonment; 1 year's deprivation of political rights, April 13, 2007[47]	• Denied access to lawyer after detention
Yao Fuxin [姚福信]	• Former worker, Liaoyang Ferroalloy Factory • Led workers in a series of protests alleging corruption in factory and demanding back pay (2002–2003)	*Charges* • **Illegal assembly and demonstration** • **Subversion of state power** *Activities alleged* • Leading approximately 2,000 workers from the Liaoyang Ferroalloy Factory, and 15,000	• Detention: March 17, 2002 • Formal arrest: March 29, 2002 • Trial: January 15, 2003, Liaoyang Intermediate People's Court • Sentence: **7 years' imprisonment; 3 years' subse-**	• Lawyer repeatedly refused access to Yao for over four months • Closed appeal hearing

NAME	BACKGROUND	CHARGES AND ACTIVITIES ALLEGED	PROCEDURAL HISTORY	PROCEDURAL PROTECTION DEROGATIONS
Yao Fuxin, *cont.*		workers from other factories, in a series of major public demonstrations with Xiao Yunliang (see above) (March 2002) · Protesting alleged corruption in the factory and demanding back pay	**quent deprivation of political rights**, May 9, 2003 · Appeal: Denied, June 27, 2003	
Ulan Shovo [乌兰少布]	· Former lecturer, Inner Mongolia University, IMAR	*Charge* · **Counterrevolutionary propaganda and incitement** *Activities alleged* · Writing two documents relating to human rights conditions in IMAR that were subsequently released abroad	· Arrest: July 31, 1991 · Trial: May 16, 1992, Hohhot Municipal Intermediate People's Court · Sentence: **5 years' imprisonment**, April 13, 1994 · Release: Reportedly late 1997	· Closed trial
Zhao Changqing [赵常青]	· Dissident from Shaanxi · Formerly imprisoned twice for participation in the 1989 democracy movement and protests against unjust local elections	*Charge* · **Inciting subversion of state power** *Activities believed to have resulted in charges* · Signing, with 191 dissidents from all over the country, an "Open Letter to the 16th Party Congress," calling, in particular, for political reforms, progress with regards to democratization, the protection of humans right in the country, the right to return for exiled Chinese politicians, and the release of prisoners of conscience	· Disappearance: November 7, 2002, authorities denied that he was in detention · Criminal detention: November 27, 2002 · Indictment: December 27, 2002 · Sentence: **5 years' imprisonment**, August 4, 2003, Xi'an Intermediate People's Court	· Closed trial

APPENDIX **III**

Incidents of Official Cover-Ups

Editors' Note:

The following table provides a collection of incidents in which the Chinese authorities, either at the local level or the central government, have attempted to control the flow of information. The chart highlights a selected number of cover-up incidents including epidemics, fatalities during natural disasters, corruption, incidents of protests and their subsequent crackdowns, and pollution. The lack of transparency and control of information that these cases illustrate has proven to have adverse effects on policy and program design, implementation, monitoring and evaluation by state and non-state actors. It hampers the ability of the Chinese government to analyze and assess situations and form relevant and useful solutions, which brings serious and harmful effects to society. For example, covering up the real scale of the impact of natural disasters could prevent the deployment of effective and efficient rescue efforts. When Typhoon Saomai, the strongest typhoon to hit China in the past half-century, swept the Fujian and Zhejiang shores, the local people were the ones to suffer due to an insufficient disaster response, while officials played down death and casualty figures.

The control of information also limits the ability of non-governmental actors, including civil society organizations, individual activists and business entities to review and assess situations, and contribute to and monitor the protection and promotion of the rights of Chinese people. All of these factors undermine the ability of the Chinese government to build meaningful partnerships with non-governmental actors in formulating relevant and useful solutions to a wide range of human rights issues. The Henan AIDS epidemic is a vivid but tragic example of the damage brought about by the control of information. In the early 1990s, thousands of Henan peasants contracted the HIV virus through selling their blood. The government not only denied the epidemic and did nothing to contain the mass contamination, but also punished individuals and NGOs trying to work on the issue. Cited in the table below are two cases related to this incident: that of Wan Yanhai, who was detained on the basis of "leaking state secrets," and the intimidation of the highly acclaimed Dr. Gao Yaojie, who criticized official conduct during the epidemic.

Lack of transparency and the control of information have also negatively affected the development of an independent media in China. Many of the cases cited in the table show that a media blackout was ordered by the authorities in order to cover up administrative wrongdoing. Press freedom is a positive force in preventing governmental abuse of power worldwide. Without press freedom, local authorities can easily hide both their own administrative wrongdoings and potentially embarrassing incidents. In real emergencies, no one will know where to turn for reliable information. The 2003 SARS outbreak has already demonstrated how cover-ups and media censorship can be lethal. An uncensored press could speedily disseminate information and potentially save lives.

INCIDENTS OF OFFICIAL COVER-UPS

DATE	EVENT	LOCATION	DESCRIPTION
1994–2002	HIV/AIDS epidemic[48]	Henan Province	• 1994: First case of HIV discovered among Henan blood sellers. • Health authorities (including the Ministry of Health, the Henan Province Department of Health and county health bureaus) hid information. • Blackouts on official websites and in newspapers concerning the seriousness of the AIDS epidemic and the blood-selling network in Henan. The government claimed that it had made great progress in strengthening management of medical organizations and ensuring the safety of the blood supply. • 2000–2002: Some international and domestic journalists who tried to visit the province detained and expelled. • Outspoken critics of the blood collection scandal, including retired Dr. Gao Yaojie (高耀洁), reported harassment by local officials, and were ordered not to speak to the press about Henan's AIDS epidemic. • Police questioned NGO workers offering help and confiscated tapes containing interviews with villagers. • August 2002: AIDS activist Wan Yanhai spent a month in custody on **state secrets** charges for delivering a government report on the spread of AIDS in Henan to people, the media, and on websites.
2000–present	Avian flu epidemic[49]	Nationwide	• Pre-2003: Chinese officials deny avian flu is present in China. • July 2003: Avian flu pandemic declassified. • 2004: Monitoring and information dissemination system on the disease established. • 2005: *Caijing Magazine* lists bird flu research in China that took place before 2003, illustrating that the official line was inaccurate. • December 2005: University of Hong Kong virologist accuses authorities of a cover-up because human cases of bird flu have been reported in areas that never announced an outbreak. Only one government-controlled laboratory is officially allowed to conduct bird flu tests, and its findings are not openly shared with foreign experts. • March 6, 2006: 9-year-old girl diagnosed with avian flu dies, Anji, Zhejiang Province. She is the tenth victim in the epidemic. No cases of avian flu reported in Zhejiang, although there are several accounts of infection and death there. • March 18, 2006: at a press conference, National Chief Veterinary Officer and the Director General of Veterinary Bureau says China has adopted a stringent reporting system regarding avian flu and has not covered up incidents. However, several suspected cover-ups are reported at this time, including the discovery of an H5N1-positive chicken smuggled into Hong Kong, suggesting a possible avian flu outbreak in Guangdong Province. Post-press conference, there are repeated pledges of transparency, but cover-up attempts continue to be documented, including: • April 2006: Approximately 8,000 chickens culled at a poultry farm in a village in Laixi City, Shandong Province, following the deaths of 400 chickens there. Farm-owner says officials told him not to talk about the cull because of **state secrets** concerns. Shandong Bird Flu Control Office official subsequently denied a bird flu outbreak.

INCIDENTS OF OFFICIAL COVER-UPS, *cont.*

DATE	EVENT	LOCATION	DESCRIPTION
2000–present	Avian flu epidemic	Nationwide	• April 26, 2006: *The Wall Street Journal* reports that China's bird flu fatalities may be higher than the 12 reported by the central government, as local officials may have concealed suspected cases of avian flu. • June 2006: A letter to the *New England Journal of Medicine* by eight Chinese researchers reveals that a Beijing man classified as having died of SARS in November 2003 in fact died of H5N1 avian influenza. One researcher is later asked to withdraw the letter. • November 2006: Hong Kong and U.S. researchers publish a paper in the "Proceedings of the National Academy of Science," stating that a new H5N1 virus sub-lineage, "the Fujian-like variant," may have broken out in Hong Kong and Southeast Asia in 2005. Ten days after the release of the findings, the head of the Veterinary Bureau at the Ministry of Agriculture refutes the report findings, saying the data was false and collected without official approval. • November 2006: China is criticized for its slow approach to supplying samples of new strains to the WHO for analysis.
March 2001	School blast[50]	Wanzai County, Jiangxi Province	• March 6, 2001: At least 42 children and teachers die in a blast at Fanglin Primary School. • Villagers claim that pupils were forced to make fireworks during school hours to fund their education. Authorities initially blame a "madman" who allegedly entered the school with explosives and set off the blast. • Villagers also claim that telephone lines were cut immediately after the explosion and police roadblocks were set at the only road into the village. • Sina.com shuts down its chat room in response to a flood of angry comments accusing the government of covering up the explosion. • Premier Zhu Rongji initially denies that fireworks were made at the school, relying on police reports. Ten days after the blast, he revokes his previous statement and orders the Public Security Ministry to send a taskforce to investigate the explosion.
December 2002– July 2003	Severe Acute Respiratory Syndrome (SARS) outbreak[51]	Nationwide	• November 2002: First SARS case appears in China. To date, SARS has infected thousands of people and killed nearly 800 worldwide. In China, the deadly virus claimed 348 lives and infected more than 5,300 people. Hong Kong registered 298 deaths out of 1,755 infections. • February 2003: When Hong Kong officials try to confirm media reports on SARS, a Guangdong health official says there is a legal requirement that infectious diseases have to be classified as **state secrets.** • February 10, 2003: Guangdong health authorities first publicly acknowledge a SARS outbreak. The first case had surfaced in December 2002 in Heyuan, and an investigative team compiled a report at that time, but no one was notified other than the central authorities. • April 10, 2003: When SARS reaches Beijing, local authorities cover it up, especially when the National People's Congress is

DATE	EVENT	LOCATION	DESCRIPTION
			in session. Military doctor Jiang Yanyong (蒋彦永) writes letter to the media and exposes the cover-up in the capital, leading to the dismissal of Health Minister Zhang Wenkang and Beijing mayor Meng Xuenong. The government subsequently admits that the real number of SARS cases is 10 times higher than official numbers. Meng re-emerges as a top official overseeing the South-North Water Transfer Project in October 2003.
November 2004– February 2005	Bacterial meningitis outbreak[52]	Nationwide	• November 2004: Cases of meningitis are reported, but covered up. • End of January 2005: Ministry of Health issues an emergency notice calling on the whole country to step up preventive measures against the disease. The Ministry of Health is criticized for withholding information on the outbreak until the epidemic had affected 24 provinces, with 546 reported cases and a death toll of 16.
June 2005	Flood[53]	Xinshao, Hunan Province	• May 31–June 6, 2005: Torrential rain sparks flooding in Xinshao. • June 7, 2005: The *Chongqing Morning Post* cites county government sources indicating that the number of fatalities resulting from the Xinshao flood could be in the hundreds, despite official statements that the total death count stood at only 40. The reported number had been scaled down because officials did not want to scare off foreign investment.

July 2005–present	Attempted removal of Taishi village head[54]	Panyu District, Guangdong Province	• Villagers in Taishi press for the removal of their village chief, who was charged with embezzling public funds. The villagers block the village office where the evidence in account books is kept, and go on a hunger strike in front of the district government office.
			• Officials seize the account books during a confrontation and break up the hunger strike. Thugs suspected of having connections with the authorities are hired to guard the entrances to the village.
			• Foreign journalists and grassroots activists, including Lü Banglie (吕邦列), who tried to enter the village, are beaten up. Yang Maodong (杨茂东), a lawyer who assisted the villagers, is detained for four months and continued to suffer from beatings and harassment after his release. Web sites with information on the beating are blocked, and discussions are deleted in some online forums. Due to the harassment and intimidations, a majority of the villagers who originally supported the removal of their village chief withdrew their support.
			• Crackdowns continue after villagers drop the motion to remove the village head:
			  • February 2006: Taishi villagers claim they are harassed and receive death threats if they attempt to leave the village following the visit by Yang Maodong.
			  • 2005 and late June, 2006: Taishi villager He Jinchao, who

INCIDENTS OF OFFICIAL COVER-UPS, *cont.*

DATE	EVENT	LOCATION	DESCRIPTION
			put other villagers in touch with activists and foreign reporters, is detained for 105 days in 2005 and taken into custody again in late June 2006 for driving without a license and riding an unlicensed motorcycle. • 2006: A *South China Morning Post* reporter is detained for eight hours in a police station and strip-searched for not carrying an identification document. However, the journalist claims that the real reason she is detained is to prevent her from reporting on the first anniversary of the Taishi incident. • September 28, 2006: Yang Maodong is formally arrested for running an illegal business.
November 2005	Pollution of the Songhua River resulting from a petrochemical plant blast[55]	Jilin Province	• November 13, 2005: An explosion at a petrochemical plant in Jilin releases more than 100 tons of toxic chemicals, including benzene, subsequently polluting the Songhua River. Water is cut off to nine million residents in Harbin, and the polluted water flows across the Russian border. The blast itself is not a secret, but the contamination of the Songhua River is covered up. • November 14, 2005: The Jilin government says the surrounding environment has not been contaminated, but simultaneously states that water has been released from a nearby reservoir in order to dilute the effects of any spillage of toxins. • November 18, 2005: The Jilin government notifies Heilongjiang. The Harbin city government initially says the water supply is only being suspended for maintenance, and only publicizes the contamination nine days after the spill. • November 23, 2005: The State Environmental Protection Administration admits serious pollution of the Songhua River. Environmental Minister Xie Zhenhua is dismissed and Wang Wei, a vice-mayor in charge of environmental protection and production safety of Jilin city, is reported to have committed suicide.
November–December 2005	Reporting deaths to the national health surveillance network[56]	Nationwide	• August 17, 2006: A Ministry of Health report reveals that mainland hospitals failed to report about a third of all deaths to the national health surveillance network; the notification failure rate peaked at 86% in one unnamed province. • Authorities delayed submitting data to the ministry in an average of 27% of instances, and 25% of causes of death were not pinpointed. • The survey was conducted in 130 local medical institutions in 29 provinces, autonomous regions and municipalities.
December 2005	Shooting at protesters[57]	Shanwei, Guangdong Province	• December 6, 2005: Police open fire to disperse protestors in Dongzhou, who were rallying against the construction of a power plant and inadequate compensation for confiscated land. The Shanwei government says three people were killed, while villagers put the toll as high as 20. • December 2005: Hundreds of paramilitary police, traffic

DATE	EVENT	LOCATION	DESCRIPTION
			• police, public security officers and border control officers are deployed to seal the village, and media coverage is limited to a few articles published by the official Xinhua News Agency and local Guangdong papers. • December 2005: The commanding officer that ordered the police to open fire is dismissed and three other senior law enforcement officials are reprimanded. • May 24, 2006: 12 residents are jailed for up to seven years for illegally manufacturing explosives, illegal assembly and disturbing public order.
January 2006	Cadmium pollution of the Xiang River[58]	Hunan Province	• January 6, 2006: The Xiang River in Hunan Province is contaminated with toxic cadmium during a silt cleaning operation. Workers at the Water Conservancy Company of Zhuzhou City mistakenly diverted river water into two basins used to separate cadmium discharged by a smelting factory. The water overwhelmed the basins and washed back into the Xiang River, which supplies potable water to Xiangtan City and the provincial capital Changsha. • January 8, 2006: The Hunan Environmental Protection Bureau states that the water supply is still drinkable, but an emergency report sent from the Xiangtan Environmental Protection Bureau to the provincial environmental protection bureau is exposed by the media; the report states that the cadmium level was 22 to 40 times above safe levels.
January 2006	Police clash with villagers over protests against unreasonable land compensation[59]	Sanjiao Township, Guangdong Province	• January 14, 2006: Several thousand policemen indiscriminately attack approximately 10,000 to 20,000 people, including protesters and passers-by, on a large highway. Villagers had been negotiating with the Sanjiao Township government for reasonable compensation after farmland in seven villages in the area was confiscated in order to build a highway and a factory for a Hong Kong-owned textile group. • Villagers state that a 15-year-old schoolgirl was beaten to death; her family later allegedly receives 130,000 *yuan* from the local government to say that their daughter had died after a heart attack. • Xinhua reports on the incident, stating that no one died in the protest and that two policemen and three villagers were injured due to stones and firecrackers that were thrown by village protesters. • February 24, 2006: Zhongshan party secretary Cui Guozhao denies the violence, arguing, "Where did you see police beating people? There was no such thing. . . . The [media] is irresponsible." Cui continued by stating that the farmers were not protesting over the requisition of their land but were rather seeking unreasonable compensation.
July–August 2006	Deadly clindamycin phosphate glucose injections[60]	Nationwide	• August 2006: Six people from Heilongjiang, Hubei, Hebei, Shaanxi, Sichuan and Hunan are confirmed dead from clindamycin phosphate glucose (CPG) and over 80 cases of severe reactions were reported from over 10 provinces after

INCIDENTS OF OFFICIAL COVER-UPS, *cont.*

DATE	EVENT	LOCATION	DESCRIPTION
			people received injections produced by the Anhui Huayuan Worldbest Biopharmaceutical Company. • July 29, 2006: The State Food and Drug Administration admits receiving a report about an adverse reaction case in Qinghai, but it did not issue a warning or a recall of the drug until a week later. The agency also denies cover-up attempts and defends its decision to keep the case from public knowledge to prevent "disrupting normal social life and causing unnecessary panic in society." • November 4, 2006: 10 victims, including four who had already died and were represented by their family members, file a lawsuit against the drug maker. The Shanghai Pudong New District People's Court reject the lawsuit on the grounds that the drug maker does not fall within Shanghai's jurisdiction and that Shanghai Worldbest and China Worldbest did not directly produce the drug.
August 2006	Typhoon Saomai death toll cover-up[61]	Southeast China	• August 2006: More than 400 people die and up to 4 million people lose their homes when Saomai, the strongest typhoon in the past half-century, sweeps through Fujian and Zhejiang provinces. Locals criticize the government's rescue efforts as being too little too late and insist that the death toll is much higher than official figures. • Immediately after the typhoon, a local newspaper puts the death toll at two, despite the massive destruction everywhere. Online sources say that they needed to rely on overseas media to report on the magnitude of the destruction.
August–November 2006	Lead and zinc poisoning[62]	Gansu Province	• August 2006: Media first reports on lead poisoning from factories in Gansu province. People from Xinxi village and its six neighboring villages with a population of around 5,000 have repeatedly complained, petitioned and protested about lead poisoning from factories in their area. Protesters are often detained by the police for questioning. • Soon after these reports, authorities order closure of the polluting factories, but villagers tell Radio Free Asia that six or seven factories still continued to pump out large quantities of black smoke and release untreated toxic sludge laden with heavy metals. • October 2006: Authorities put the number of people suffering from lead poisoning to just over 300, but local residents say the real figure is probably 2,000–3,000.
January–December 2006	Environmental statistics[63]	Nationwide	• 2006: The State Environment Protection Administration (SEPA) identifies a 2% discrepancy in its own annual calculations on nationwide carbon dioxide and sulfur dioxide emissions as compared to figures submitted by local governments. The environmental watchdog suspects that it had received fake data, as local governments had been under great pressure to meet clean air targets.

Appendices Notes

1. "PRC: Human Rights Defenders at Risk," Amnesty International, December 6, 2004, http://web.amnesty.org/library/Index/ENGASA170452004?open&of=ENG-CHN. "China Jails Uyghur Journalists for 'Separatism,'" Radio Free Asia, July 30, 2004, http://www.rfa.org/english/news/politics/2004/07/30/142490/.

2. "China Convicts 50 to Death in 'Terror Crackdown,'" July 30, 2004, Radio Free Asia. Available at Uyghur Human Rights Project, http://uhrp.org/articles/154/1/China-convicts-50-to-death-in-quotterror-crackdownquot/China-Jails-Uyghur-Journalist-For-quotSeparatismquot.html.

3. *State Secrets: A Pretext for Repression*, Amnesty International, 1996, http://www.amnesty.org/ailib/intcam/china/china96/secret/secret5.htm.

4. CASS and the Ministry of Foreign Affairs refused to confirm the sentence.

5. Chen Meng, "Man Who Exposed 'Blacklist' Ill in Prison," *China Rights Forum*, March 31, 1999, http://www.hrichina.org/public/contents/article?revision%5fid=2638&item%5fid=2637.

6. Shenzhen Municipality Intermediate People's Court Ruling No. 33, June 19, 1997. Available at Human Rights Watch, http://www.hrw.org/press/1999/apr/shenzhen.htm.

7. Ibid.

8. "The Sixth Political Prisoner Archive" (政治犯档案之六), Yangjianli.com, http://www.yangjianli.com/digest/zhangsanyiyan20031112f.htm; "Prisoner Information: He Zhaohui," Laogai.com, http://www.laogai.org/dissent/show.php?code=363&n=.

9. John Wilson Lewis and Hua Di, "China's Ballistic Missile Programs: "Technologies, Strategies, Goals," *International Security*, Vol. 17, No. 2 (Fall 1992).

10. "China, Cuba, Two African Nations Are Top Jailers of Journalists," *The Panama News*, http://www.thepanamanews.com/pn/v_11/issue_24/opinion_03.html.

11. "Hua's Second Conviction, 10-year Sentence Dismay Colleagues" (被指泄露国家机密华棣判十年), Standard University News Service, February 7, 2001, http://news-service.stanford.edu/news/2001/february7/huadi-27.html.

12. Ibid.

13. "In Custody," *China Rights Forum*, No. 4 (2003).

14. In response to this protest, on July 22, 1999 the Chinese government officially banned the Falun Gong.

15. "In Custody," *China Rights Forum*, No. 2 (2003).

16. "In Custody," *China Rights Forum*, No. 4 (2003).

17. In response to this protest, on July 22, 1999 the Chinese government officially banned the Falun Gong.

18. "In Custody," *China Rights Forum*, No. 2 (2003).

19. "Protestant House Church Member Liu Fenggang Released from Prison" (北京地下教会人士刘凤钢获释）, Radio Free Asia, February 4, 2007, http://www.rfa.org/mandarin/shen-rubaodao/2007/02/04/liufenggang.

20. "CPC Sentences Gao Zhan and Two Others to 10 Years' Imprisonment or More for Spying" (中共以间谍罪名判处高瞻等叁人至少十年徒刑）, *Central News Agency*, July 25, 2001.

21. HRIC Press Release, "Trial Date Set for Hangzhou Environmentalist," *Human Rights in China*, May 12, 2006.

22. "Prisoner Profile: Tohti Tunyaz", Human Rights in China, February 17, 2003, http://www.hrichina.org/public/contents/1899.

23. "No Word For Wife on Jailed Uyghur Writer's Fate,'" Radio Free Asia, June 19, 2006. Available at http://uhrp.org/articles/172/1/No-Word-For-Wife-On-Jailed-Uyghur-Writers-Fate/No-Word-For-Wife-On-Jailed-Uyghur-Writers-Fate.html.

24. "In Custody," *China Rights Forum*, No. 4 (2003).

25. In response to this protest, on July 22, 1999 the Chinese government officially banned the Falun Gong.

26. "In Custody," *China Rights Forum*, No. 2 (2003).

27. "House Church Leader's Sentence Wrongfully Prolonged," HRIC Press Release, February 3, 2006, http://www.hrichina.org/public/contents/26775.

28. "Update on Xu Zerong's Court Appeal," *Dialogue*, no. 11 (Spring 2003): 7, The Dui Hua Foundation, http://www.duihua.org/our_work/publications/newsletter/nl_pdf/nl_11_1.pdf.

29. "In Custody," *China Rights Forum*, No. 4 (2003).

30. In response to this protest, on July 22, 1999 the Chinese government officially banned the Falun Gong.

31. "Zhao Yan Appeals Against Three-year Sentence on Fraud Charge," Reporters Without Borders, September 4, 2006, http://www.rsf.org/article.php3?id_article=18663.

32. Ibid.

33. "MacKay Confident China Won't Execute Canadian Citizen," Initiative in to Save Huseyin Celil, November 20, 2006, http://www.huseyincelil.com/mackay_death_peanlty.html.

34. "Ministry Refuses to Send Charged Uygur to Canada," *South China Morning Post*, December 13, 2006.

35. "Prisoner Profile: Huseyin Celil," *China Rights Forum*, No. 4 (2006): 114.

36. Geoffrey York, "Celil's Desperate Family Had Given up Hope", *Globe and Mail*, February 8, 2007, http://www.theglobeandmail.com/servlet/story/RTGAM.20070208.w2celil0208/BNStory/International/home.

37. "Human Rights Watch Urges China to Release Rights Activist Chen Guangcheng" (人权观察呼吁释放维权人士陈光诚), Voice of America, July 19, 2006, http://www.voanews.com/chinese/archive/2006-07/w2006-07-19-voa45.cfm.

38. "Ching Cheong Appeals Spying Conviction" (程翔要對間諜罪判決上訴), BBC, September 1, 2006, http://news.bbc.co.uk/chinese/trad/hi/newsid_5300000/newsid_5304500/5304530.stm.

39. "Ching Cheong Transferred to Guangzhou Prison to Serve Out Spying Sentence (程翔已经转移至广州监狱服刑)," BBC, February 9, 2007, http://news.bbc.co.uk/chinese/trad/hi/newsid_6340000/newsid_6345000/6345075.stm.

40. "China Gives Rights Lawyer Suspended Sentence," Reuters (via Yahoonews), December 22, 2006, http://news.yahoo.com/s/nm/20061222/wl_nm/china_lawyer_dc_2.

41. "Case Profile—Hada," Human Rights in China, April 16, 2001, http://www.hrichina.org/public/contents/2541.

42. "Tenzin, Delek Rinpoche: Vital Statistics and Chronology," Tibet Online, http://www.tibet.org/itsn/campaigns/lithang/reports/ustc/ustc-factsheetside1.doc.

43. "China: Death Sentence of Tenzin Deleg Rinpoche," Project on Extrajudicial Executions, Center for Human Rights and Global Justice, New York University School of Law, http://www.extrajudicialexecutions.org/communications/china.html.

44. "Tibetan Religious Leader Sentenced to Life in Prison; ICT Calls for the Immediate Release of Tenzin Delek Rinpoche," International Campaign for Tibet, January 26, 2005, http://www.savetibet.org/news/newsitem.php?id=700.

45. Beijing No.1 Intermediate People's Court, Verdict on Xu Wenli (北京市第一中級人民法院刑事判決書). Available at 64memo.com, http://www.64memo.com/b5/7642_5.htm.

46. "Yan Zhengxue Indicted for 'Participating in a Hostile Organization,' Says He Will Commit Suicide If Given Long Sentence" (律师会见严正学说案有重大隐情严将以死抗争), Radio Free Asia, February 5, 2007, http://www.rfa.org/mandarin/shenrubaodao/2007/02/05/yan.

47. "Yan Zhengxue Sentenced to 3 Years' Imprisonment for Inciting Subversion", (严正学被浙江法院以煽动颠覆罪判刑三年) Radio Free Asia, April 13, 2007, http://www.rfa.org/cantonese/xinwen/2007/04/13/china_dissident_trial.

48. Wan Yanhai, "China Health News and the Henan Province Health Scandal Cover-Up" (万延海，"河南人民健康的遮羞布"), *Aizhixing Institute Beijing*, January 30, 2001, http://www.aizhi.org/news/jkb2.htm (English summary available at: http://www.usembassy-china.org.cn/sandt/ChinaHealthNews-criticism.html). "AIDS Activist Freed after Confession," *South China Morning Post*, September 21, 2002. Brad Adams, "China's Other Health Cover-up," *The Asian Wall Street Journal*, June 12, 2003. "China Says It's Caring for Henan HIV/AIDS Villagers," Reuters, March 8, 2006.

49. Cao Haili, Zhang Fan, Chang Hongxiao, Li Yan, Lou Yi and Ji Minhua, "The Lethal Avian

Flu,"（曹海丽，张帆，常红晓，李琰，楼夷，季敏华，"致命禽流感"），*Caijing Magazine*, October 17, 2005: 51. "Expert Says China Hiding Bird Flu, WHO Disagrees," *Reuters*, December 9, 2005, http://asia.news.yahoo.com/051209/3/2c5tq.html. "Jia Youling: To Date No Cover-ups of Avian Flu Found, But If Found They Will Be Severely Punished （"贾幼陵：至今未发现瞒报疫情现象一旦发现严处"），*China News Agency*, March 18, 2006. "UNFPA: Smuggled Live Chickens With Avian Flu Prompted WHO to Trace Their Origins （"联国粮农：粤可能已出事 港揭走私禽流鸡 世卫查源头"），*Hong Kong Economic Times*, February 3, 2006. "Hong Kong Bird Flu Finds Raise New Fears About China Reporting," *Agence France Presse*, February 2, 2006, "Authorities Covered up Parasitic Infection in Chickens in Guangzhou, Said Chicken Farm Owner"（"死鸡鸡场东主指当局 隐瞒"），*Apple Daily*, March 3, 2006. "Hong Kong Doctor Urges Banning Import of Mainland Chickens After Hawker in Guangzhou Market Dies of Suspected Human Avian Flu" （"港医生促即禁止内地鸡只输港 街市工作穗汉染禽流感死"），*Apple Daily*, March 4, 2006. "9-year-old Zhejiang Girl Dies of Avian Flu After Visiting Anhui（"浙江九岁女染禽疫死 曾探安徽养病鸡亲戚"），*Orisun*, March 9, 2006. "News Ban for Guangzhou's Suspected Second Bird Flu Case, Sources Say," *South China Morning Post*, April 11, 2006. Kevin Huang, "8,000 Birds Culled in Shandong, Says Villagers," *South China Morning Post*, April 18, 2006. "China's Bird Flu Toll May Be Higher," *United Press International*, April 26, 2006, http://pda.physorg.com/lofi-news-reported-flu-officials_65331429.html. Mary Ann Benitez and Josephine Ma, "Beijing SARS Case H5N1, Doctors Say," *South China Morning Post*, June 23, 2006. Patsy Moy, "Bird Flu Project Constrained by Mainland, Says Expert," *South China Morning Post*, June 26, 2006. "Chinese Minister Refutes Reports on New H5N1 Strain," *Xinhua News Agency*, November 10, 2006. Lindsay Beck, "China Shares Bird Flu Samples, Denies New Strain Report," *Reuters*, November 10, 2006. Jane Cai, "Bird Flu Whistle-blower Detained, Sparking Fears of Revenge," *South China Morning Post*, December 6, 2005. Jane Cai, "Lawyer Kept away from Farmer Who Blew Whistle," *South China Morning Post*, December 8, 2005. Xu Xiang, "China Plagued by Bird-flu Coverups," *Asia Times Online*, June 8, 2006, http://www.atimes.com/atimes/China/HF08Ad01.html. Jane Cai, "Bird Flu Whistle-blower Gets Jail for Graft," *South China Morning Post*, July 10, 2006.

50. "Madman Blamed for Blast," *South China Morning Post*, March 9, 2001. "Blast Girl: We Made Fireworks for Four Years," *South China Morning Post*, March 10, 2001. Tom Mitchell, "Isolated and Powerless, Blast Village Awaits News," *South China Morning Post*, March 12, 2001. Vivien Pik-kwan Chan, "Pupils 'Did Make Fireworks'," *South China Morning Post*, March 16, 2001. "Zhu Promise to Widen Blast Probe Welcomed," *South China Morning Post*, March 17, 2001.

51. Josephine Ma, "Beijing Has 10 Times More Cases Than Reported," *South China Morning Post*, April 21, 2003. Allen T. Cheng, "Sackings Will Help Foster Openness, Analysts Predict," *South China Morning Post*, April 21, 2003. Bill Savadove, "Sars Cover-up Emboldens Mainland Journalists to Seek out the Truth," *South China Morning Post*, June 9, 2003. "Deadly 'Cover-up'," *The Standard*, June 19, 2003. Nailene Chou Wiest, "Rapid Return to the Top for Sacked Beijing Mayor," *South China Morning Post*, October 2, 2003. Mary Ann Benitez, "Health Chief Was Told Outbreak a State Secret," *South China Morning Post*, January 13, 2004.

52. Mary Ann Benitez and Jane Cai, "HK Seeks Facts About Deadly Outbreak", *South China Morning Post*, February 1, 2005.

53. "Cover-up of Actual Fatality in the Flood in Hunan"（"湖南爆隐瞒灾情疑云 被指恐损形象 少报死难者 当局否认"），*Hong Kong Economic Times*, June 7, 2005.

54. Siew-ying Leu, "Riot Police Broke up Panyu Hunger Strike, Arresting 18," *South China Morning Post*, September 1, 2005. Siu-sin Chan, "Panyu Clears Village Chief of Corrup-

tion," *South China Morning Post*, October 1, 2005. "Chinese Protest Lawyer 'Arrested'," *BBC News*, October 6, 2005. Siew-ying Leu, "Censors Close Website of Pro-Taishi Professor," *South China Morning Post*, October 7, 2005. "Two Journalists Intending to Investigate Taishi Incident Beaten Up" ("两名外国记者前往太石村采访被打"), *Radio Free Asia*, October 10, 2005. Leu Siew Ying, "State of Fear Returns to Taishi," *South China Morning Post*, February 10, 2006. Leu Siew Ying, "We Will Not Be Bowed or Broken," *South China Morning Post*, September 13, 2006. Leu Siew Ying, "Detained Rights Activist and Lawyer Formally Arrested," *South China Morning Post*, October 3, 2006.

55. Shi Jiangtao and Josephine Ma, "'Serious Pollution' of River After Blast Finally Admitted," *South China Morning Post*, November 24, 2005. Richard McGregor, "China's Response to Disasters Impeded by Secrecy," *Financial Times*, November 27, 2005. Jiangtao Shi, "More Heads to Roll over Chemical Spill," *South China Morning Post*, December 4, 2005. Jiangtao Shi, "Vice-mayor of Spill City Kills Himself," *South China Morning Post*, December 8, 2005.

56. Sun Xiaohua, "Hospitals Fail to Report Deaths," *China Daily*, August 17, 2006. Vivien Cui, "Mainland Hospitals Keep Mum over Deaths," *South China Morning Post*, August 18, 2006.

57. Minnie Chan, "Villagers Reportedly Shot Dead During Land Dispute," *South China Morning Post*, December 8, 2005. "Riot Village Sealed off in Hunt for Protesters," *South China Morning Post*, December 10, 2005. Audra Ang, "China Detains Commander in Protest Deaths," *Associated Press via Yahoo! News*, December 11, 2005. Jane Cai, "Media Muted on Shanwei Incident," *South China Morning Post*, December 12, 2005. "China Steps up 'Patriotic Education' as Dongzhou Mourns its Dead," *Radio Free Asia*, April 6, 2006. Leu Siew Ying and Kristine Kwok, "Prison Terms for Dongzhou Rioters," *South China Morning Post*, May 25, 2006.

58. Zhuang Pinghui, "In a Grim Irony, Cleanup Spills Cadmium into Yangtze Tributary," *South China Morning Post*, January 9, 2006. Hung Kafei, "Who's Lying: the Pollution of Xiang River by Heavy Dose of Cadmium" (洪克非，"谁在说谎¾湘江镉污染事件内幕追踪"), *China Youth Daily*, January 10, 2006. "Hunan Officials Covered-up Cadmium Pollution of Xiang River Forced 600,000 Residents to Drink Poisonous Water (湖南隐瞒湘江镉污染60万人饮毒水)", *Orisun*, January 12, 2006. Edward Cody, "A Stand Against China's Pollution Tide," *Washington Post*, January 12, 2006.

59. "Scores Injured as China Police Quell Protest: Residents," AFP (via Yahoonews), January 15, 2006; "Traffic Blockade Ends in Guangdong," Xinhuanet via Chinaview.cn, January 15, 2006, http://news.xinhuanet.com/english/2006-01/15/content_4055529.htm; "Dozens Injured as Over 10,000 Police and Villagers Clash in Zhongshan" (中山逾萬警民衝突數十傷), Ming Pao, January 16, 2006; "Police in China Hurt Villagers, Protesters Say," New York Times, January 17, 2006; "Family of Dead Teen Paid to Keep Quiet: Villagers," *South China Morning Post*, January 17, 2006. Leu Siew Ying, "Zhongshan Party Chief on Defensive over Clashes," South China Morning Post, February 24, 2006.

60. Kevin Huang, "Shaanxi Women Believed to Be the Fourth Victim of Deadly Antibiotic," *South China Morning Post*, August 8, 2006. Vivien Cui, "Drug Watchdog Denies Cover-up over Deadly Antibiotic Scandal," *South China Morning Post*, August 9, 2006. "One More Dead from Deadly Antibiotic" ("欣弗死亡人数再增1人"), *Apple Daily*, August 9, 2006. Ng Tze-wei, "Court Rejects Lawsuits by Victims of Fatal Antibiotic," *South China Morning Post*, December 13, 2006.

61. "Fujian Government Criticized for Covering up Saomai Death Toll" (福建风灾死者骤增至138 网民批政府隐瞒), *Ming Pao*, August 15, 2006. Chow Chung Yan, "Saomai's Trail of Shattered Lives," *South China Morning Post*, August 20, 2006.

62. "China Villages Battle Lead, Zinc Poisoning," Radio Free Asia, November 29, 2006.

63. "Watchdog Probing Chinese Pollution Data," Associated Press via Yahoo! News, December 28, 2006.

Glossary

I. GENERAL TERMS

CHINESE	PINYIN	ENGLISH
保守国家秘密	baoshou guojia mimi	protection of state secrets
保密	baomi	protected secret; also an abbreviation for 保守国家秘密
保密 (工作) 部门	baomi (gongzuo) bumen	state secrets bureau (not national-level)
保密范围	baomi fanwei	the scope of state secrets protection
保密工作	baomi gongzuo	the work of protecting state secrets
管制	guanzhi	public surveillance
国防保密	guofang baomi	protection of state secrets in national defense
机密	jimi	highly secret
解密	jiemi	declassify
较大影响	jiaoda yingxiang	[cases of] relatively high significance
绝密	juemi	top secret
劳动教养	laodong jiaoyang	reeducation through labor
劳教人员	laojiao renyuan	reeducation-through-labor inmates
密干	migan	secret agent
密级	miji	security classification
秘密保卫员	mimi baoweiyuan	state secrets protection personnel
秘密	mimi	secret (level)
内部	neibu	internal

CHINESE	PINYIN	ENGLISH
情报	qingbao	intelligence
少年管教	shaonian guanjiao	juvenile rehabilitation
少管所	shaoguansuo	juvenile rehabilitation facility
审查	shencha	investigate, examine, check
审核	shenhe	examine/check and verify
审批	shenpi	examine/check and approve
特别重大影响	tebie zhongda yingxiang	[cases of] very high significance
特情	teqing	special agent
为境外的机构、组织、人员窃取、刺探、收买、非法提供国家秘密、情报	wei jingwai de jigou, zuzhi, renyuan qiequ, citan, shoumai, feifa tigong guojia mimi, qingbao	stealing, gathering, procuring or illegally providing state secrets or intelligence outside of the country
宣传口径	xuanchuan koujing	circulation guidelines
预审	yushen	prejudication, pre-trial
舆论监督	yulun jiandu	public opinion supervision
直辖市	zhixiashi	directly-administered municipality
重大影响	zhongda yingxiang	[cases of] high significance

II. STATE BODIES

CHINESE	PINYIN	ENGLISH
保密委员会	Baomi Weiyuanhui	Committee on the Protection of State Secrets
国防部	Guofangbu	Ministry of National Defense
国防科技工业保密委员会	Guofang Keji Gongye Baomi Weiyuanhui	Committee on the Protection of State Secrets for the Science and Technology Industry, under the Ministry of National Defense
国家保密局	Guojia Baomiju	National Administration for the Protection of State Secrets (NAPSS)
国家保密工作部门	Guojia Baomi Gongzou Bumen	National State Secrets Bureau (i.e. NAPSS)

CHINESE	PINYIN	ENGLISH
国家科技监督局	Guojia Keji Jianduju	State Bureau of Technology Supervision
科技保密机构	Keji Baomi Jigou	Protection of State Secrets Agency for Science and Technology
企事业单位保密委员会	Qishiye Danwei Baomi Weiyuanhui	Committee on the Protection of State Secrets for Businesses and Enterprises
审判委员会	Shenpan Weiyuanhui	Sentencing Committee
市保密局	Shi Baomiju	Municipal State Secrets Bureau
外事保密机构	Waishi Baomi Jigou	Protection of State Secrets Agency for Foreign Affairs
中央保密委员会办公室	Zhongyang Baomi Weiyuanhui Bangongshi	General Office of the Committee on the Protection of State Secrets
主管部保密委员会	Zhuguanbu Baomi Weiyuanhui	Committee on the Protection of State Secrets of the Department in Charge
专职保密机构	Zhuanzhi Baomi Jigou	Protection of State Secrets Agency for Particular Professions
最高人民法院保密委员会	Zuigao Renmen Fayuan Baomi Weiyuanhui	Committee on the Protection of State Secrets of the Supreme People's Court

III. PRC STATE SECRETS LAWS AND REGULATIONS CITED IN THIS REPORT

CHINESE NAME	ENGLISH NAME	ABBREVIATION USED (IF ANY)	PROMULGATION (P) & EFFECTIVE (E) DATES
中华人民共和国保守国家秘密法	Law on the Protection of State Secrets of the People's Republic of China	State Secrets Law	September 5, 1988 (P) May 1, 1989 (E)
中华人民共和国保守国家秘密法实施办法	Measures for Implementing the Law on the Protection of State Secrets of the People's Republic of China	Implementation Measures	May 25, 1990 (P)
保守国家机密暂行条例	Provisional Regulation on Protecting State Secrets		June 1951 (P)

CHINESE NAME	ENGLISH NAME	ABBREVIATION USED (IF ANY)	PROMULGATION (P) & EFFECTIVE (E) DATES
公安工作中国家秘密及其密级具体范围的规定	Regulation on State Secrets and the Specific Scope of Each Level of Secrets in Public Security Work	MPS Regulation	March 28, 1995 (P) May 1, 1995 (E)
检察工作中国家秘密及其密级具体范围的规定	Regulation on State Secrets and the Specific Scope of Each Level of Secrets in the Work of the People's Procuratorates	SPP Regulation	January 15, 1996 (E)
人民法院工作中国家秘密及其密级具体范围的规定	Regulation on State Secrets and the Specific Scope of Each Level of Secrets in the Work of the People's Courts	SPC Regulation	July 31, 1995 (P) August 8, 1995 (E)
司法行政工作中国家秘密及其密级具体范围的规定	Regulation on State Secrets and the Specific Scope of Each Level of Secrets in Judicial Administration Work	MOJ Regulation	August 31, 1995 (P) October 15, 1995 (E)
新闻出版保密规定	Regulation on the Protection of State Secrets in News Publishing		June 13, 1992 (P) October 1, 1992 (E)
社会科学研究工作中国家秘密及其密级具体范围的规定	Regulation on State Secrets and the Specific Scope of Each Level of Secrets in Social Science Research Work		April 21, 1995 (P)
劳动和社会保障工作中国家秘密及其密级具体范围的规定	Regulation on State Secrets and the Specific Scope of Each Level of Secrets in Labor and Social Security Work		January 27, 2000 (P)
工会工作中国家秘密及其密级具体范围的规定	Regulation on State Secrets and the Specific Scope of Each Level of Secrets in Trade Union Work		May 27, 1996 (P)
环境保护工作中国家秘密及其密级具体范围的规定	Regulation on State Secrets and the Specific Scope of Each Level of Secrets in Environmental Protection Work		December 28, 2004 (P)
土地管理工作中国家秘密及其密级具体范围的规定	Regulation on State Secrets and the Specific Scope of Each Level of Secrets in Managing Land and Resources Work		May 14, 2003 (P)
计划生育工作中国家秘密及其密级具体范围的规定	Regulation on State Secrets and the Specific Scope of Each Level of Secrets in Family Planning Work		May 16, 1995 (P)

CHINESE NAME	ENGLISH NAME	ABBREVIATION USED (IF ANY)	PROMULGATION (P) & EFFECTIVE (E) DATES
文化工作中国家秘密及其密级具体范围的规定	Regulation on State Secrets and the Specific Scope of Each Level of Secrets in Cultural Work		July 21, 1995 (P)
民政工作中国家秘密及其密级具体范围的规定	Regulation on State Secrets and the Specific Scope of Each Level of Secrets in Civil Affairs Work		February 29, 2000 (P)
卫生工作中国家秘密及其密级具体范围的规定	Regulation on State Secrets and the Specific Scope of Each Level of Secrets in Public Health Work		January 23, 1996 (P)
妇女工作中国家秘密及其密级具体范围的规定	Regulation on State Secrets and the Specific Scope of Each Level of Secrets in Women's Work		April 24, 1991 (P)
民族工作中国家秘密及其密级具体范围的规定	Regulation on State Secrets and the Specific Scope of Each Level of Secrets in Ethnic Work		March 17,1995 (P)
宗教工作中国家秘密及其密级具体范围的规定	Regulation on State Secrets and the Specific Scope of Each Level of Secrets in Religious Work		October 12, 1995 (P)
国家秘密保密期限的规定	Regulation on the Time Limits of State Secrets		September 19, 1990 (P)
最高人民法院关于审理为境外窃取、刺探、收买、非法提供国家秘密、情报案件具体应用法律若干问题的解释	The Supreme People's Court's Interpretation of Certain Issues Regarding the Specific Application of the Law When Trying Cases of Stealing, Gathering, Procuring or Illegally Providing State Secrets or Intelligence Outside of the Country	SPC Interpretation of Certain Issues	November 20, 2000 (P) January 17, 2001 (E)

Bibliography

I. CHINESE LANGUAGE SOURCES

"百姓网站换址重开 继续与读者互动." 《自由亚洲电台》, 2006年91月13日 ["Website of Magazine Baixing Reopened, Continues Interacting with Readers." Radio Free Asia, September 13, 2006].

"保密法修订草案稿将尽快上报国务院." 《法制日报》, 2006年12月5日 ["Revisions to the State Secrets Law Soon to be Submitted to the State Council." *Legal Daily*, December 5, 2006].

"北京大学保密委员会举办《保密责任书》签订仪式". 北京大学网站, 2005 年5月25日 ["Peking University Protection of State Secrets Committee Holds Ceremony to Issue Protection of State Secrets Responsibility Book." Peking University, May 25, 2005]. http://72.14.203.104/search?q=cache:VQOSkwnpDcEJ:www.research.pku.edu.cn/ displaynews.asp%3Fid%3D506+%E5%8C%97%E4%BA%AC%E5%A4%A7%E5%A D%A6%E6%B6%89%E5%AF%86%E4%BA%BA%E5%91%98%E7%AE%A1%E7%9 0%86%E6%9A%82%E8%A1%8C%E8%A7%84%E5%AE%9A&hl=en&lr=lang_ zh-CN.

"北京地下教会人士刘凤钢获释." 《自由亚洲电台》, 2006年9月13日 ["Protestant House Church Member Liu Fenggang Released from Prison." Radio Free Asia, February 4, 2007.] http://www.rfa.org/mandarin/shenrubaodao/2007/02/04/liufenggang.

"北江镉量降英德急截水 村民斥当局隐瞒." 《太阳报》, 2005年12月22日 ["North River Cadmium Level Drops, Yingde Cut Water Supplies; Villagers Blamed the Authorities for Covering Up." *Orisun*, December 22, 2005].

"不满兄被抓 粤汉率众杀警." 《文汇报》, 2006年2月14日 ["Angry Guangdong Villager Killed Police Officer for Summoning His Brother." *Wenweipo*, February 14, 2006].

曹海丽, 张帆, 常红晓, 李琰, 楼夷, 季敏华. "致命禽流感." 《财经》, 2005年10月17 日, 51页 [Cao Haili, Zhang Fan, Chang Hongxiao, Li Yan, Lou Yi and Ji Minhua. "The Lethal Avian Flu," *Caijing Magazine*, October 17, 2005, 51].

"彻底调查：政府信息公开条例的台前幕后." 《法制日报》, 2002年11月05日 ["A Thorough Investigation: The Inside Story on the Regulation on Making Government Information Public." *Legal Daily*, November 5, 2002].

"陈光诚二审料将书面审理 律师称证据多疑点应开庭" 《自由亚洲电台》, 2007年1月5日 ["Chen Guangcheng's Appeal Trial to Be Held on Paper Only, Lawyer Still Calls for Public Trial". Radio Free Asia, January 5, 2007.] http://www.rfa.org/mandarin/shenru baodao/2007/01/05/chen.

陈南轩(主编). 《绝对秘密：泄密、窃密案例集萃》. 北京：金城出版社，2001 [Chen Nanxuan, ed. *Absolute Secrets: A Selection of Cases Involving the Disclosure and Theft of State Secrets*. Beijing: Jincheng Publishing House, 2001].

陈绍基. "深入贯彻落实《保密法》 创工作新局面." 《南方日报》，2003年9月5日 [Chen Shaoji. "Thorough Implementation of the Law on the Protection of State Secrets Creates New Working Conditions." *Southern Daily,* September 5, 2003].

"程翔已经转至广州监狱服刑." BBC 中文广播，2007年2月9日 ["Ching Cheong Transferred to Guangzhou Prison to Serve Out Spying Sentence." BBC (Chinese Web site), February 9, 2007]. http://news.bbc.co.uk/chinese/trad/hi/newsid_6340000/newsid_6345000/6345075.stm.

成梅. "94.8％的公众确认近年来我国环境问题严重." 《中国青年报》，2006年11月20日 [Cheng Mei. "China's Environmental Problems are Grave, Say 94.8% in a Survey." *China Youth Daily*, November 20, 2006]. http://zqb.cyol.com/content/2006-11/20/content_1580181.htm.

"重庆法院秘密审理异见人士许万平." 自由亚洲电台网站，2005年11月3日 ["Chongqing Court Holds Secret Trial for Dissident Xu Wanping." Radio Free Asia, November 3, 2005]. http://www.rfa.org/cantonese/xinwen/2005/11/03/china_dissident.

"到2010年中国审计结果除涉国家机密等将全部公开." 新华网，2006年9月22日，["China's Audit Results Will be Made Public Until 2010 Unless They Contain State Secrets", Xinhua, September 22, 2006]. http://news.xinhuanet.com/lianzheng/2006-09/22/content_5124374.htm.

"地方官常瞒报死伤数字." 《苹果日报》，2005年6月14日 ["Officials Usually Hide Number of Causalities." *Apple Daily*, June 14, 2005].

董智慧. "从立法基础的演变看修《保密法》的必要性." 《保密工作》2003年7月：15页 [Dong Zhihui. "The Need to Look at Amending the State Secrets Law from the Basis of Evolving Legislation." *Protection of State Secrets Work* (July 2003): 15].

杜萌. "最高检确定今年侦查监督重点." 《法制日报》，2005年5月17日 [Du Meng. "Supreme People's Procuratorate Confirms Emphasis of Investigative Supervision This Year," *Legal Daily*, May 17, 2005]. http://202.99.23.215:8080/search/detail.jsp?dataid=39167&tableclassid=4_0.

"毒奶案亦隐瞒 港商北闯忧信息不通." 《香港经济日报》，2003年4月9日 ["Soymilk Poisoning Case Is Covered Up; Hong Kong Merchants Worry About Information Blockade While Doing Business in China." *Hong Kong Economic Times*, April 9, 2003].

"非法采煤发生塌冒事故 房山大安山矿难非法矿主被捕." 《北京娱乐信报》，2006年6月8日 ["Mine Owners Arrested for Accident by Illegal Mining." *Beijing Daily Messenger*, June 8, 2006].

"佛山邮政亏空案禁报导," 《明报》，2006年9月4日 ["Media Blackout on Foshan Postal Saving Embezzlement." *Ming Pao*, September 4, 2006].

"福建风灾死者骤增至138 网民批政府隐瞒." 《明报》，2006年8月15日 ["Fujian Government Criticized for Covering up Saomai Death Toll." *Ming Pao*, August 15, 2006].

"甘肃炼钢厂隐瞒漏煤气." 《头条日报》，2006年3月3日 ["Gansu Steel Mill Covered up Gas Leak." *Hong Kong Headline*, March 3, 2006].

"港医生促即禁止内地鸡只输港 街市工作穗汉染禽流感死." 《苹果日报》，2006年3月4日 ["Hong Kong Doctor Urges Banning Import of Mainland Chickens After Hawker in Guangzhou Market Dies of Suspected Human Avian Flu." *Apple Daily*, March 4, 2006].

"官员多为仕途「造数」." 《苹果日报》，2005年6月7日 ["Officials Will Make Things up for Better Career ." *Apple Daily*, June 7, 2005].

"关于信息公开问题的思考，" 中国人民大学信息资源管理学院，2005年7月8日 ["Some Thoughts About the Problems of Making Information Public," The School of Information Resource Management of Renmin University of China, July 8, 2005]. http://www. irm.cn/?q=node/210.

"广电一局瞒报五宗死亡事故，" 《大公报》，2005年4月6日 ["The No.1 Engineering Bureau of Guangdong Electronic Industrial Bureau Covered up Five Industrial Accidents in Five Months." *Tai Kung Po*, April 6, 2005].

广东省人民政府. 《广东省保守国家秘密实施细则》. 暨南大学网站 [Guangdong Province People's Government. "Detailed Rules on How to Implement the Protection of State Secrets in Guangdong Province," Jinan University]. http://zzb.jnu.edu.cn/show.asp? ArticleID=345.

"贵阳市'三五'普及保密法制宣传教育考核试卷." 贵阳市国家保密局网站. ["Examination Paper for Propaganda Education on Guiyang City's '3–5' Widespread Protection of State Secrets System," Guiyang City State Secrets Bureau]. http://www.gybmj.gov.cn/ zs/zcwd/wd-1.htm.

国家保密局. 《中华人民共和国保守国家秘密法实施办法》. 1990年发 [National Administration for the Protection of State Secrets. "Measures on Implementing the Law on the Protection of State Secrets of the People's Republic of China," promulgated 1990].

———. 《新闻出版保密规定》. 1992年6月13日发 [National Administration for the Protection of State Secrets. "Regulation on the Protection of State Secrets in News Publishing," promulgated June 13, 1992).

———. 《保密知识读本》. 北京：金城出版社，1999年 [National Administration for the Protection of State Secrets, ed. *Manual of State Secrets Protection Knowledge*. Beijing: Jincheng Publishing House, 1999].

———. 《国家秘密及其密级具体范围的规定选编 》（修订本）（机密）. 北京： 金城出版社，1997年 [National Administration for the Protection of State Secrets, ed. *Selected Regulations on State Secrets and the Specific Scope of Each Level of Secrets* (Revised Edition, Classified as "Highly Secret"). Beijing: Jincheng Publishing House, 1997].

"国家保密局调整方向，专家称：国家不能有太多秘密." 《瞭望东方周刊》. 2005年9月20日 ["National Administration for the Protection of State Secrets Corrects Direction, Expert Says 'Our Country Can't Have Too Many Secrets.'" *Oriental Outlook*, September 20, 2005]. http://cn.news.yahoo.com/050920/1005/2f3eh.html.

国家保密局法规处、天津市保密局（编）. 《我国有关保守国家秘密的法律规定选编》. 北京：金城出版社，2001年 [Legal Regulations Office of the Administration for the Protection of State Secrets and the Tianjin Municipality State Secrets Bureau, ed. *Selection of Laws and Regulations Related to the Protection of State Secrets in China*. Beijing: Jincheng Publishing House, 2001].

"国家保密局副局长丛兵指出：要加强信息安全保密管理工作." 《信息安全与通信保密》第11期，（2004年）：第6–8页 ["Zhang Congbing, Assistant Bureau Chief of the National Administration for the Protection of State Secrets, Says: We Must Strengthen the Management of Information Security and the Protection of State Secrets." *China Information Security Magazine* 11 [2004]: 6–8].

"国家保密局涉密信息系统安全保密测评中心介绍",《计算机安全》第3期, 2003年: 第53–54页 ["An Introduction to the National Administration for the Protection of State Secrets' Information System for Secret Matters' Secure Protection of Secrets Survey and Analysis Center." *Computer Security* 3 (2003): 53–54].

国家保密局宣传教育处（编）. 《违反保密法律法规承担的法律责任》. 北京：金城出版社，1999 [National Administration for the Protection of State Secrets' Propaganda Education Bureau, ed. *The Legal Liability that One Must Bear for Violating Protection of State Secret Laws.* Beijing: Jincheng Publishing House, 1999].

"国务院法制办：'政府信息公开条例' 草案完成."《中国青年报》. 2004年6月1日 ["State Council Completes Draft of 'Regulation on Making Government Information Public," *China Youth Daily*, June 1, 2004].

"国务院法制办介绍《突发事件应对法(草案)》." 中国网, 2006年7月3日 ["State Council's Legislative Affairs Office Introduces *Draft Law on Emergency Response* ." China.com, July 3, 2006]. http://news.china.com/zh_cn/domestic/945/20060703/13444571.html.

"国务院原则通过政府信息公开条例(草案)."《法制日报》, 2007年1月17日 ["State Council Passes Draft Open Government Information Disclosure Regulation." *Legal Daily*, January 17, 2007].

"国新办就水污染防治情况举行新闻发布会." 搜狐新闻网站，2005年11月24日 ["State Council's National Administration on Press and Publications Holds Press Conference to Give Information on Efforts to Control Water Pollution," Sohu.com, November 24, 2005]. http://news.sohu.com/20051124/n227586623.shtml.

韩大元，杨福忠，"试论我国政府信息公开法治化,"《国家行政学院学报》, 年第2期, 2004：第58–62页 [Han Dayuan and Yang Fuzhong, "On the Politicization of the Law on Making Government Information Public," *Journal of China National School of Administration* 2 (2004): 58–62].

"河北 "谁是真凶" 疑案引人关注."《法制日报》, 2005年3月17日 ["Who's the Real Murderer in Hebei? Doubts on the Case Cause Concern." *Legal Daily*, March 17, 2005]. http://legaldaily.com.cn/xwzx/2005-03/18/content_197214.htm.

何清涟.《中国人权研究报告：中国政府如何控制媒体》. 纽约：中国人权，2005年 [He Qinglian. *Media Control in China: A Report by Human Rights in China.* New York: Human Rights in China, 2005].

洪克非. "谁在说谎：湘江镉污染事件内幕追踪."《中国青年报》, 2006年1月10日 [Hong Kefei. "Who's Lying: the Pollution of Xiang River by Heavy Dose of Cadmium." *China Youth Daily*, January 10, 2006].

"湖南爆隐瞒灾情疑云 被指恐捐形象少报死难者 当局否认."《香港经济日报》, 2005年6月7日 ["Cover-up of Actual Fatality in the Flood in Hunan." *Hong Kong Economic Times*, June 7, 2005].

"湖南隐瞒湘江镉污染60万人饮毒水."《太阳报》, 2006年1月12日 ["Hunan Cover-up of Cadmium Pollution of Xiang River Forced 600,000 Residents to Drink Poisonous Water." *Orisun*, January 12, 2006].

胡舒立. "假如灾难即将来临."《财经》, 2005年10月17日 [Hu Shuli. "Facing Future Disasters." *Caijing Magazine*, October 17, 2005].

湖南省长沙市中级人民法院，《刑事判决书(师涛)》，（2005）长中刑一初字第29号 [Changsha Intermediate People's Court of Hunan Province, Changsha Intermediate People's Court Criminal Ruling (for Shi Tao), Changsha First Trial Docket No. 29, 2005]. The Chinese verdict with an accompanying English translation is available online at: http://www.globalvoicesonline.org/2005/09/06/warning-yahoo-wont-protect-you/.

湖南省怀化市中级人民法院，《刑事判决书（张善光)》，（1998) [Huaihua City Intermediate People's Court of Hunan Province, Criminal Court Ruling (for Zhang Shanguang), December 27, 1998]. An English translation is available online at HRIC: http://hrichina.org/public/contents/2853.

怀化市中级人民法院. "湖南省怀化市中级人民法院刑事判决书." 1998年12月27日 [Huaihua City Intermediate People's Court. "Criminal Ruling of the Huaihua City Intermediate People's Court of Hunan Province," December 27, 1998].

黄桐华、张子学，"政府信息公开与保密管理.《秘书》，（2005年5月)：第5–6页 [Huang Tonghua and Zhang Zixue. "Making Government Information Public and the Management of Protecting State Secrets." *Secretary* (May 2005): 5–6].

"吉林省长公开道歉：谁为松花江流域污染买单？" 多维新闻网，2005年11月24日 ["Jilin Mayor Publicly Apologizes and Asks, Who Will Pay for the Pollution of the Songhua River?" Duowei News, November 24, 2005]. http://www1.chinesenewsnet.com/MainNews/SinoNews/Mainland/2005_11_24_1_51_48_311.html.

"吉林市暂未公布水污染消息 寄希望于放水稀释." 雅虎资讯，2005年11月25日 ["Jilin Not Yet Announcing News of River Spill, Hoping Diluting Water Will Help," Yahoo News, November 25, 2005]. http://cn.news.yahoo.com/051125/1055/2g8lg.html.

"加强办案保密工作的建议"，《人民检察》，（1997年8月)：35–36页 ["Suggestions on Strengthening Protection of Secrets Work When Handling Cases." *People's Procuratorate* (August 1997): 35–36].

"加强保密法制建设 依法管理保密工作." 《信息网络安全》，2005年3月，第9–10页 ["Strengthening the Establishment of a System to Protect State Secrets and Doing the Administration of Protection of State Secrets Work According to Law." *China Net Information Security* (March 2005): 9–10].

"贾幼陵：至今未发现瞒报疫情现象一旦发现严处." 中国新闻社，2006年3月18日 ["Jia Youling: To Date No Cover-ups of Avian Flu Found, But If Found They Will Be Severely Punished." China News Agency, March 18, 2006].

"家属：程翔被转送北京天河监狱." BBC 中文广播，2007年1月4日 ["Jailed Journalist Ching Cheong Has Been Transferred to Tianhe Prison in Beijing, Family Says." BBC, January 4, 2007.] http://news.bbc.co.uk/chinese/trad/hi/newsid_6220000/newsid_6229700/6229749.stm.

蒋美仕、杨如、任树言. "市场化、网络化条件下科技保密管理体系的结构优化." 《中国科技论坛》，2005年，第 4 期 [Jiang Meishi, Yang Ru, and Ren Shuxin. "How to Optimize the Science and Technology Protection of State Secrets Management System Given the Current Developments in Marketization and Networking." *Forum on Science and Technology in China 4* (2005). Available at: http://www.jhskj.net/web_info09/info2005-9-7/0859@1611053.html.

"交警队为评先瞒报420起事故." 《北京晨报》，2006年5月30日 ["Traffic Police Covered up 420 Accidents for a Higher Rank." *Beijing Morning Post*, May 30, 2006].

"禁采访半世纪最大矿难." 《苹果日报》，2005年2月16日 ["Press Coverage on the Worst Ever Coal Mine Blast in Liaoning Forbidden." *Apple Daily*, February 16, 2005].

"京报封锁抗议杀狗消息." 《明报》，2006年11月13日 ["Beijing Newspapers Block Rally Against Dog-killing." *Ming Pao*, November 13, 2006].

"京封杀《财经》杂志." 《明报》，2003年6月25日 ["Beijing Clamps Down on Outspoken Magazine *Caijing*." *Ming Pao*, June 25, 2003].

景涛. "广州：清理解密十万馀项　为信息公开提供保障." 《保密工作》（2003年5月）：6–7页 [Jing Tao. "Guangzhou: To Guarantee That Information is Made Public, More Than 100,000 of Secrets Get Declassified." *Protection of State Secrets Work* (May 2003): 6–7].

"拒絕公开信息市民可打行政官司." 《法制日报》，2006年12月3日 ["Citizens Can Sue Local Government for Refusal to Disclose Information." *Legal Daily*, December 3, 2006].

"老总停职新京报编辑部怠工　中宣部著眼「政治安全」下令改组." 雅虎资，2005年12月29日 ["Reporters on Strike after Chief Editor Sacked and Party Propaganda Unit Order an Overhaul to Ensure Political Correctness," Yahoo News, December 29, 2005]. http://hk.news.yahoo.com.

李友丰. "党委办公室要带头做好保密工作" 《秘书工作》7期（2003年）：第31–32页 [Li Youfeng. "Party Committee Office Must Lead the Work of Protecting State Secrets." *Secretarial Work* 7 (2003): 31–32].

李志东（主编）.《中华人民共和国保密法全书》（本书仅供各级保密部门、组织、人员使用）. 长春：吉林人民出版社，1999 [Li Zhidong, ed. *Compendium of Laws of the People's Republic of China on the Protection of State Secrets* (Circulation limited to departments, organizations and personnel doing state secrets protection work). Changchun: Jilin People's Press, 1999].

"联国粮农：粤可能已出事　港揭走私禽流鸡　世卫查源头." 《香港经济日报》，2006年2月3日 ["UNFPA: Smuggled Live Chickens With Avian Flu Prompted WHO to Trace Their Origins." *Hong Kong Economic Times*, February 3, 2006].

"两名外国记者前往太石村采访被打." 《自由亚洲电台》，2005年10月10日 ["Two Journalists Intending to Investigate Taishi Incident Beaten Up." Radio Free Asia, October 10, 2005].

"两会期间死伤报细数." 《苹果日报》，2005年3月4日 ["Death Toll Watered Down Before NPC Session." *Apple Daily*, March 4, 2005].

辽宁省国家保密局, 辽宁省无线电管理委员会办公室. "辽宁省国家保密局、宁省无线电管理委员会办公室文件，" 2005年3月12日 [Liaoning Province State Secrets Bureau and the Liaoning Province Wireless Administration Committee Office. "Documents from the Liaoning Province State Secrets Bureau and the Liaoning Province Wireless Administration Committee Office," March 12, 2005].

"六盘水副市长撒谎案被督办." 《北京青年报》，2006年11月22日 ["Vice-mayor Disciplined for Lies." *Beijing Youth Daily*, November 22, 2006].

刘坚. "司法行政保密工作要处理好4个关系." 《中国司法》第2期，1998年：第8页 [Liu Jian. "The Four Relationships that Must Be Dealt With in Judicial Administration Protection of Secrets Work." *China's Judiciary* 2 (1998): 8].

刘志才（主编），《保密法概论》. 北京：金城出版社，1996 [Liu Zhicai, ed. *Overview of the Law on the Protection of State Secrets*. Beijing: Jincheng Publishing House, 1996].

"律师会见严正学说案有重大隐情严将以死抗争." 《自由亚洲电台》，2007年2月5日 ["Yan Zhengxue Indicted for 'Participating in a Hostile Organization,' Says He Will Commit Suicide If Given Long Sentence." Radio Free Asia, February 5, 2007]. http://www.rfa.org/mandarin/shenrubaodao/2007/02/05/yan/.

"罗干强调进一步做好新形势下的保密工作. "《法制日报,》 2001年8月31日 ["Luo Gan Emphasizes Going Forward with Protection of State Secrets Work Under New Conditions." *Legal Daily*, August 31, 2001]. http://www.legaldaily.com.cn/gb/content/2001 08/31/content_23454.htm.

"罗干指出: 以 "三个代表" 为指导进一步做好新形势下的保密工作, " 人民网, 2001年8月30日 ["Luo Gan Says: We Should Go Forward with Protection of State Secrets Work Under New Conditions Using the 'Three Represents' as Our Guide." People.com.cn, August 30, 2001]. http://www.people.com.cn/GB/shizheng/16/20010830/ 548104.html.

"莫少平: 中国刑事立法执法弊端多. " 美国之音中文网, 2005年10月12日 ["Mo Shaoping: Abuses Abound in China's Criminal Legislation." Voice of America, October 12, 2005]. http://www.voanews.com/chinese/archive/2005-10/w2005-10-14-voa40.cfm? CFID=41958943&CFTOKEN=22569578.

"目前全国31个省（自治区、直辖市）政府建立政务公开管理制度. " 新华网, 2006年12月10日 ["Currently Across China There Are 31 Jurisdictions with Open Government Information Initiatives." Xinhua News, December 10, 2006]. http://news.xin-huanet.com/lianzheng/2006-12/10/content_5466668.htm.

"南丹礦難玩忽職守 河池專員被判徒刑. "《人民日報(海外版)》, 2004年2月20日 ["Official Jailed for Negligence at Nandan Mine Accident." *People's Daily* (Overseas), February 20, 2004].

《宁夏回族自治区党委: 自治区党委贯彻中共中央关于加强新形势下保密工作的决定的意见》, 宁夏回族自治区党委发, 资源天下网站, 2005年8月1日 ["Ningxia Hui Autonomous Region Party Committee: Opinion on the Autonomous Region Party Committee's Implementation of the CPC Central Committee's Decision to Strengthen Protection of State Secrets Work Under New Conditions," issued by the Ningxia Hui Autonomous Region Party Committee. Fortune Space, August 1, 2005].http://lib. fortunespace.net/Article/HTML/107492.shtml.

"农业大学5人染肺痨. "《明报》, 2005年4月5日 ["Five Tuberculosis Cases Confirmed at the University of Agriculture," *Ming Pao*, April 5, 2005].

皮纯协, 刘飞宇. "论我国行政公开制度的现状及其走向. "《法学杂志》第1期, （2002年）: 第8–12页 [Pi Chunxie and Liu Feiyu. "On the Reality and Direction of Our Country's Public System of Administration." *Law Science Magazine* 1 (2002): 8–12].

"聂树斌死刑案官方首次表态 律师可能提出国家赔偿, " 《人民日报》, 2005年 3 月18日 ["Authorities Indicate that Compensation May Be Available in the Wrongful Execution Case of Nie Shubin," *People's Daily*, March 18, 2005], http://legal.people.com.cn/GB/ 42733/3252380.html.

"器官移植: 加快规制的地带. "《财经》, 2005年11月28日 ["Organ Transplants: An Area That Needs to Be Quickly Regulated." *Caijing Magazine*, November 28, 2005]. http:// caijing.hexun.com/text.aspx?sl=2304&id=1423058.

"全国保密工作先进集体先进工作者表彰大会在京召开. " 安全保密新干线网, 2004年8月5日 ["Outstanding Collectives and Workers Nationwide in Protection of State Secrets Field Receive Awards at Conference Held in Beijing." Secure Protection of State Secrets New Network, August 5, 2004]. http://218.28.24.195/news3.3/33/20048511 5126.htm.

全国人大常委会. 《中华人民共和国保守国家秘密法》, 1989年 [Standing Committee of the National People's Congress, *Law on the Protection of State Secrets of the People's Republic of China*, 1989].

全国人大常委会法制工作刑法室及中国高级律师高级公证员培训中心编著.《中华人民共和国法律集注 (修订本)》. 北京：法律出版社，1992年 [Office of Law Drafting of the Standing Committee of the National People's Congress and the Training Center for Senior Level Notary Publics and Senior Level Lawyers, ed. *Legal Focus of the People's Republic of China* (Revised edition). Beijing: Legal Publishing House, 1992].

全国人民代表大会常务委员会.《中华人民共和国治安管理处罚法》，2005年8月20日发布，2006年3月1日生效 [Standing Committee of the National People's Congress, *Law on Punishing Public Order Management Crimes in the People's Republic of China,* issued August 20, 2005, implemented March 1, 2006].

"人权观察呼吁释放维权人士陈光诚." 美国之音中文网，2006年7月19日 ["Human Rights Watch Urges China to Release Rights Activist Chen Guangcheng." Voice of America, July 19, 2006]. http://www.voanews.com/chinese/archive/2006-07/w2006-07-19-voa45.cfm.

"陕西上下串通瞒矿难 上周致14死伤遗属获赔20万私了." 《太阳报》，2005年9月20日 ["Victims' Families Received 200,000 Yuan for Keeping Their Mouth Shut," *Orisun*, September 20, 2005.]

"山西临汾发生矿难隐瞒死亡人数案省委严令彻查." 《中新网》，2003年1月14日 ["Provincial Party Chief Called for Investigation of Mine Blast Cover up." Chinanews.com, January 1, 2003]. http://www.chinanews.com.cn/n/2003-01-14/26/263287.html.

上海市第二中级人民法院.《刑事判决书 (郑恩宠)》，（2003）沪二中刑初字第136号 [Shanghai No. 2 Intermediate People's Court. Shanghai No. 2 Intermediate People's Court Criminal Verdict (for Zheng Enchong), Shanghai Criminal Docket No. 136, 2003]. English translation is available online at: http://www.hrichina.org/public/contents/3471.

"是否刑讯逼供 警察出庭质证：四川规定两种情况下翻供成立."《法制日报》，2005年6月7日 ["Police Testify as to Whether or Not Torture Was Used to Extract Confessions: Sichuan Stipulates Two Situations Under Which Confessions May Be Retracted." *Legal Daily*, June 7, 2005]. http://www.legaldaily.com.cn/xwzx/2005-06/07/content_150861.htm.

深圳市中级人民法院. "广东省深圳市中级人民法院刑事裁定书." 1997年6月19日 [Shenzhen Intermediate People's Court. "Criminal Ruling of the Shenzhen Intermediate People's Court of Guangdong Province," June 19, 1997].

"水危机与政府的负责."《中国新闻周刊》，2005年11月28日 ["The Water Crisis and the Government's Responsibility." *China Newsweek*, November 28, 2005].

"死鸡鸡场东主指当局隐瞒."《苹果日报》，2006年3月3日 ["Authorities Covered up Parasitic Infection in Chickens in Guangzhou, Said Chicken Farm Owner." *Apple Daily*, March 3, 2006].

"四川4官瞒疫情撤职."《明报》，2005年8月7日 ["Four Officials Sacked for Hiding Swine Flu Epidemic." *Ming Pao*, August 7, 2005].

四川省高级人民法院. "四川省高级人民法院刑事裁定书，川刑终字第43号（2004）[Sichuan Higher People's Court. Sichuan Higher People's Court Criminal Ruling (on Li Zhi), No. 43 (2004), February 26, 2004].

四川省高级人民法院、四川省人民檢察院、四川省公安厅. "关于规范刑事证据工作的若干意见," 5月1日2005年 [Sichuan Higher People's Court, the Sichuan People's Procuratorate, and the Sichuan Department of Public Security. "Several Opinions Regarding the Standardization of Criminal Evidence Work," May 1, 2005].

"突发事件应对法已送人大审议 如无意外明年将出台." 中国网， 2006年9月22日 ["Draft Law on Emergency Response Submitted to NPC for Review and Likely to be Made Public Next Year." *China.com*, September 22, 2006]. http://www.china.com.cn/law/txt/2006-09/22/content_7182459.htm.

万延海. "河南人民健康的遮羞布." 爱知行动网站，2001年1月30日 [Wan Yanhai. "China Health News and the Henan Province Health Scandal Cover-up." Aizhixing Institute Beijing, January 30, 2001]. http://www.aizhi.org/news/jkb2.htm (English summary available at: http://www.usembassy-china.org.cn/sandt/ChinaHealthNews-criticism.html).

"王刚：保密工作部门要切实做好保密工作." 中国网，2003年1月16日 ["Wang Gang: Departments that Do Protection of State Secrets Work Should Do Their Work Conscientiously." China.com.cn, January 16, 2003]. http://www.china.org.cn/chinese/PI-c/263061.htm.

王守信. 《保密工作管理概论（修订版）》（内部发行）. 北京：金城出版社 ，1999 [Wang Shouxin. *Overview of the Management of State Secrets Protection Work* [Revised Edition, for Internal Circulation Only]. Beijing: Jincheng Publishing House, 1999].

"为境外窃取、非法提供国家秘密 席世国被判处无期徒刑." 《人民日报》，1999年8月30日 ["Xi Shiguo Sentenced to Life Imprisonment for Stealing and Illegally Providing State Secrets Outside of the Country," *People's Daily*, August 30, 1999].

"我国保密制度重置底线." 《新京报》，2005年9月20日 ["The Bottom Line of China's State Secret System." *The Beijing News*, September 20, 2005].

"我国大力推行政务公开 保密制度重置底线." 新闻中心，2006年9月20日 ["Our Country Pushes Ahead with Making Civil Affairs Public; the Baseline is Reset for the System of Protecting State Secrets." *Beijing News*, September 20, 2006]. Available at http://news.sina.com.cn/c/p/2005-09-20/03227811050.shtml.

"我国起草政府信息公开法 采访被拒记者可告官." 《法制晚报》，2004年10月9日 ["Our Country Drafts Law on Making Government Information Public; Journalists Turned Down for Interviews Can Report Officials." *Legal Daily* (evening edition), October 9, 2004].

"我国首次宣布解密国家秘密事项 因灾死亡人数不再是国家秘密." 《中国青年报》，2005年9月13日 ["Our Country's First Announcement of the Declassification of State Secret Matters; The Number of Deaths by Natural Disasters Will No Longer Be a State Secret." *China Youth Daily*, September 13, 2005.] http://zqb.cyol.com/content/2005-09/13/content_1175471.htm.

"我国因自然灾害死亡人数不再是国家秘密." 《中国青年报》， 网大论坛，2005年9月13日 ["The Number of Those Killed in Natural Disasters in Our Country is no Longer a State Secret," *China Youth Daily*, September 13, 2005.] Available at: http://forum.netbig.com/bbscs/read.bbscs?bid=1&id=6553677&page=27.

"武汉大学保密委员会工作职责." 武汉大学 ["The Work Responsibilities of the Wuhan University Protection of State Secrets Committee." Wuhan University]. http://sub.whu.edu.cn/benet/bumenzize/zizebaomiweiyuanhui.htm.

萧坊. "修改保密法，为制定信息公开法作准备." 《检察日报》，2005年9月26日 [Xiao Fang. "Amending State Secrets Law Is a Preparation for Drafting Law on Public Disclosure of Information." *Procuratorial Daily*, September 26, 2005]. http://www.jcrb.com/n1/jcrb843/ca416853.htm.

"行政机关提供政务信息不得收费." 《法制日报》，2006年12月5日 ["Administrative Bodies Cannot Charge Fees for Disclosing Government Information." *Legal Daily*, December 5, 2006].

徐潜（主编）．《保密工作实务全书》．吉林：吉林音像出版社，2004 [Xu Qian, ed. *Encyclopedia of Protection of State Secrets Work*. Jilin: Jilin Audio-Visual Publishing House, 2004].

"严正学被浙江法院以煽动颠覆罪判刑三年．"《自由亚洲电台》，2007年4月13日 ["Yan Zhengxue Sentenced to 3 Years' Imprisonment for Inciting Subversion." Radio Free Asia, April 13, 2007.] http://www.rfa.org/cantonese/xinwen/2007/04/13/china_dissident_trial/.

叶保强．"世界最危险的职场—中国煤矿坑．"《信报财经新闻》，2005年1月8日 [Yip Po-kueng. "The World's Most Dangerous Occupation—Mining in China." *Hong Kong Economic Journal*, January 8, 2005].

叶边鱼．"对事故数字瞒报真是公开的秘密？"《法制晚报》，2006年5月30日 [Ye Bianyu. "Is Covering Up Statistics Really an Open Secret?" *Fazhi Wanbao*, May 30, 2006].

"欣弗死亡人数再增1人，"《苹果日报》，2006年8月9日 ["One More Dead from Deadly Antibiotic." *Apple Daily*, August 9, 2006].

于志刚（编）．《危害国家安全罪》．北京：中国人民公安大学出版社，1999 [Yu Zhigang, ed. *Crimes of Endangering State Security*. Beijing: Chinese People's Public Security University Publishing House, 1999].

"粤北数百人骚乱冲击镇政府瑶民杀警官．"《苹果日报》，2006年2月14日 ["Hundreds Demonstrated Against Local Government in North Guangdong, Killed a Police Officer." *Apple Daily*, February 14, 2006].

张栋．"律师在保密工作中的角色 也谈于萍案件．"《律师文摘》，2002年12月，64–67页 [Zhang Dong. "The Role of Lawyers in Protection of Secrets Work and a Discussion of the Yu Ping Case." *Lawyers' Digest* (December 2002): 64–67].

赵国俊．"关于进一步完善我国党政机关公文处理法规建设问题的几点考．"《工商／经济管理论文》，2004年12月13日 [Zhao Guojun, "Several Points to Consider Regarding Going Forward with Completion of the Regulation on How Party Administration Organs Should Handle Public Documents," Business/Economic Management Forum, December 13, 2004].

"浙江九岁女染禽疫死 曾探安徽养病鸡亲戚．"《太阳报》，2006年3月9日 ["9-year-old Zhejiang Girl Dies of Avian Flu After Visiting Anhui." *Orisun*, March 9, 2006].

郑保卫．"试论我国新闻舆论监督的制度建与规范管理．"《新闻记者》（2005年 10月）：第11–14页 [Zheng Baowei. "Discussion on Establishing a System of Public Opinion Supervision of the News and the Specifics of its Administration." *The Journalist Monthly* (October 2005): 11–14].

"政府信息公开的难点何在？—访国家信息中心副主任胡小明．"《信息化建设》第12期（2003年）：第4–7页 ["What Are the Problems With Making Information Government Public? An Interview with Hu Xiaoming, Assistant Director of the State Information Center," *Informatization Construction* 12 (2003): 4–7].

"政府信息公开法规早该出台．" 新华网，2005年9月14日 ["Regulation on Disclosure of Government Information to Be Enacted Soon." Xinhua News, September 14, 2005]. http://news.xinhuanet.com/comments/2005-09/14/content_3484447.htm.

"政府信息公开条例草案文本之不足．"《中国青年报》，2002年9月25日 ["Why the Text of the Draft Regulation on Making Government Information Public is Insufficient." *China Youth Daily*, September 25, 2002].

"政府信息公开条例目前已完成草案起草和说明稿并上报至国务院"，《法制日报》，2005年1月18日 ["Regulation on Making Government Information Public' Recently Completed and Draft Handed in to State Council." *Legal Daily*, January 8, 2005].

"政府信息公开条例起草工作遇难题. " 新华社, 2002年9月24日 ["Work on Drafting the 'Regulation on Making Government Information Public' Encounters Difficulties," Xinhua News, September 24, 2002].

"政府信息何时'解除封锁': 政府信息公开与个人信息保护立法并进, "《财经》, 2005年2月7日, 第102页 ["When Will Government Information Be 'Released of Restrictions'? Legislation on Protecting Government Information and Personal Information Go Hand-in-Hand," *Caijing Magazine*, February 7, 2005: 102].

"政治犯档案之六. " 杨建利救援会, 2003年11月12日 ["The Sixth Political Prisoner Archive." Yang Jianli Support Group, November 12, 2003]. http://www.yangjianli.com/digest/zhangsanyiyan20031112f.htm.

"中科院三院士厦门车祸　北京高层高度关注. "《亚洲周刊》, 2006年10月8日 ["Three Academics from CASS in Hospital After Traffic Accident; Top Beijing Leaders Express Concern." *Yazhou Zhoukan*, October 8, 2006].

中华人民共和国人民代表大会常务委员会,《中华人民共和国治安管理处罚法》. 2006年3月1日 [Standing Committee of the National People's Congress of the PRC. *Law on Punishing Public Order Management Crimes in the PRC*. March 1, 2006. Available at: http://www.mps.gov.cn/gab/flfg/info_detail.jsp?infoId=221.

"中共中央关于加强新形势下保密工作的决定"（内部发行）. 1996年中发16号 ["The Central Party Committee's Decision on Strengthening the Work of Protecting State Secrets Under New Trends" (Internal Circulation Only). Document 16 of the Central Party Committee of the Communist Party of China, 1996].

"中共中央直属机构. " 新华网, 2002年11月15日 ("Departments and Institutions Under the CPC Central Committee." Xinhua News, November 15, 2002]. http://news.xinhuanet.com/ziliao/2002-11/15/content_630715.htm.

"中国保密制度重置底线 政府信息公开进立法程序. " 人民网, 2005年9月20日 ["Baseline of the Protection of State Secrets System Redefined." People.com.cn, September 20, 2005]. http://gov.people.com.cn/BIG5/46737/3709800.html.

"中国上周安全生产呈8特点　煤矿重大事故时有发生. "《中国新闻社》, 2006年5月30日 ["Frequent Coal Mine Accidents over Past Week in China." China News Service, May 30, 2006].

"中国修改保密法　媒体析称为制定信息公开法准备. " 中国新闻网, 2006年12月5日 ["China Amends State Secrets Law, Media Considers it a Standard for Drafting Law on Public Disclosure of Information." China News.com, September 26, 2005]. http://www.chinanews.com.cn/news/2005/2005-09-26/8/631072.shtml.

中华人民共和国国务院.《中华人民共和国政府信息公开条例》. 2007年1月17日公布, 2008年5月1日施行 [State Council of the People's Republic of China. "Regulation on Open Government Information of the People's Republic of China." Issued January 17, 2007, effective May 1, 2008]. Available at http://www.gov.cn/zwgk/2007-04/24/content_592937.htm.

"中央保密委检查到本市检查保密工作. "《北京日报》, 2005年8月27日 ["CPC's Committee on the Protection of State Secrets Investigates Protection of State Secrets Work in This City." *The Beijing News*, August 27, 2005]. http://www.ben.com.cn/BJRB/200508 27/GB/BJRB%5E19083%5E2%5E27R226.htm.

中央纪委.《信息公开指导纲要》（内部发行）, 2005年9月19日 ["Summary of Instructions on the Public Disclosure of Information" (Internal Circulation Only). Issued by the Central Discipline Inspection Committee, September 19, 2005].

中央纪委法规室（编）.《中国共产党纪律处分条例》. 北京：中国方正出版社，1997年 [Office of the Central Discipline Inspection Committee, ed. *Chinese Communist Party Rules on Disciplinary Action.* Beijing: China Fangzheng Publishing House, 1997].

"中央文献：全国保密工作会议（1996年12月11–13日）." 北京党建网站. ["Important Documents from the Central Authorities: National Conference on State Secrets Protection Work (December 11–13, 1996), Website of Beijing's Party-Building Committee], http://www.bjdj.gov.cn/article/detail.asp?UNID=7688.

"中共以间谍罪名判处高瞻等叁人至少十年徒刑." 中央通讯社，2001年7月25日 ["CPC Sentences Gao Zhan and Two Others to 10 Years' Imprisonment or More for Spying." Central News Agency, July 25, 2001].

最高人民检察院.《人民检察院刑事诉讼规则》，1999 年 [Supreme People's Procuratorate. *Criminal Procedure Regulation of the People's Procuratorate,* 1999].

最高人民法院.《关于进一步做好死刑第二审案件开庭审理工作的通知》，214号（2005）[Supreme People's Court. *Notice Regarding Further Improving Open Court Session Work in Second Instance Death Penalty Cases,* Doc. 214 (2005)].

———.《最高人民法院关于进一步做好死刑第二审案件开庭审理工作的通知 》，2005年12月7日， [Supreme People's Court. "Supreme People's Court's Notice Regarding Further Improving Open Court Session Work in Second Instance Death Penalty Cases." December 7, 2005].

———.《最高人民法院关于执行中华人民共和国刑事诉讼法若干问题的解释》，1998 年 [Supreme People's Court. *Supreme People's Court's Interpretation of Certain Issues Regarding Implementing the Criminal Procedure Law of the People's Republic of China,* 1998].

最高人民法院，最高人民检察院，公安部，国家安全部， 司法部，全国人大常委会.《最高人民法院，最高人民检察院，公安部，国家安全部，司法部，全国人大常委会法制工作委员会关于刑事诉讼法实施中若干问题的规定》，1998 年 [Supreme People's Court, Supreme People's Procuratorate, Ministry of Public Security, Ministry of State Security, Ministry of Justice, and Standing Committee of the National People's Congress. *Joint Regulation Concerning Several Issues in the Implementation of the Criminal Procedure Law,* 1998].

最高人民法院、最高人民检察院、公安部、司法部、卫生部、民政部.《关于利用死刑罪犯尸体或尸体器官的暂行规定》，1984 年 [Supreme People's Court, Supreme People's Procuratorate, Ministry of Public Security, Ministry of Justice, Ministry of Public Health, and the Ministry of Civil Affairs. *Provisional Regulation on the Use of the Body Parts or Organs from Executed Criminals,* 1984].

II. ENGLISH LANGUAGE SOURCES

The 6th Global Forum on Reinventing Government. The Seoul Declaration on Participatory and Transparent Governance. Seoul: May 27, 2005.

"Accident Fallout." *Shanghai Daily*, July 6, 2006.

Adams, Brad. "China's Other Health Cover-up," *The Asian Wall Street Journal*, June 12, 2003.

"AIDS Activist Freed after Confession." *South China Morning Post*, September 21, 2002.

Amnesty International. "Annual Death Penalty Report Reveals 20,000 on Death Row Worldwide." Amnesty International news, April 20, 2006. http://www.amnesty.org.uk/news_details.asp?NewsID=16920.

———. "China: Fear of Torture and Ill-treatment/Arbitrary Detention: Chen Guangcheng." Amnesty International urgent action, October 14, 2005. http://web.amnesty.org/library/Index/ENGASA170372005?open&of=ENG-CHN.

———. "PRC: Human Rights Defenders at Risk." December 6, 2004. http://web.amnesty.org/library/Index/ENGASA170452004?open&of=ENG-CHN.

———. *State Secrets: A Pretext for Repression.* Chapter V: The Victims, 1996. http://www.mnesty.org/ailib/intcam/china/china96/secret/secret5.htm.

"Amnesty: Record Rise in Executions." CNN, April 5, 2005. http://edition.cnn.com/2005/POLITICS/04/05/amnesty.death/.

Ang, Audra. "China Detains Commander in Protest Deaths." Associated Press via Yahoo! News, December 11, 2005.

"Arrest Rise as Hopes Grow Dim for Miners." *Shanghai Daily*, May 27, 2006.

"Avoid Graft Case, Journalists Told." *South China Morning Post*, June 16, 2003.

Beck, Lindsay. "China Shares Bird Flu Samples, Denies New Strain Report." Reuters, November 10, 2006.

Benitez, Mary Ann. "Health Chief Was Told Outbreak a State Secret." *South China Morning Post*, January 13, 2004.

Benitez, Mary Ann and Jane Cai. "HK Seeks Facts About Deadly Outbreak." *South China Morning Post*, February 1, 2005.

Benitez, Mary Ann and Josephine Ma. "Beijing SARS Case H5N1, Doctors Say." *South China Morning Post*, June 23, 2006.

"Bird Flu Whistle-blower Gets Jail Term for Graft." *South China Morning Post*, July 10, 2006.

Birkinshaw, Patrick. *Freedom of Information: the Law, the Practice, and the Ideal.* 3rd ed. London: Butterworths, 2001.

"Blackmailer Held." *Shenzhen Daily*, December 8, 2005. Available at http://my.tdctrade.com/airnewse/index.asp?id=13837&w_sid=99&w_pid=196&w_nid=1757&w_cid=489825&w_idt=2005-12-13. PDF available at: http://pdf.sznews.com/szdaily/pdf/200512/1208/s051208.pdf.

"Blast Girl: We Made Fireworks for Four Years." *South China Morning Post*, March 10, 2001.

Bodeen, Christopher. "China Cuts off Water Along Poisoned River." Associated Press, November 28, 2005.

Bok, Sissela. *Secrets: On the Ethics of Concealment and Revelation.* New York: Pantheon Books, 1982.

Cai, Jane. "Bird Flu Whistle-blower Detained, Sparking Fears of Revenge." *South China Morning Post*, December 6, 2005.

———. "Bird Flu Whistle-blower Gets Jail for Graft." *South China Morning Post*, July 10, 2006.

———. "Death Toll at Mine Rises to 166." *South China Morning Post*, December 3, 2005.

———. "Lawyer Kept away from Farmer Who Blew Whistle." *South China Morning Post*, December 8, 2005.

———. "Media Muted on Shanwei Incident," *South China Morning Post*, December 12, 2005.

———. "Quake in Yunnan Adds to Trail of Storm Destruction." *South China Morning Post*, July 24, 2006.

Chan, Alex. "From Propaganda to Hegemony: Jiaodian Fangtan and China's Media Policy." *Journal of Contemporary China* 11, no. 30 (2002): 35–51.

Chan, Minnie. "Cover-up of Pollution in Guizhou." *South China Morning Post*, October 15, 2006.

———. "Mass Protest over Ban on Motorized Tricycles." *South China Morning Post*, June 29, 2006.

———. "Villagers Reportedly Shot Dead During Land Dispute." *South China Morning Post*, December 8, 2005.

Chan, Vivien Pik-kwan. "Pupils 'Did Make Fireworks.'" *South China Morning Post*, March 16, 2001.

Chan, Siu-Sin. "Lifting of Secrecy Veil Sheds Light on Worst Dam Tragedy." *South China Morning Post*, October 2, 2005. http://www.probeinternational.org/tgp/index.cfm?DSP=content&ContentID=13830.

———. "Panyu Clears Village Chief of Corruption." *South China Morning Post*, October 1, 2005.

Chan, Siu-sin. "Lifting of Secrecy Veil Sheds Light on Worst Dam Tragedy." *South China Morning Post*, October 2, 2005. http://www.probeinternational.org/tgp/index.cfm?DSP=content&ContentID=13830.

Chen, Meng. "Man Who Exposed 'Blacklist' Ill in Prison." *China Rights Forum*, March 31, 1999. http://www.hrichina.org/public/contents/2637.

Chen, Zhiwu. "Free Press Could Help China's Economy." *Financial Times*, September 19, 2005. http://news.ft.com/cms/s/97db5d0e-293f-11da-8a5e00000e2511c8,ft_acl=_ftalert_ftarc_ftcol_ftfree_ftindsum_ftmywap_ftprem_ftspecial_ftsurvey_ftworldsub_ftym_ftymarc_ic_ipadmintool_nbe_poapp_printedn_psapp_reg,s01=1.html.

Cheng, Allen T. "Sackings Will Help Foster Openness, Analysts Predict." *South China Morning Post*, April 21, 2003.

"China Amends Law to Limit Death Sentence." *China View*, October 31, 2006. http://news.xinhuanet.com/english/2006-10/31/content_5272422.htm.

"China Announces New Measures to Avoid Cover Up of Disasters." *Press Trust of India*, February 7, 2006.

"China Convicts 50 to Death in 'Terror Crackdown.'" Radio Free Asia, July 30, 2004. Available at http://uhrp.org/articles/154/1/China-convicts-50-to-death-in-quotterror-crackdownquot/China-Jails-Uyghur-Journalist-For-quotSeparatismquot.html.

"China Cover-up Official Executed." BBC News, February 20, 2004. http://news.bbc.co.uk/2/hi/asia-pacific/3507067.stm.

"China: Death Sentence of Tenzin Deleg Rinpoche." Project on Extrajudicial Executions, Center for Human Rights and Global Justice, New York University School of Law. http://www.extrajudicialexecutions.org/communications/china.html.

"China Denies U.N. Claim of Widespread Torture." MSNBC News Services, December 8, 2005. http://www.msnbc.msn.com/id/10347827/.

"China Executes 10,000 People a Year: NPC Delegate." Agence France Presse, March 15, 2004. Available at: http://www.infoshop.org/inews/article.php?story=04/03/15/3081942.

"China Hospital 'Cleared' on Death." BBC News, November 14, 2006. http://news.bbc.co.uk/2/hi/asia-pacific/6146362.stm.

"China Issues Landmark Decree to Encourage Gov't Transparency." Xinhua News Agency, April 24, 2007. http://news.xinhuanet.com/english/2007-04/24/content_6017635.htm.

"China Jails Uyghur Journalists for 'Separatism.'" Radio Free Asia, July 30, 2004. http://www.rfa.org/english/news/politics/2004/07/30/142490/.

China Labour Bulletin. "CLB Calls for Immediate Release of Internet Writer Detained for Publicizing Recent Mass Protests by Chongqing Steel Workers." China Labour Bulletin press release, October 27, 2005. http://www.clb.org.hk/public/contents/18067.

————. "The Liaoyang Four Have Been Detained For Almost Seven Months—With No Formal Charges." China Labour Bulletin, October 16, 2002. http://www.china-labour.org.hk/public/contents/news?revision%5fid=4853&item%5fid=4852.

"China Promotes Recording, Videotaping of Interrogations." Xinhua News, May 16, 2006. http://news.xinhuanet.com/english/2006-05/16/content_4554452.htm.

"China Publishes Resolution on Building Harmonious Society." Xinhua News, October 18, 2006. http://news.xinhuanet.com/english/2006-10/18/content_5219143.htm.

"China Sacks Smelter Official over Toxic Spill." Reuters, December 24, 2005.

"China Says It's Caring for Henan HIV/AIDS Villagers." Reuters, March 8, 2006.

"China Steps up 'Patriotic Education' as Dongzhou Mourns its Dead." Radio Free Asia, April 6, 2006.

"China Stops Planned Jiangxi Protest." Radio Free Asia, October 30, 2006. http://www.rfa.org/english/news/2006/10/30/china_jiangxi/.

"China Suffers Another Toxic Waste Spill." Associated Press via Taipei Times, February 21, 2006.

"China: Swine Flu Cover-up—China's Stiff Warning." *The Straits Times*, August 2, 2005.

"China's Bird Flu Toll May Be Higher." United Press International, April 26, 2006. http://pda.physorg.com/lofi-news-reported-flu-officials_65331429.html.

"China's Harbin Slammed for Toxic Spill 'Cover-up.'" Radio Free Asia, November 29, 2005.

"China Villages Battle Lead, Zinc Poisoning." Radio Free Asia, November 29, 2006.

"Chinese Minister Refutes Reports on New H5N1 Strain." Xinhua News Agency, November 10, 2006.

"Chinese Protest Lawyer 'Arrested.'" BBC News, October 6, 2005.

"Chinese Web Site Shut Down for Publishing Beating Death of Villager, Editor Says." *International Herald Tribune*, September 7, 2006.

"Christian Sect Leader Secretly Executed," *South China Morning Post*, November 30, 2006.

Chow, Chung Yan. "Five Held After Clash over Illegal Sluice Gates." *South China Morning Post*, April 14, 2006.

———. "Saomai's Trail of Shattered Lives." *South China Morning Post*, August 20, 2006.

Cody, Edward. "A Stand Against China's Pollution Tide." *Washington Post*, January 12, 2006.

———. "China Puts Journalist on Trial; Writer Had Supported Official Who Denounced Party Members' Graft." *Washington Post*, January 20, 2006.

Cohen, Jerome A. *Written Statement to the Congressional-Executive Commission on China's Hearing on Human Rights and Rule of Law in China*. September 20, 2006. http://www.cecc.gov/pages/hearings/2006/20060920/cohen.php.

Committee to Protect Journalists. "China, Cuba, Two African Nations Are Top Jailers of Journalists." December 13, 2005. http://www.cpj.org/Briefings/2005/imprisoned_05/imprisoned_05.html.

Cui, Vivien. "2 Jailed for Covering up Tragedy in Gold Mine." *South China Morning Post*, October 25, 2003.

———. "Drug Watchdog Denies Cover-up over Deadly Antibiotic Scandal." *South China Morning Post*, August 9, 2006.

———. "Mainland Hospitals Keep Mum over Deaths." *South China Morning Post*, August 18, 2006.

"Deadly 'Cover-up.'" *The Standard*, June 19, 2003.

Dehua, Liu and Wang Jing. "Certain Opinions on Standardizing Criminal Evidence Work." *China Rights Forum* 2 (2005): 46–50.

"Deputy Procurator-General Urges Protection of Suspects' Rights." Xinhua News, November 19, 2006. http://news3.xinhuanet.com/english/2006-11/20/content _5350883.htm.

Dickie, Murie. "China Refuses to be Open on Transparency." *Financial Times*, January 18, 2007. http://www.ft.com/cms/s/00b6dd82-a74b-11db-83e4-0000779e2340,dwp_uuid= 9c33700c-4c86-11da-89df-0000779e2340.html.

———. "Justice Remains the Great Brick Wall of China." *Financial Times*, April 22, 2006.

———. "Murder Case Puts the Chinese Legal System on Trial." *Financial Times*, April 13, 2005.

"Dissident's Health Worsening, Says Wife." *South China Morning Post*, January 2, 2007.

Donghaisong. "On the Unjust Nature of Article 105." *China Rights Forum* 2 (2005): 57–62.

Eckholm, Erik. "Aides for Times Revealed Secrets, China Charges." *The New York Times*, October 22, 2005.

Economy, Elizabeth. "The Lessons of Harbin: Government Inaction Means Millions Are Paying for Prosperity with Their Health." *Time Asia*, November 27, 2005. http://www.time.com/time/asia/magazine/article/0,13673,501051205-1134809,00.html.

Embassy of the People's Republic of China in the Kingdom of Nepal, *Summary of Opinions on Relationship Between Human Rights and Social Development and Stability*, Oct. 27, 2004.

"Expert Says China Hiding Bird Flu, WHO Disagrees." Reuters, December 9, 2005. http://asia.news.yahoo.com/051209/3/2c5tq.html.

Fairbank, John, and Ssu-yu Teng. *Ch'ing Administration: Three Studies*. Cambridge, Mass: Harvard University Press, 1961.

"Families, Media Kept from Mine." *South China Morning Post*, October 25, 2004.

"Family of Dead Teen Paid to Keep Quiet: Villagers." *South China Morning Post*, January 17, 2006.

Ford, Peter. "Ahead of Olympics, China Lifts Foreign Media Restrictions." *The Christian Science Monitor*, December 1, 2006.

Forney, Mattew and Susan Jakes. "Behind a Chinese Cover-up." *Time Magazine*, December 1, 2005.

French, Howard W. "20 Reported Killed as Chinese Unrest Escalate." *The New York Times*, December 9, 2005.

———. "Letter From China: Beijing Fails to Deliver on Promise of Honesty." *The International Herald Tribune*, December 1, 2005. http://www.iht.com/bin/print_ipub.php?file=/articles/2005/11/30/news/letter.php.

Fu, Hualing. "Creating a Support Structure for Rights: Legal Aid and the Rule of Law in China," A Report Prepared for Asia Foundation, December 2005. http://asiafoundation.org/pdf/CH_legalaid.pdf.

Fu, Hualing and Richard Cullen. *Media Law in the People's Republic of China. Hong Kong : Asia Law & Practice*, 1996.

Fu, Jing. "134 Miners Confirmed Dead in Explosion." *China Daily*, November 29, 2005.

———. "Mine Cover-up: County Chiefs Sacked." *China Daily*, May 29, 2006.

"Fudging on Leak Let Rumours Fuel the Fears." *South China Morning Post*, November 24, 2005.

Gen, Cao. "We are All Nie Shubin." *China Rights Forum* 2 (2005): 54.

Genyuan. "The Paradox of the "Perfect Conviction Rate." *China Rights Forum* 2 (2005): 55–56.

"Harassment Continues After Prison." China Aid Association, February 13, 2006. http://www.persecutedchurch.com/SOS/Current/SOS-06-02-13.html.

He, Qinglian. *The Fog of Censorship: Media Control in China*. Human Rights in China: New York, Hong Kong and Brussels (forthcoming summer 2007).

Holz, Carsten A. "China' Reform Period Economic Growth: How Reliable Are Angus Maddison's Estimates?." *Review of Income and Wealth*, Vol. 52, No. 1 (March 2006): 85–119.

"Hong Kong Bird Flu Finds Raise New Fears About China Reporting." *Agence France Presse*, February 2, 2006.

Horsley, Jamie P. "China's Pioneering Foray Into Open Government." *China Business Review*, July–August 2003. http://www.chinabusinessreview.com/public/0307/horsley.html.

———. "The Democratization of Chinese Governance Through Public Participation and Open Government Information." in *Political Civilization and Modernization in China*, Vol. 3, The Political Context of China's Transformation. Beijing: Renmin University, 2004.

———. "Shanghai Advances the Cause of Open Government Information in China." Freedom Info, April 20, 2004. http://www.freedominfo.org.

Hu, Shuli. "Moments of Disaster Call for Moments of Truth." *Caijing Magazine* (English online edition), November 28, 2005. http://caijing.hexun.com/english/current.aspx?issue=147.

Huang, Kevin. "21 Held Liable for Qiqihar Drugs Scandal." *South China Morning Post*, July 20, 2006.

———. "8,000 Birds Culled in Shandong, Says Villagers." *South China Morning Post*, April 18, 2006.

———. "Shaanxi Women Believed to Be the Fourth Victim of Deadly Antibiotic." *South China Morning Post*, August 8, 2006.

"Hua's Second Conviction, 10-year Sentence Dismay Colleagues." Stanford University News Service, February 7, 2001. http://news-service.stanford.edu/news/2001/february7/huadi-27.html.

Human Rights in China. "Case Profile—Hada." April 16, 2001. http://www.hrichina.org/public/contents/2541.

————. "China's Foreign News Rules Spell Trouble for an Open Olympics." HRIC Statement, September 11, 2006. http://www.hrichina.org/public/contents/30669.

————. "Christian Face Long Sentences in Secret Trial." HRIC Press Release, March 16, 2004. http://www.hrichina.org/public/contents/9444.

————. "Empty Promises: Human Rights Protections and China's Criminal Procedure Law in Practice." HRIC report, March 2001. http://www.hrichina.org/fs/view/downloadables/pdf/downloadable-resources/Empty_Promises_Text.pdf.

————. "House Church Leader's Sentence Wrongfully Prolonged." HRIC Press Release, February 3, 2006. http://www.hrichina.org/public/contents/26775.

————. "Implementation of the Convention on the Elimination of All Forms of Discrimination Against Women in the People's Republic of China: A Parallel NGO Report by Human Rights in China." June 26, 2006, http://hrichina.org/public/PDFs/HRIC-CEDAW-REPORT.6.26.2006.pdf.

————. "Setback for the Rule of Law—Lawyers Under Attack in China." HRIC Trends Bulletin, August 28, 2006. http://hrichina.org/public/contents/30425.

————. "Trial Delay in Yan Zhengxue's Subversion Case." HRIC Press Release, February 12, 2007. http://www.hrichina.org/public/contents/32355.

————. "Trial Date Set for Hangzhou Environmentalist." HRIC Press Release, May 12, 2006.

Human Rights in China and China Labour Bulletin. "Labour and State Secrets." *China Rights Forum* 3 (2004): 23–33.

Human Rights Watch. Shenzhen Municipality Intermediate People's Court Ruling. http://www.hrw.org/press/1999/apr/shenzhen.htm.

"In Custody." *China Rights Forum* 2 (2003).

"In Custody." *China Rights Forum* 4 (2003).

Information Office of the State Council of the People's Republic of China. *China's 'White Paper' on Progress in China's Human Rights Cause in 2003*, March 30, 2004. http://english.peopledaily.com.cn/whitepaper/hr2004/hr2004.html.

Jiang, Zhuqing. "19 Die in Colliery Flooding. 9 Still Missing." *China Daily*, March 25, 2006.

Jiang, Zemin. *Speech at the Millennium Summit of the United Nations*, September 8, 2000, *in* Ambassador Shen Guofang, Deputy Permanent Representative of China to the UN, *Statement to the Third Committee of the 55th Session of the G.A on the Issue of Human Rights*, 2000. http://www.china-un.org/eng/zghlhg/jjhshsw/rqwt/t29315.htm.

Jiao, Guobiao. "China's Information Pigsty." *China Rights Forum* 3 (2005): 85–97.

Johnson, Tim. "China Dealing with Bird Flu Outbreaks." Knight Ridder/Tribune Information Services, November 4, 2005.

————. "China Police Under Scrutiny for Forcing Murder Confessions from the Innocent." *Knight Ridder Newspapers*, April 8, 2005.

Ka-ching, Poon and Martin Wong. "Woman Believed Dead in Bomei Clashes Seriously Injured." Radio Free Asia, April 18, 2006.

Keller, Perry. "Privilege and Punishment: Press Governance in China." *Cardozo Arts and Entertainment Law Journal* 21 (2003): 87.

"Key Suspect in Coal Mine Disaster Cover-up Caught." *China Daily*, May 27, 2006.

"'Kinder' Policy Targets Executions." *South China Morning Post*, March 10, 2004.

Kuhn, Anthony. "The New Spin." Far *Eastern Economic Review*, July 15, 2004: 33.

Kwan, Daniel. "Cover-up of Mine Disaster Shakes Xinhua Journalists Received Money and Gold in Return for Playing down Seriousness of Accident." *South China Morning Post*, September 28, 2003.

Kwok, Kristine. "Don't Play Down Death Tolls, Warn Officials." *South China Morning Post*, July 22, 2006.

"Labor and State Secrets." *China Rights Forum* 3 (2004): 23–33.

Lam, Agnes. "Health Chief in the Dark of Ant Outbreak." *South China Morning Post*, January 26, 2005.

"Leaders Resign in Mine Scandal." *Shanghai Daily*, June 5, 2006.

Lelyveld, Michael. "China's 'Green GDP' Estimate Disputed." Radio Free Asia, September 22, 2006.

Leu, Siew-ying. "Censors Close Website of Pro-Taishi Professor." *South China Morning Post*, October 7, 2005.

———. "Riot Police Broke up Panyu Hunger Strike, Arresting 18." *South China Morning Post*, September 1, 2005.

———. "Zhongshan Party Chief on Defensive over Clashes." *South China Morning Post*, February 24, 2006.

Leu, Siew Ying and Kristine Kwok. "Prison Terms for Dongzhou Rioters." *South China Morning Post*, May 25, 2006.

Lewis, John Wilson and Hua Di. "China's Ballistic Missile Programs: Technologies, Strategies, Goals." *International Security*, Vol. 17, No. 2 (Fall 1992).

Li, Yuwen. "Court Reform in China: Problems, Progress and Prospect." In *Implementation of Law in the People's Republic of China*, ed. Chen Jianfu, Li Yuwen and Jan Michiel Otto. The Hague and Boston: Kluwer Law International (2002): 55–84.

Liebman, Benjamin L. "Watchdog or Demagogue? The Media in the Chinese Legal System." *Columbia Law Review* 105, no.1 (January 2005). http://www.columbialawreview.org/pdf/Liebman-Web.pdf .

Liu, Li. "Wrongly Jailed Man Freed After 11 Years." *China Daily*, April 14, 2005. http://www.chinadaily.com.cn/english/doc/2005-04/14/content_434020.htm.

Loh, Christine, ed. *At the Epicenter: Hong Kong and the SARS Outbreak*. Hong Kong: Hong Kong University Press, 2004.

Ma, Josephine. "Beijing Has 10 Times More Cases Than Reported." *South China Morning Post*, April 21, 2003.

———. "Supreme Court to Keep Check on Death Sentences." *South China Morning Post*, March 11, 2004.

"MacKay Confident China Won't Execute Canadian Citizen." Initiative to Save Huseyin Celil, November 20, 2006. http://www.huseyincelil.com/mackay_death_peanlty.html.

"Madman Blamed for Blast." *South China Morning Post*, March 9, 2001.

Magnier, Mark. "China's High Court to Review Death Sentences." *L.A. Times*, November 1, 2006. http://www.latimes.com/news/nationworld/world/la-fg-death1nov01,1,3315103. story?coll=la-headlines-world.

McDonald, Joe, "Residents: Chinese City Shut Down Water." Associated Press, December 21, 2005.

McGregor, Richard. "Asia-Pacific: Economists Cast Doubts on China's GDP Data." *Financial Times*, July 12, 2004.

———. "China's Response to Disasters Impeded by Secrecy." *Financial Times*, November 27, 2005.

———. "Chinese Media Open Up in Aftermath of Chemical Spill." *Financial Times*, November 26, 2005.

"Media Told to Downplay Demise of Party Boss," *South China Morning Post*, September 27, 2006.

Meng, Tiexia. "Death Report Not Accepted." *Shanghai Daily*, April 14, 2003.

"Mine Bosses Arrested as Death Toll Hits 161." *Shanghai Daily*, December 1, 2005.

"Mine Explosion in China Kills at Least 25." United Press International, November 13, 2006. http://www.upi.com/NewsTrack/view.php?StoryID=20061113-105600-8588r.

Ministry of Health, Joint United Nations Programme on HIV/AIDS and World Health Organization. *2005 Update on the HIV/AIDS Epidemic and Response in China*, January 2006.

"Ministry Refuses to Send Charged Uygur to Canada." *South China Morning Post*, December 13, 2006.

Mitchell, Tom. "Isolated and Powerless, Blast Village Awaits News." *South China Morning Post*, March 12, 2001.

Mosher, Stacy, ed. "Prisoner Profile: Zheng Enchong." *China Rights Forum* 4 (2003): 124–129.

Moy, Patsy. "Bird Flu Project Constrained by Mainland, Says Expert." *South China Morning Post*, June 26, 2006.

Nathan, Andrew, and Perry Link, eds. *The Tiananmen Papers.* Compiled by Zhang Liang. New York: PublicAffairs, 2001.

"New Chemical Spills Threaten Water Supply for Millions in China." Agence France-Presse via Terradaily, January 8, 2006.

"News Ban for Guangzhou's Suspected Second Bird Flu Case, Sources Say." *South China Morning Post*, April 11, 2006.

Ng, Tze-wei. "Court Rejects Lawsuits by Victims of Fatal Antibiotic." *South China Morning Post*, December 13, 2006.

"No Word For Wife On Jailed Uyghur Writer's Fate." Radio Free Asia, June 19, 2006. http://www.rfa.org/english/news/politics/2006/06/19/uyghur_writer/.

Office of the United Nations High Commissioner for Human Rights, *Frequently Asked Questions on a Human Rights-Based Approach to Development Cooperation*; HR/PUB/06/8, NY and Geneva 2006. http://www.ohchr.org/english/about/publications/docs/FAQ_en.pdf.

"Official: Regulations to Balance Public Right to Know Against State Secrets." Xinhua News, December 12, 2006. http://news.xinhuanet.com/english/2006-12/12/content_5474470.htm.

Oksenberg, Michel. "Methods of Communication Within the Chinese Bureaucracy." *The China Quarterly* 143, no. 57 (January–March 1974): 1–39.

Organisation for Economic Co-operation and Development, Development Assistance Committee. *Issues Brief: Equal Access to Justice and the Rule of Law*, 2005. www.oecd.org/dataoecd/26/51/35785471.pdf.

Pan, Philip P. "Internal Times Memo Key to China's Case—Paper Uncertain How Copy Was Obtained." *Washington Post*, October 5, 2005, A18.

———. "Chinese Whistle-Blower Gets Life Sentence in Bribery Case; Local Party Official Gained Prominence with Letter on Internet." *Washington Post*, November 11, 2005.

———. "Who Controls the Family." *Washington Post*, August 27, 2005.

———. "Chinese Officials Sought to Hide Toxic Spill." *Washington Post*, November 26, 2005.

Pei, Minxin. *China's Trapped Transition: The Limits of Developmental Autocracy*. Harvard University Press, 2006.

———. "The Dark Side of China's Rise." *Foreign Policy* (March/April 2006): 32–40.

Peters, B. Guy. *The Politics of Bureaucracy*. 5th ed. Routledge: London and New York, 2001.

Pomfret, John. "China Closes Beijing Newspaper in Media Crackdown." *Washington Post*, June 20, 2003.

"Prisoner Information: He Zhaohui," Laogai Research Foundation, February 7, 2007. http://www.laogai.org/dissent/show.php?code=363&n=.

"Prisoner Profile: Huseyin Celil." *China Rights Forum* 4 (2006): 114.

Pun, Pamela. "First PRC Lawyer Jailed for Leaking State Secrets." *Hong Kong iMail*, 15 May 2001. Available at http://www.fas.org/sgp/news/2001/05/hk051501.html.

"Punishment Metered out Following Illegal Shanxi Gold Mine Explosion." Interfax News, September 22, 2003.

Qiao, Xinsheng. "Who Controls China's Courts?" *China Rights Forum* 2 (2005): 40–41.

"Rebiya Kadeer's Son Sentenced to Seven Years; Another Fined; Another Feared Tortured." Uyghur Human Rights Project, November 27, 2006. http://uhrp.org/articles/351/1/Rebiya-Kadeers-son-sentenced-to-seven-years-another-fined-another-feared-tortured/rabiye.html.

"Review of Procedure Laws Raises Hopes for Justice." *China Rights Forum* 2 (2005): 43–50.

"Riot Village Sealed off in Hunt for Protesters." *South China Morning Post*, December 10, 2005.

Rosenthal, Elisabeth. "Doctor Says China Lied About SARS in Beijing." *International Herald Tribune*, April 11, 2003.

Savadove, Bill. "Sars Cover-up Emboldens Mainland Journalists to Seek out the Truth" *South China Morning Post*, June 9, 2003.

"Several Injured in South China Protest over Land." Reuters, January 15, 2006.

Shi, Jiangtao. "200 Pupils Dead in Flooding, Parents Claim." *South China Morning Post*, June 13, 2005.

———. "Legal Threat Opens New Debate over Spill in Jilin." *South China Morning Post*, March 7, 2006.

———. "More Heads to Roll over Chemical Spill." *South China Morning Post*, December 4, 2005.

————. "Nightmare for Safety Troubleshooter." *South China Morning Post*, December 9, 2005.

————. "Vice-mayor of Spill City Kills Himself." *South China Morning Post*, December 8, 2005.

Shi, Jiangtao and Josephine Ma. "'Serious Pollution' of River After Blast Finally Admitted." *South China Morning Post*, November 24, 2005.

Shimizu, Katsuhiko. "Jailed Uyghur Student Has Todai on His Side." *The Asahi Shimbun*, August 30, 2006. http://www.asahi.com/english/Herald-asahi/TKY200608300110.html.

Shurmann, Franz. *Ideology and Organization in Communist China*. Berkeley and Los Angeles: University of California Press, 1968.

"Sichuan: Thousands Protest Against Hospital that Left Poor Boy to Die." AsiaNews.it, November 13, 2006. http://www.asianews.it/view.php?l=en&art=7730.

"Son of Rebiya Kadeer Sentenced to Nine Years in Prison on Charges of 'Secessionism.'" Uyghur Human Rights Project, April 17, 2007. http://uhrp.org/articles/465/1/Son-of-Rebiya-Kadeer-sentenced-to-nine-years-in-prison-on-charges-of-quotsecessionismquot/index.html.

"Soymilk Poisons Thousands, Kills Three." *Shanghai Daily*, April 9, 2003.

Sturcke, James and agencies. "China Pledges Transparency over Bird Flu." *The Guardian*, November 1, 2005.http://www.guardian.co.uk/birdflu/story/0,14207,1606149,00.html.

Sun, Xiaohua. "Hospitals Fail to Report Deaths." *China Daily*, August 17, 2006.

"Tenzin, Delek Rinpoche: Vital Statistics and Chronology." Fact Sheet, Tibet Online. http://www.tibet.org/itsn/campaigns/lithang/reports/ustc/ustc-factsheetside1.doc.

"Tibetan Religious Leader Sentenced to Life in Prison; ICT Calls for the Immediate Release of Tenzin Delek Rinpoche." International Campaign for Tibet, January 26, 2005. http://www.savetibet.org/news/newsitem.php?id=700.

"Trapped Miners 'Could Still Be Alive.'" *China Daily*, May 25, 2006.

United Nations. "Joint Declaration." (Adopted on 6 December 2004 by Ambeyi Ligabo, Special Rapporteur on the Right to Freedom of Opinion and Expression, Miklos Haraszti, the OSCE Representative on Freedom of the Media, and Eduardo Bertoni, the OAS Special Rapporteur on Freedom of Expression.) UN Doc. E/CN.4/2006/55.

————. "Report of the Special Rapporteur on Promotion and Protection of the Right to Freedom of Opinion and Expression," Special Rapporteur, Abid Hussain. U.N. Doc. E/CN.4/1995/32 (1994).

————. "Report of the Special Rapporteur on the Protection and Promotion of the Right to Freedom of Opinion and Expression." January, 1999. Available at http://www.hri.ca/fortherecord1999/documentation/commission/e-cn4-1999-64.htm.

————. "Report of the Special Rapporteur on the Question of Torture and Other Cruel, Inhuman or Degrading Treatment or Punishment to the General Assembly." UN Doc. A/56/156 (2001).

————. "Report of the Special Rapporteur on Torture and Other Cruel, Inhuman or Degrading Treatment or Punishment—Mission to China," prepared by Manfred Nowak. UN Doc. E/CN.4/2006/6/Add.6 (2006). http://ap.ohchr.org/documents/dpage_e.aspx?m=103.

————. "Report of the Working Group on Arbitrary Detention, Addendum: Mission to China." UN Doc. E/CN.4/2005/6/Add.4 (2004). Available at http://daccessdds.un.org/doc/UNDOC/GEN/G05/102/74/PDF/G0510274.pdf?OpenElement.

————. "Special Rapporteur on Extrajudicial, Summary or Arbitrary Executions' Annual Report 2006." UN Doc. E/CN.4/2006/53 (2006).

————. "The Johannesburg Principles on National Security, Freedom of Expression and Access to Information." UN Doc. E/CN.4/1996/39 (1996).

United Nations' Committee Against Torture. "Third Periodic Reports of States Parties Due in 1997: China." UN Doc. CAT/C/39/Add.2 (2000). http://www.unhchr.ch/tbs/doc.nsf/ (Symbol)/CAT.C.39.Add.2.En?OpenDocument.

United Nations' Human Rights Committee. "General Comment 6, The Right to Life." http:// www.ohchr.org/english/bodies/hrc/comments.htm.

————. "General Comment 29, Derogations During a State of Emergency." http://www.ohchr. org/english/bodies/hrc/comments.htm.

————. "General Comment 21, Replacing General Comment 9 Concerning Humane Treatment of Persons Deprived of Liberty," April 10, 1992.

————. "General Comment 10, Article 19, "Compilation of General Comments and General Recommendations Adopted by Human Rights Treaty Bodies," UN Doc. HRI/GEN/1/Rev.6 at 132 (2003).

United Nation's Economic and Social Council. "Implementation of the Safeguards Guaranteeing Protection of the Rights of Those Facing the Death Penalty," Resolution 1989/64 (1989). Available at http://hei.unige.ch/~clapham/hrdoc/docs/ecosocresolutiondeathpen1989.html.

"Update on Xu Zerong's Court Appeal." *Dialogue*, no. 11 (Spring 2003): 7. The Dui Hua Foundation, http://www.duihua.org/our_work/publications/newsletter/nl_pdf/nl_11_1.pdf.

US Congressional-Executive Commission on China. "Freedom of Expression in the United States: The Doctrine of Prior Restraint." http://www.cecc.gov/pages/virtualAcad/exp/expuspriorrestraint.php.

————. CECC Annual Report 2005, III(b) "Rights of Criminal Suspects and Defendants," http://www.cecc.gov/pages/annualRpt/annualRpt05/2005_3b_criminal.php.

————. "International Agreements and Domestic Legislation Affecting Freedom of Expression: International Treaties, Covenants, and Agreements." http://www.cecc.gov/pages/virtualAcad/exp/explaws.php#priorrestrain.

————. "Selected Legal Provisions of the People's Republic of China Affecting the Free Flow of Information." http://www.cecc.gov/pages/selectLaws/freeFlow/index.php.

————. "Defense Lawyers Turned Defendants: Zhang Jianzhong and the Criminal Prosecution of Defense Lawyers in China." May 27, 2003. http://cecc.gov/pages/virtualAcad/crimjustice/index.php.

"Uyghur Dissident's Sons Detained, Beaten in Front of Children." Radio Free Asia, June 1, 2006, http://www.rfa.org/english/uyghur/2006/06/01/uyghur_kadeer/.

"Villagers Clash with China Police." BBC News, January 15, 2006.

"Villagers Riot over Land Dispute in Shandong." *South China Morning Post*, November 15, 2006. http://china.scmp.com/chitoday/ZZZ0JAM47UE.html.

"Voices of the Poor: Crying Out for Change." The World Bank Report, New York, 2000. http:// www1.worldbank.org/prem/poverty/voices/reports.htm#crying.

Wang, Heyuan. "A Quoi Servent les Publications Internes de l'Agence Xinhua ["What Purpose Do the Internal Publications of the New China News Agency Serve?"]. *Perspectives Chinoises* 5–6 (July–August 1992): 10–16.

Wang, Yi. "Human Rights Lawyers and the Rule-of-Law Camp." *China Rights Forum* 3 (2006): 21–26.

"Watchdog Probing Chinese Pollution Data." *Associated Press*, December 28, 2006.

Weber, Max. *Economy & Society*. Berkeley: University of California Press, 1979.

Wiest, Nailene Chou. "Rapid Return to the Top for Sacked Beijing Mayor." *South China Morning Post*, October 2, 2003.

"Weiquan Online." *China Rights Forum* 3 (2006): 17–20.

Woo, Margaret Y.K. "Law and Discretion in the Contemporary Chinese Courts." *Pacific Rim Law and Policy Journal* 8, no. 3 (September 1999): 581–605.

World Bank. *World Development Report 2006: Equity and Development*. Washington DC (2005).

Wu, Silas. *Communication and Imperial Control in China: Evolution of the Palace Memorial System*. Cambridge: Harvard University Press, 1970.

Wu, Vivan. "Bureau Denies It Sold Rotten Rice." *South China Morning Post*, August 14, 2006.

Xia Li, Lollar. "Assessing China's E-Government: Information, Service, Transparency and Citizen Outreach of Government Websites." *Journal of Contemporary China* 15, no. 46 (2006): 31–41.

Xin, Dingding. "Not a Grain of Truth in Rice Rumours: City Gov't," *China Daily*, October 3, 2006.

Xu, Jianxin. "Justice and the Need for Legal Aid NGOs in China," *China Rights Forum* 3 (2005): 71–73.

Xu, Xiang. "China Plagued by Bird-flu Coverups." *Asia Times*, June 8, 2006. http://www.atimes.com/atimes/China/HF08Ad01.html.

Yan, Alice. "Four Arrested over Blast That Killed 148 Workers." *South China Morning Post*, December 2, 2004.

Yan, Ming and Jiadai Yang, trans. Luisetta Mudie. "Media Blackout as Pig-borne Disease Spreads to 10 Chinese Cities." Radio Free Asia, August 3, 2005.

Yardley, Jim. "China Tried to Keep Benzene Spill Secret." *The New York Times*, November 25, 2005.

———. "Rising Death Toll in China Storm Raises Questions of a Cover-up." *The New York Times*, July 23, 2006.

Ying, Leu Siew. "Detained Rights Activist and Lawyer Formally Arrested." *South China Morning Post*, October 3, 2006.

———. "State of Fear Returns to Taishi." *South China Morning Post*, February 10, 2006.

———. "We Will Not Be Bowed or Broken." *South China Morning Post*, September 13, 2006.

York, Geoffrey. "Celil's Desperate Family Had Given up Hope." *Globe and Mail*, February 8, 2007. http://www.theglobeandmail.com/servlet/story/RTGAM.20070208.w2celil0208/BNStory/International/home.

———. "Death-penalty Debate Grips China After Wrongful Execution." *Globe and Mail*, March 18, 2005. http://www.theglobeandmail.com/servlet/ArticleNews/TPStory/LAC/20050318/CHINA18/Front/Idx.

———. "Virus Hunters," *Globe and Mail*. December 10, 2005. http://globecareers.workopolis.com/servlet/Content/fasttrack/20051210/BIRD10?section=Science.

Zhang, Yaojie. "State Secrets and Omerta," *China Rights Forum* 2 (2005): 63–65.

"Zhao Yan Appeals Against Three-year Sentence on Fraud Charge." Reporters Without Borders, September 4, 2006. http://www.rsf.org/article.php3?id_article=18663.

"Zhejiang Bans Police Extortion of Confession through Torture." Xinhua News Agency, 23 September 2003.

"Zhu Promise to Widen Blast Probe Welcomed." *South China Morning Post*, March 17, 2001.

Zhuang, Pinghui, "In a Grim Irony, Cleanup Spills Cadmium into Yangtze Tributary." *South China Morning Post*, January 9, 2006.